MODERNITY'S MIST

Sara Guyer and Brian McGrath, series editors

Lit Z embraces models of criticism uncontained by conventional notions of history, periodicity, and culture, and committed to the work of reading. Books in the series may seem untimely, anachronistic, or out of touch with contemporary trends because they have arrived too early or too late. Lit Z creates a space for books that exceed and challenge the tendencies of our field and in doing so reflect on the concerns of literary studies here and abroad.

At least since Friedrich Schlegel, thinking that affirms literature's own untimeliness has been named romanticism. Recalling this history, Lit Z exemplifies the survival of romanticism as a mode of contemporary criticism, as well as forms of contemporary criticism that demonstrate the unfulfilled possibilities of romanticism. Whether or not they focus on the romantic period, books in this series epitomize romanticism as a way of thinking that compels another relation to the present. Lit Z is the first book series to take seriously this capacious sense of romanticism.

In 1977, Paul de Man and Geoffrey Hartman, two scholars of romanticism, team-taught a course called Literature Z that aimed to make an intervention into the fundamentals of literary study. Hartman and de Man invited students to read a series of increasingly difficult texts and through attention to language and rhetoric compelled them to encounter "the bewildering variety of ways such texts could be read." The series' conceptual resonances with that class register the importance of recollection, reinvention, and reading to contemporary criticism. Its books explore the creative potential of reading's untimeliness and history's enigmatic force.

MODERNITY'S MIST

British Romanticism and the Poetics of Anticipation

Emily Rohrbach

Forham University Press

New York   2016

Fordham University Press has no responsibility for the persistence or accuracy of
URLs for external or third-party Internet websites referred to in this publication
and does not guarantee that any content on such websites is, or will remain,
accurate or appropriate.

Fordham University Press also publishes its books in a variety of electronic
formats. Some content that appears in print may not be available in electronic
books.

Visit us online at www.fordhampress.com.

Library of Congress Cataloging-in-Publication Data

Rohrbach, Emily.
    Modernity's Mist : British Romanticism and the poetics of anticipation / Emily
Rohrbach. — First edition.
        pages cm. — (Lit Z)
    Includes bibliographical references and index.
    ISBN 978-0-8232-6796-5 (hardback)
    ISBN 978-0-8232-6797-2 (paper)
    1. Romanticism—Great Britain. 2. English literature—18th century—History
and criticism. 3. Literature and history—Great Britain—History—18th century.
4. Time in literature. 5. English literature—19th century—History and criticism.
6. Literature and history—Great Britain—History—19th century. 7. Poetics—
History—18th century. 8. Poetics—History—19th century. I. Title.
PR447.R65 2015
820.9'145—dc23

                                                                    2015008869

Printed in the United States of America

18 17 16   5 4 3 2 1

First edition

to David Wagenknecht

Contents

Acknowledgments

When I approached Fordham University Press with this book in the summer of 2013, the late Helen Tartar responded with warmth and encouragement; I am extraordinarily lucky to have had her as a reader who found value in the manuscript and was willing to send it forward. Throughout the process, Tom Lay, as assistant editor and then editor, has been the stuff of dreams: insightful, savvy, prompt, and supportive. I am deeply grateful to Fordham University Press as well as to Tres Pyle and the anonymous reader for their knowledgeable, rigorous, and constructive reports. I am honored that the co-editors of the new Lit Z series, Sara Guyer and Brian McGrath, accepted the book for their list.

At Northwestern, I landed in a department of astonishingly fine readers and generous colleagues for whom I count my lucky stars. I was especially warmly welcomed (over grits and eggs at regular Dixie Kitchen breakfasts) by the junior faculty, including Katy Breen, Nick Davis, Evan Mwangi, Susie Phillips, Helen Thompson, and Ivy Wilson. Since then, the arrival of Harris Feinsod, Jim Hodge, Rebecca Johnson, Andrew Leong, Juan Martinez, and Shaun Myers has assured me that amazing colleagues are a tradition in University Hall. Each of them has contributed substantially to the pleasures—and the genuine sense of fun—I've enjoyed in everyday teaching and research, and they've helped me through all sorts of intellectual, professional, and practical challenges as well. Chris Herbert, Chris Lane, Carl Smith, and Julia Stern have read and commented generously on my work. Jules Law and Viv Soni read nearly every page of the book manuscript at least once and gave invaluable feedback; I cannot thank them enough. My early career has been rich in remarkably supportive department chairs: Katie Kodat at Hamilton College, Susan Manning, and Chris Herbert. Most recently, Laurie Shannon has been the department chair extraordinaire.

I've enjoyed stimulating interdisciplinary conversations with César Braga-Pinto, Clare Cavanagh, Jorge Coronado, Anna Parkinson, and Michelle M. Wright, and my work was enriched by a full year of my immersion in such exchanges thanks to a Faculty Fellowship at the Alice Kaplan Institute for the Humanities. With her incisive questions and brilliant leadership throughout that year, Director Holly Clayson taught me much about interdisciplinary thought.

For their inspiring conversation and resonant writing, I am deeply grateful to a number of Romanticists, many of whom I meet most often at the North American Society for the Study of Romanticism (NASSR) conferences: Matt Borushko, Tim Campbell, Mark Canuel, Kevis Goodman, Eric Lindstrom, Jonathan Mulrooney, Anahid Nersessian, Onno Oerlemans, Chuck Rzepka, and Emily Sun. Jonathan Gross and Piya Pal-Lapinski gave generously of their time and their expertise on Byron by reading Chapter 5 and helping me see what needed to be done. On all things narrative theory and beyond, Peter Rabinowitz has been a genial and supportive interlocutor. Ian Balfour read several chapters in very rough form, intervening at a crucial stage with helpful suggestions and encouragement. In my work-in-progress seminar at NASSR 2013, Marjorie Levinson delivered the formal response to a version of Chapter 2 with characteristic rigor and generosity of spirit. Among other acts of generosity, Brian McGrath, with sensitivity and insight, read the entire work in its final stages and offered much-needed advice.

Many friends have made my time in Chicago warm and wonderful as I've worked to bring this book to conclusion. The brilliant friendship of Helen Thompson has sustained me. Anna Kornbluh has been a most excellent reader and pal. I cannot imagine where I would be without Nathalie Bouzaglo, Kasey Evans, Jane Springer, and Jade Werner. How are we not sisters? John Alba Cutler has been the most lovely human being with whom to share a train car on the tenure tracks. My father and stepmother, Barton and Nancy Rohrbach, have been supportive of my work. My mother, JoAnn Scott, takes on my desires as her own, and I know that she will be happy, above all, that the book is finished. My brother and sister, Geoff and Susie, have always had my back. This book owes something, too, to my dog Rosie, who dutifully woke me at dawn every morning of my fellowship year so I could get to work.

Tacita Dean answered my wildest dreams by granting me permission to use her image of the salty book "The Book End of Time" for the cover. A very early version of the argument of Chapter 4 appeared as "Austen's Later Subjects," in *SEL: Studies in English Literature 1500–1900* 44.4 (Autumn 2004): 737–52. About a third of Chapter 2 was published as "Reading the Heart, Reading the World: Keats's Historiographical Aesthetic," in *European Romantic Review* 25.3 (June 2014): 275–88.

At the University of Miami, Kathryn Freeman and Frank Stringfellow introduced me to Jane Austen's novels in courses on Romanticism and on the nineteenth-century European novel, respectively. That is to say that I was not part of D. A. Miller's "[a]ll of us who read Jane Austen early—say, at eleven or twelve." When, as an undergraduate, I did encounter her novels, she was taught alongside the Shelleys and Byron, in the first case, and Stendhal, Fontane, and Turgenev, in the second. Those courses made it second nature for me to treat Austen with philosophical seriousness and to put her in conversation with a wide range of authors. I am grateful for what was then—and to a degree still is now—an unorthodox introduction.

At Boston University, David Wagenknecht once asked if it worried me that I might end up in a corner talking to myself. He warmly encouraged this project in its inception with his singular humor and helped it develop with his perspicacious ability to gently steer my more idiosyncratic literary obsessions toward important critical insights and interventions. In those years, I despaired more than once about my capacity to participate effectively in academic conversations, and I know that I owe any success on that front to the sense, all along, that he never had doubts.

INTRODUCTION:
ON BEING IN A MIST

> This Chamber of Maiden Thought becomes gradually
> darken'd and at the same time on all sides of it many doors
> are set open—but all dark—all leading to dark passages—We
> see not the balance of good and evil. We are in a Mist—*We*
> are now in that state—We feel the "burden of the Mystery,"
> To this point was Wordsworth come, as far as I can conceive
> when he wrote "Tintern Abbey" and it seems to me that his
> Genius is explorative of those dark Passages.
>
> John Keats

This book explains why Romantic writers felt they could not fully know
the historical dimensions of the age in which they were living and describes
the poetic and narrative strategies they used to convey that "burden of the
Mystery." Whereas numerous critical studies have focused on the Romantic imagination of the past—describing Romanticism as a form of memory
or mourning, or as the longing elicited by ruins—the "burden" of *Modernity's Mist* comes from the Romantic propensity to imagine the present in
its relation to futurity. Romantic-period writers understood their world to
be shadowed by a dark futurity, even inhabited by it. This book focuses,
more specifically, on literary shapings of anticipation that envision the
present in the terms of an unknown and unpredictable time, yet to come.
Situating this temporal logic within an intellectual history of concepts
of time and the historiographical debates of the late eighteenth and early
nineteenth centuries, I argue that the Romantic poetics of anticipating
futurity offer a historically engaged imagination of time that accounts for
the epistemological uncertainty of the "present." For any relation to the
present, according to these writers, contained something stubbornly elusive
insofar as it had to take into account a sense of uncertainty associated with
futurity: the radical unpredictability of what was to come and of how the
present would look from that inaccessible future vantage.

The Future Anteriority of Mist

Modernity's Mist focuses primarily on the work of John Keats, Jane Austen,
and Lord Byron, with shorter readings of works by William Hazlitt and

Helen Maria Williams, among others. The kinds of anticipation that these central authors share approximate the logic and the temporal model for being in the world that, as we shall see, psychoanalytic discourse has named the *future anterior*—a thinking, with all the uncertainty attending such thoughts, of what *will have been*. But I should quickly add that, for Lacanian psychoanalysis as well as for the writers in this study, these anticipations are never reducible to a straightforward prediction of what will have been. However awkward the construction, what *might will have been* in fact may be the closest grammatical formulation for the poetics of time at stake in this study.[1] Romantic anticipations, that is, inhabit the "present," rendering it a process of unfolding that involves an unknown futurity and, at times explicitly, the imagination of futurity's backward glance. Given the many contingencies guiding that unfolding, this "present" entails also a sense of multiple, often incompatible possibilities; consequently, knowledge of the "present" appears always conditional, based on the uncertainties of how it actually will unfold. Therefore, these authors posit knowledge of the present not in absolute terms but always in provisional ones. In regard to these aspects of Romantic anticipations, the "Mist" in the epigraph to this chapter contains the germ of this entire book, for it appears as a sensory, material figure for the difficulty of knowing the present and for the provisional, fleeting quality of that knowledge when it verges on an unknown futurity.

In the epigraph, John Keats's epistolary prose begins to introduce the temporality of Romantic anticipations and their epistemological uncertainty with the image of a darkening room and dark passages. In this letter to his poet-friend J. H. Reynolds, Keats famously outlines his notion of human life as a process of transformation: a movement through "Chambers" of distinct intellectual, emotional, and ethical stages. Keats positions himself and his friend on the verge of a dark unknown that gives to the present a sense of mystery and multiple possibilities. These principles of change apply generally to what is "human," but Keats specifies with an emphatic "*We*" that he and Reynolds have arrived at the "Chamber of Maiden Thought." Wordsworth went further, Keats says, by exploring the "dark Passages," which Keats could only anticipate with some difficulty ("as far as I can conceive") in his own writing and in his own life. Nevertheless, those "passages" seem to affect even Keats's present "state," which gradually darkens "at the same time" that doors open onto the "dark Passages." With the conjunctional phrase "and at the same time," Keats avoids declaring a cause-and-effect relationship of one thing leading to another—the opening of doors as cause of the darkening of rooms. But the simultaneity, while sidestepping linear causality, still suggests a reversal of our usual sense of physics in this poetic construct, since the images open the possibility that the darkness floods into the "Chamber of Maiden Thought," diminishing its light. Without yet having explored those "dark Passages" but poised, or hovering, at their (plural) thresholds, Keats asserts, quoting Wordsworth's "Tintern Abbey": "We feel the 'burden of the Mystery.'" Anticipatory feeling lends an air of mystery (a feeling without knowing) to the "present," a time inhabited by a dark futurity.

Keats, then, compounds the obscurity of darkness with another visual source in which the two poets appear immediately embedded: a Mist. "We are in a Mist," Keats tells his friend. With the introduction of Mist, the epistolary imagery becomes a wild sensorium through which we see the *myst*ery of the present shaped by a nonlinear temporality that involves a dark futurity. I describe it as "wild" because the visually layered, simultaneous sources of obscurity (derived from mist and darkness) blur the usual boundaries between present and future. If chronological time helps organize civilized society, Keats's epistolary poetic disorganizes it. It troubles a linear understanding of time whereby present and future would appear in chronological succession. In this way, Romantic anticipations do not inhabit strictly the "time" of the present (Mist) or that of the future (dark Passages) but constitute an alternative imagining of the "now" that involves both concepts.

The mist both inhibits and feeds. It enables us to imagine a "present" that is on the move, continually on the verge of change, and, to a certain extent, elusive: a present that remains open to, or inhabited by, the potential unexpectedness of an approaching futurity. The present appears uncertain precisely because the unknown future is part of its conception. While this concept of the present appeals to a sense of futurity, it does not conceive of the present moment as continuous with the future (hence my preference for the word "futurity" over the more sharply delineated "future"). The concept and the poetics of anticipation are decidedly nonteleological. Rather than suggesting a linear movement toward a specified end point or goal, the mist of anticipation opens the present up to multiple possibilities.

Given that epistemological elusiveness is inherent to this peculiar temporality, any literary "poetics" evoking the same temporal perspective would also be inextricably embedded in uncertainty—a literature of nonmastery. In this sense, we might distinguish, by degree, the Keatsian mist from the Wordsworthian version in Book XIII of *The Prelude* (1805), where Wordsworth's mists play an equally central, though markedly different, role in respect to his poetic self-reflection. The comparison helps illustrate how

Keats's position of being embedded *in* the mist produces more readily the imaginative conditions and contingencies of multiple possibilities. Whereas for Keats (as well as for Austen and Byron), mists, blind spots, and other obscurities provide a resource for the imagination, Wordsworth characterizes the imagination in Book XIII as being consistent with an insight that comes only at the moment when, alone, the poet rises *above* the mist.

As Wordsworth's speaker is ascending Mount Snowdon, he suddenly rises out of the mist. "[L]ike a flash," the light of the Moon illuminates the "sea of mist" at his feet, and in an extended revelation, he sees in the natural world a material image of the imaginative mind that "feeds upon infinity":

> With forehead bent
> Earthward, as if in opposition set
> Against an enemy, I panted up
> With eager pace, and no less eager thoughts,
> Thus might we wear perhaps an hour away,
> Ascending at loose distance each from each,
> And I, as chanced, the foremost of the Band—
> When at my feet the ground appear'd to brighten,
> And with a step or two seem'd brighter still;
> Nor had I time to ask the cause of this,
> For instantly a Light upon the turf
> Fell like a flash: I look'd about, and lo!
> The Moon stood naked in the Heavens, at height
> Immense above my head, and on the shore
> I found myself of a huge sea of mist,
> Which meek and silent, rested at my feet: (13.29–44, 1805)[2]

The contrast between Wordsworth's and Keats's spatial orientations with respect to the mist resonates with an occasionally sharp difference between their ideas of the role of the poet as visionary. In the letter to Reynolds, Keats keeps in step with his friend, both of them equally embedded in the mist, whereas Wordsworth notably figures himself in *The Prelude* as "foremost of the Band"—emerging from the mist in a privileged position with respect to others. In his letter, Keats similarly places Wordsworth in a position more advanced than his own and that of Reynolds in that the first-generation poet has shed a light on the passages ahead, which remain dark to Keats and his friend. Jacques Rancière observes the political implications of this subtle distinction when he comments on the politics of human relations in Wordsworth's *The Excursion*: "Equality is given from on high, and the poem completes itself in a program of educating the people that mounts, like a prayer to the sky, towards 'the State's parental ear.'" For Keats, on the other hand,

> Equality ought to be thought as wholly horizontal. The indolence or passivity of the dreamer lying on a sofa or on the clover participates in this reversal. It is opposed to the gait of the walker, moving with him the "active principle" that grants equality to the passersby as sovereigns grant their people the charter.[3]

In the letter to Reynolds, although Keats anticipates—and seemingly aspires to—the visionary perspective he attributes to Wordsworth in "Tintern Abbey," in his poetry the sense of anticipation and uncertainty *at the threshold*, rather than the Wordsworthian flash of visionary insight, becomes its own aim or end. In other words, Keats's poetic project is, finally, not to find a way out of the mist but to discover how to think and imagine from within it.[4]

In the darkness and "Mist" that Keats imagines, a world that teems with *possibilities* (as in the pluralized "Passages") is the same as a world of *obscurities* (darkness and mist). The aural affiliation between *mist* and *myst*ery is a linguistic accident that Keats's imagination seizes, for both the natural phenomenon and the concept imply an element of the invisible or unknowable. But whereas the mystery associated with the gothic "dark Passages" appears foreboding, the figure of mist brings to the obscurity a positive valence of the creativity that it makes possible, in that mists in the natural world foster growth. The Keatsian imagination feeds less on infinity than on the noncomprehensiveness or partiality intrinsic to any understanding of the present.

Various forms of Romantic anticipation expand the aural affiliations and implications of my title's keyword *mist* to include the idea of a present that is—like a target that cannot be hit, as well as something that is longed for—*missed*. Something significant is absent. It eludes one's grasp when trying to get the mind around the present as a historical moment.[5] Samuel Weber nicely elucidates the temporal logic of the something missed as it has taken shape in Freudian-Lacanian psychoanalytic discourse. He focuses on one sentence in particular from Lacan's essay *The Function and Field of Speech and Language in Psychoanalysis*:

> What is realized in my history [i.e., in that of the individual subject] is not the past definite of what was, since it is no more, or even the present perfect of what has been in what I am, but the future anterior of what I shall have been for what I am in the process of becoming.[6]

As the final clause emphasizes, Lacan's "future anterior" subjectivity does not designate a static identity or state but bespeaks the ongoing-ness of a "process of becoming" and sense of incompletion that are crucial also to the future anteriority that we find in Romantic texts. As Weber explains, this perspective entails a sense of anticipation and incompletion that can never be overcome:

> In invoking the future anterior tense, Lacan troubles the perfected closure of the always-already-having-been [*Immer-schon-gewesen-Seins*] by inscribing it in the inconclusive futurity of what will-always-already-have-been [*Immer-schon-gewesen-sein-wird*], a "time" which can never be entirely remembered, since it will never have fully taken place. It is an irreducible remainder or remnant that will continually prevent the subject from ever becoming entirely self-identical . . . every attempt by the subject of the unconscious to grasp its history inevitably divides that history into a past that, far from having taken place once and for all, is always yet to come.[7]

Something—an "irreducible remainder or remnant"—will forever elude the "grasp" of any totalizing impulse to identify or know the object (here, the "self"). Weber's explication of the temporal logic connects the persistence of the "remainder or remnant" to the "time" of future anteriority. Drawing on that conceptual link, the chapters that follow pay particular attention to such "irreducible remainders" in various aspects of the texts, such as epistemological gaps and rhythmic silences, which signal aspects of a world that eludes full mental "grasp."

Modernity's Mist explores *literary* future anteriority with an approach that is both conceptual and attentive to the poetic and aesthetic dimensions not only of lyric and narrative poems but also of novels and historical writing. In that respect, I take seriously Percy Shelley's impassioned statement that the "distinction between poets and prose writers is a vulgar error."[8] By using the term "poetics," I mean to draw attention to the way literary language shapes meanings in the play between "semantics" or "reference," on the one hand, and the largely arbitrary visual and aural materiality of words as signs, on the other. The inveterate tension between these two systems is at work in Keats's reflection on the life of sensations (aural, visual, and so on) and that of thought in his 1817 letter to Benjamin Bailey. "O for a Life of Sensations rather than of Thoughts!"—so Keats declares in an oft-quoted phrase (*LJK*, 1:185). He goes on, however, to reflect that "a complex Mind—one that is imaginative and at the same time careful of its fruits," is a mind that "would exist partly on sensation partly on thought" (*LJK*, 1:186). The play between those "parts" I take to be the work of "poetics," approximately in the way Percy Shelley defines and employs the term in *A Defence of Poetry*. There, Shelley similarly sees the two parts working together in the way poetry makes meaning:

> Sounds as well as thoughts have relations, both between each other and towards that which they represent, and a perception of the order of those relations has always been found connected with a perception of the order of relations between thoughts. Hence the language of poets has ever affected a certain uniform and harmonious recurrence of sound, without which it were not poetry, and which is scarcely less indispensable to the communication of its influence, than the words themselves without reference to that peculiar order. Hence the vanity of translation. (514)

To analyze lyric and narrative poetry from this double perspective of material "sound" and conceptual "thought" would seem obvious, but my readings of Austen's rhythmic silences in *Persuasion*, in particular, aim to extend a poetic sensibility to prose, in that those silences "do" something; they shape meanings in ways that cannot be explained by the referential function of language. As Giorgio Agamben writes in *The End of the Poem*, "All poetic institutions participate in this noncoincidence, this schism of sound and sense—rhyme no less than caesura."[9] My readings in the following pages pay particular attention to moments in which poetic experience comes into tension with—or even exceeds—referential meaning. Critics of poetry often draw, whether overtly or not, on statements such as Keats's and Shelley's when they describe this tension as a convergence and divergence of acoustic phenomena and signifying sounds that we process visually and acoustically as well as cognitively.[10] That relation between sense and the senses (meaning and sensation) within language is important to this study because it is where one frequently finds the "remainders" of future anteriority. But whereas some critics, such as Mutlu Blasing, restrict the significant operation of this kind of tension to lyric poetry, in the spirit of Shelley's *Defence of Poetry*, *Modernity's Mist* extends its potential field of play beyond lyric poetry to comic epic (Byron's *Don Juan*) and the novel (Austen's *Persuasion*).

I am following Percy Shelley when I mostly do not distinguish between "poetics" and "aesthetics" but envision these two terms, starting with Romanticism, as forming part of the same creative enterprise. If, as Forest Pyle has recently put it, aesthetics, and more specifically aesthetic experience, involves "a radical engagement with the very processes by which the world is not merely known, but felt—and felt as an effect of representation" and, as such, it is a confronting of "the aporias between perception and sensation, on the one hand, and cognition and conceptualization, on the other" ("the aporias out of which the aesthetic as a 'domain' is constituted in the first place"), then Shelley's Romantic conception of "poetry" involves what we call "aesthetics."[11] It involves a conspicuous awareness of the play between those two dimensions as well as an awareness that neither one is reducible or easily resolvable into the other. That critics such as Agamben and Blasing—neither of whom is a specialist in Romanticism—refer to the noncoincidence between these two dimensions as aspects of poetics, without using the term "aesthetic," attests to the Romantic perspective having won out and become normative within the study of poetics today. That influence has been buoyed, no doubt, by the residual force of de Manian deconstruction. "Poetics," for many critics working now, is not restricted to describing the technical and grammatical aspects of poems but involves rigorous close reading with an attention to the rifts between, say, the phenomenological experience of poetry and the idea of metaphysics or a hermeneutical explanation—a legacy of deconstruction for whom Percy Shelley's poetry took center stage.

In this study, I refer to "form" when the concept and readerly expectations of what a sonnet, a novel, an ode, or an epic entails would seem to make various effects possible. An early nineteenth-century novel, for instance, promises resolutions in marriage of the central (typically social) plot conflicts and encourages readers' anticipations. The expectation that a sonnet whose octave is in Petrarchan form will not involve an English quatrain in the last six lines makes Keats's rhyme patterns in "On Sitting Down to Read *King Lear* Once Again" notably jarring. An epic calls for a heroic male protagonist, making Byron's Don Juan appear conspicuously insufficient or deviant. Aspects of form and poetics overlap at many points in my analyses, but form (sonnet, ode, novel, epic) distinguishes the works in the chapters that follow from one another, in that they elicit distinct expectations, whereas concepts of time, and even certain poetic effects, can be traced across these different forms. Austen uses the poetics of caesura as effectively as Keats or Byron does.

Modernity, Temporality, and Historiographical Crisis

The literary texts in this study respond to a historical crisis that emerged toward the end of the eighteenth century. For Keats, Austen, and Byron develop a temporal logic that is both *historicizing* (offering a theoretical framework for "thinking" the present in view of the modern dilemma) and *historical* (deeply engaged with the historiographical crisis specific to the early nineteenth-century moment). The crisis to which I am referring emerged from a paradox in intellectual history: namely, just as the rise of periodization isolated the present from the past—calling on historians, philosophers, and artists to define it as the most recent historical age—the sense of a radically uncertain, impending futurity made that project of historical definition seem all but impossible. Historian Reinhart Koselleck refers to this paradox as a "crisis of historism."[12] By the end of the eighteenth century,

> the difficulty of apprehending one's own time grew, since the course that it would follow could no longer be derived from previous history. The future became a challenge, a puzzle. . . . It was this fact, that the course of past time was obviously different from that of the present and the future, which robbed the annalistic "onward-writing" of present incidents of its previous certainty. One could no longer rely on the conviction of an eye-witness to establish which events would matter, or which would have an impact.[13]

For British Romantic-period writers, rapidly changing political circumstances at home and abroad heightened the urgency, and thus the awareness of the difficulty, of comprehending the historical dimensions of the present—"which events would matter, or which would have an impact." From this dilemma follows the question (without a clear answer) of how to imagine the present as history.

In Anna Barbauld's epistolary instructions to a young pupil titled "On the Uses of History," for instance, this crisis accounts for the text's internal contradictions. First published posthumously in 1826, Barbauld's epistolary essay ponders the possibility of historical prediction, initially expressing serious doubts in light of recent events that appear to "mock all power of calculation."[14] The idea of the incalculability of recent events in the French Revolution leads Barbauld to declare the inevitable unpredictability of a host of other political and social events of late:

> The deepest politician, with all his knowledge of the revolutions of past ages, could probably no more have predicted the course and termination of the French revolution, than common man. The state of our own national debt has baffled calculation, the course of past ages has presented nothing like it. Who could have pronounced that the struggle of the Americans would be successful—that of the Poles unsuccessful? (286)

Barbauld associates the *unpredictability* of recent events with their quality of being *unprecedented*: "the course of past ages has presented nothing like it." The essay goes on, however, to contradict this historical account when the author makes room for the possibility of contemporary political prediction: "let the circumstances be known and the characters upon the stage [rulers], and history will tell [the politician] what to expect from them. It will tell him with certainty, for instance, . . . that if the church and the monarch are united they will oppress" (287). Moreover, if one reads history, Barbauld instructs, one will learn that all events have precedents:

> A well-informed person will not be apt to exclaim at every event out of the common way, that nothing like it has ever happened since the creation of the world, that such atrocities are totally unheard of in any age or nation;—sentiments we have all of us so often heard of late on the subject of the French revolution: when in fact we can scarcely open a page of [French] history without being struck with similar and equal enormities. (290)

How do we account for this contradiction in Barbauld's assessment of the French Revolution? In "On the Uses of History," the late eighteenth-century history of changing and competing forms of historiography informs the author's dilemma about the French Revolution but in ways of which she appears unaware, or at least in ways of which she gives no synthesizing account.

Although Barbauld refers to "history" as if it were an unmediated object, her thinking about the French Revolution shifts between two very different philosophies of history—two ways of mediating history—in these two passages: exemplary history in the latter passage and, in the former, the sense of history emerging circa 1800 that Koselleck describes as an increasing distance between the "space of experience" and the "horizon of expectation."[15] Koselleck associates that distance with the rise of philosophical history, which tells the story not of historical repetition or even of political prognosis but of cultural progress. Older history books (written, say, from the Renaissance to the mid-eighteenth century) of French history (or any Western history) most often had the purpose of instruction, proceeding on the assumption that all contemporary events have precedents from which one could learn how to act in the present.[16] From the perspective of that epistemological frame, therefore, any recent event in France would be understood as a repetition or variation of some previous historical event(s). In the mid-eighteenth century, with the rise of philosophical history, these two models came into tension with one another.[17] By Barbauld's time, history was being written in a great variety of forms—but rarely in the exemplary form drawn from classical models.

Barbauld's apparent confusion about how to understand the historicity of the French Revolution attests to a widely felt historiographical dilemma:

the need to define the historical dimensions of the present age at the very moment that its distinctiveness seemed to become especially difficult to characterize. Capacious and searching thought about time distinguishes writing after the French Revolution, when a significant accumulation of literary and historical discourses bearing the phrase "spirit of the age" began to appear.[18] This phrase flourished not because everyone knew what that "spirit" was but because the distinctive character of the present epoch seemed so elusive. That elusiveness derived, in part, from the fact that the modern age—the present age circa 1800—was defined by its sense of break with the past, and so philosophers, cultural critics, and historians could not rely on patterns or epistemologies of the past in order to comprehend and define the present. As Jürgen Habermas puts it:

> Modernity can and will no longer borrow the criteria by which it takes its orientation from the models supplied by another epoch; *it has to create its normativity out of itself.* Modernity sees itself cast back upon itself without any possibility of escape. This explains the sensitiveness of its self-understanding, the dynamism of the attempt, carried forward incessantly down to our time, to "pin itself down."[19]

Habermas's critique describes the challenges faced by those who felt the urgency of understanding the time in which they lived both on its own terms and as a historical epoch. Deriving the models for understanding an object (the historical epoch) from the object itself robs the project of a privileged, outside position from which to observe and judge a complete picture.

A conceptual counterpart to this Romantic urgency to define the *present* as a historical period is the new sense of *futurity* that, according to recent scholars, becomes integral to historical thinking. Fredric Jameson explains: "it is the present's responsibility for its own self-definition of its own mission that makes it into a historical period in its own right and that requires the relationship to the future fully as much as it involves the taking of a position on the past. History is to be sure both dimensions."[20] Although early modern historians arguably understood their age as "new" particularly with respect to scientific developments, recent scholarship suggests they did not write about history with the concept of periodization that characterizes modern historiography, circa 1800 to the present. What most notably distinguishes Romantic concepts of time and history from those of earlier moments are new ways of imagining futurity that are crucial to thinking of the present as a *singular* historical period in its own right.[21] According to late twentieth- and twenty-first-century scholars, the present age in the early modern period was not imagined to give way—at some unpredictable future moment—to yet another paradigmatically new age; one's thought about how to act thus could be guided by lessons from the past without the concern that lessons of history were obsolete.[22] Put another way, the early modern historiographical imagination from the perspective of the present and from that of the future (if one in the sixteenth century were to worry about that vantage) might have amounted roughly to the same thing.[23] Based on this distinction, Jameson argues that modernity's "consciousness of history and of being historical" depends on a "new attitude towards the present": "the judgment of the future on the present." "I am tempted to argue," Jameson writes, "that the present cannot feel itself to be a historical period in its own right without this gaze from the future."[24] For that gaze to be significant to the historical imagination, the future had to be conceived as a time paradigmatically different from the present.

Two distinct qualities characterize this new conception of time as it marks late eighteenth- and early nineteenth-century discourse: an unprecedented sense of speed or acceleration (with which major historical events take place in succession, for instance) and the idea of an unknowable, unpredictable future.[25] As Habermas notes: "The *Zeitgeist*, or spirit of the age, one of the new words that inspired Hegel, characterizes the present as a transition that is consumed in the consciousness of a speeding up and in the expectation of the differentness of the future."[26] A sense of accelerated history marks, for instance, the *London Times*' announcement of the Fête de la Fédération on July 20, 1790: "Such a magnificent association of FREE MEN, emancipated from the shackles of despotism within so short a space of time, is hitherto unparalleled in the annals of History."[27] Given that "so short a space of time" for the change from despotism to emancipation appears "unparalleled," the sense of speed itself appears to have struck the journalist as the unpredictable and unpredicted event.

From the 1790s onward, that journalist was scarcely alone in sensing the speed with which major events were happening in rapid succession. When William Wordsworth, impressed by the chronological compression of recent large-scale historical events, notes in his preface to *Lyrical Ballads* "the great national events which are daily taking place," historical acceleration, a key contributing factor to the historiographical crisis, features prominently and suggests the rapidly shifting grounds of the present.[28] When Chateaubriand went to write those historical events down, it was precisely this compression, opening onto an unknown futurity, which frustrated the historiographical task of writing about the present. For Chateaubriand "drew up while in emigration in 1797 a parallel of the new and the old revolutions, whence he drew conclusions from the past for the future in the usual manner. But he was soon forced to realize that whatever he had written during the day was by night-time already overtaken by events."[29] It was not just the speed but also the unpredictability of events that thwarted the historiographical task. Whether in Wordsworth's Britain or Chateaubriand's France, the epistemological frame of exemplary history failed to offer comprehensive explanations for the course of recent events. Reliance on past examples no longer sufficed to explicate the present or prognosticate the future. Nor was it obvious which of the emerging historiographical models would substitute to provide a comprehensive picture of the contemporary historical age.[30]

As we shall see in more detail in Chapter 1, the prevailing modes of historiography were not equipped to narrate the present while taking into account the unpredictability of the future. The central claim of this book is that the works of Keats, Austen, and Byron developed a sense of temporality—a future anteriority or what *might will have been*—that does just that: it elicits an imagining of the present as a historical age whose apparent trajectory might be disrupted by some dark, unpredictable futurity. In this respect, Romantic anticipations emphatically depart from the notion of progress. Although philosophical history, whose assumptions rested on the idea of progress, became the dominant paradigm for thinking about futurity in the eighteenth century, it could not accommodate the notion of paradigm-shifting historical surprise. Articulating an important temporal distinction, Jürgen Habermas has critiqued Reinhart Koselleck's celebration of progress as the most radical form of intellectual rupture with respect to the future. Habermas explains, "Koselleck overlooks the fact that the notion of progress served not only to render eschatological hopes profane and open up the horizon of expectation in a utopian fashion but also to close off the future as a *source* of disruption with the aid of teleological constructions of history."[31] The eighteenth-century idea of progress opens up a "horizon of expectation," but the very delineation of that "horizon" works to "close off" a potentially disruptive future. Put another way, "progress" eliminates the possibility of paradigm-shifting historical surprise because it develops out of, rather than displaces, the past.[32] By contrast, the Romantic anticipations that I shall describe in the following pages appear remarkably sensitive to that possibility of surprise.

How Romantic Anticipations Imagine the Implications of Modernity

In the title of this study, the term "Modernity," as may already be apparent, refers not to a particular material condition or even political development, such as print culture or democratic politics, but rather to something like the trope of rewriting that Fredric Jameson describes in *A Singular Modernity*.[33] It is less an object of culture than an "explanatory feature," as Jameson puts it, or, as this project emphasizes, a particular poetics of temporality and a structuring of the time of reading.

More specifically, the literary works by Keats, Austen, and Byron all present a certain kind of rewriting trope in the form of an unendingly revisionary sense of history. This revisionary quality arises from a "present" that is inflected by anticipations of unknown futurity; it is the shadows cast on the present by futurity in a world in which the future is perceived as fast-approaching, yet unknown and unknowable. Keats's poetry and letters, Austen's *Persuasion*, and Byron's *Don Juan* all reflect the ideas and develop the implications of modernity in two key ways: first, the sense of the future, toward which the literary works so often turn, appears radically unpredictable; second, as a logical consequence of that uncertain futurity, the present teems with multiple possibilities, since future retrospection may dramatically revise what or how this "present" means. Keats's poetry and letters show how integral a sense of disorientation is to reading a world that is always on the verge of an unknown and, ultimately, to inhabiting and even shaping it. Like Keats's poetry, Austen's *Persuasion* incorporates the ideas of unpredictability and multiple possibilities, while her narrative temporality emphasizes as well the necessarily provisional status of historical knowledge that comes with a revisionary paradigm; history becomes available not as an *object* of narration but through a continual narrative *process* of knowing, or trying to know. This knowledge thus is endlessly subject to revision. Byron's *Don Juan* pursues the most radical conclusion of modernity's unknowable, impending futurity by committing itself to an insistent "presentness," teeming with narrative and interpretive possibilities. Its poetics of unpredictability emphasizes the moment-to-moment writing process of its narrator-author, as if the narrative developments to come were wholly inaccessible and even the author had no imaginative control over where his poem was heading. Byron's radical solution amounts to an embeddedness in the sensuous materiality of the present and the narrator-author's constant encounters with the unpredictability of the creative process. In various ways—Keats's disorientation as a means of finding a place; Austen's provisional reckonings and understanding of history as process; and Byron's radical presentness—these writers pursue the implications of modernity for imagining the present. They think through some of the problems of comprehending the historical dimensions of the present, offering tropes and reading experiences that promise to bring us closer to a newly elusive historical world, unmoored from the historical epistemologies of the past and devoid of guarantees.

By situating these texts in relation to the history of concepts of time and futurity, to the conditions of modernity circa 1800, and to modernity's historiographical crisis, *Modernity's Mist* argues that these Romantic literary concepts of time constitute a historical engagement and that the poetic forms and stylistic techniques the texts use to convey the implications of modernity are crucial to their distinctive historiographical force.

Aesthetics and/of Historical Engagement in Recent Romantic Studies

Modernity's Mist contributes to Romantic studies, and to literary studies more broadly, by envisioning anew the role that poetic forms and stylistic techniques play—that is, helping shape an experience and concept of time—in the way Romantic literature engages with history. It shows not only that Romantic literature engages with the demands specific to its historical world but also that the inextricably "literary" dimensions of texts are crucial to the kinds of engagement these texts create and facilitate. In recent years, the question of *whether or not* Romanticism directly engages with the historical world has changed to that of *how* it does. Following a broad New Historicist portrayal of Romanticism as enacting a rigid divide between literature and history (or politics)—that is, Romanticism as aspiring to timelessness or a refuge from history—Romantic studies in the 1990s largely sought to align Romantic "texts" with recovered cultural "contexts," which the political language or ideas positively reflected. That shift toward a more expansive critical understanding of historically specific "culture(s)" revised our sense of Romanticism by showing how the language and ideas of poets engaged with the historical and political climates of the day. Consequently, "Romanticism" was no longer the name for the poetics of a politically suspect attempt to evade history. Nicholas Roe's extraordinary research into Keats's education at the progressive Enfield School, for example, became the basis for his book *John Keats and the Culture of Dissent*, which showed how Keats's poetry reflected the political culture of dissent alive in the pedagogical world that he enjoyed there.[34] In this vein, these kinds of cultural studies tend to suggest that the political or historical implications of literary works can be verified sufficiently by tracing a correspondence between their language or ideas and a material or cultural "context," a world of material conditions or political views already in place. They have shown that Romantic literature engaged in various ways with such political and historical contexts, and much insight has been gained from the vast historical research that has gone into this critical body of work. However, the literary text, in such studies, often appears reactive to cultural climates rather than, as *Modernity's Mist* claims, as a climate or creative force of its own—a "context"—for shaping experience. These studies tend to have little to say about how the play of thought and sensation, rhythmic slowness and speed, as well as form and self-reflexivity, help shape distinctive kinds of literary engagements with history.

Attending to the singular poetic experiences that works by Keats, Austen, and Byron bring about, this book argues that their literary works do not simply reflect political or historical contexts; rather, by shaping historical experience—that is, by making these singular conceptions and experiences of time and history available—they enact creative agency. Hence, the term "poetics" of the title, characterizing the literary less as a process of representing than as an act of *making*.

Methodologically, whereas cultural studies approaches tend to start from a cultural context and then situate literature in relation to it, *Modernity's Mist* proceeds in the opposite direction. Let me illustrate the implications of this reversal via a comparison with one book-length cultural study of Romantic anticipations, Andrew Bennett's *Romantic Poets and the Culture of Posterity*.[35] Bennett's study surveys the conditions of print culture and Romantic-period statements about literary culture available in nonfiction prose writing in order to establish the grounds of a Romantic culture of posterity—a culture, he contends, that shapes poetry's relations to futurity in crucial ways:

> It is my suggestion that the particular predicament of early nineteenth-century poetry publication not only allowed for but, for certain writers and for a certain culture of writing, demanded deferred reception. Once the conditions of publication and the market for books have given poetry audiences a certain anonymity, and once the democratization of the readership has allowed a certain degradation and, by association, a *feminization* of reading to become credible as a narrative of reception, then poets begin to figure reception in terms of an ideal audience—masculine, generalised and anonymous—deferred to an unspecified future. (2–3)

The grammar of Bennett's claims drives home the point that writers and their works occupy the receiving end of cultural agency. "[T]he particular predicament of early nineteenth-century poetry publication" and "the conditions of publication and the market for books" hold the place of actors;

they act as causal forces. *"Once" cultural conditions are like this, "then" poetry will be like that*, Bennett seems to say.

Bennett astutely identifies a sharp gender bias in early nineteenth-century literary culture, which establishes the basis for his study's repetition of that cultural division between the literary works of men and women writers. "An examination of women's poetry in the period should then disclose certain alternative trajectories to Romantic posterity," Bennett argues, since the "Romantic culture of posterity" constitutes "a specifically masculine phenomenon" (66). However much one may wish to contest his assumptions about the investments of the individual literary works themselves, his assessment of broad trends of sexism in Romantic-period literary culture would seem undeniable. A study that proceeds from literary culture to literary texts thus would logically discover little shared ground between the works of men and women writers.

Modernity's Mist moves methodologically in the opposite direction, insofar as the associations I discover between texts—and thus the logic of selecting the works that concern the following pages—originated in readings of the literary texts themselves with an attention to the way they shape, in the poetic experience, an understanding of time. Consequently this study focuses primarily on Keats, Austen, and Byron—authors who do not routinely sit still together for a critical portrait. In the process of pursuing a logic to this alignment beyond a shared poetics of temporality, I then discovered the rich relevance of the conditions of intellectual history and historiography at the turn of the nineteenth century. In this study, therefore, Romantic anticipations come to be thought of not as cultural phenomena or symptoms but as active intellectual and historical engagements that do not respect the normative cultural boundaries between gender and genre. Across authorial genders and a range of genres and formal procedures, these texts participate, however unwittingly, in a shared project of imagining anew the predicaments of modernity.

Attention to poetic and narrative strategies, as we shall see, is key to how that imagining offers a relation to the historical world. For it is often in a rhythmic silence or an epistemological gap, and in the tensions between what a text "says" and what it "does," that these literary works offer access to peculiarly modern temporalities—to an experience of a shifting grounds of knowing, a paradoxical anticipation of the unpredictable, and an encounter with a not fully knowable present. That resistance to complete knowledge, as we saw via Samuel Weber's analysis of the future anterior, prevents a complete or perfect sense of self-knowledge or identity.

The self—and by implication historical knowledge—can never be fixed or complete if it is constantly unfolding in a historical process of (self-) knowing. In this respect we find, through these texts, an understanding of history as process, which is to say an understanding that is at odds with an assumption underlying cultural-historicist studies that aim to retrieve the past *as it was*. For instance, as Jeffrey Cox puts it in *Poetry and Politics in the Cockney School*, the historicist project values "the work undertaken both in attempting to remove the accumulations of temporal junk, the material and mental barriers between us and the past, and in seeking to reintroduce to our sense of the past lost populations, lost groups."[36] That project has undoubtedly enriched our knowledge of the conditions of literary production and reception, as well as our readings of works and the scope of the literary canon. At the same time, however, the historical logic of future anteriority that takes shape in these texts comes into tension with such a recovery project, since not only do these texts tell us that history is a dynamic process of unfolding, unfixed in time, enriched and shaped, perhaps even realized, by the imagination of "temporal junk," but also one aspect of that historical past that these writers imagined is that the historical dimensions of their moment were already, to some extent, "lost" on them.

Asserting this self-consciously historical and historicizing dimension to Romantic-period texts, *Modernity's Mist* is deeply indebted to James Chandler's magisterial *England in 1819*. In that study of early nineteenth-century historicity, Chandler demonstrated the intense "historical self-representation" of literary activity in 1819, focusing on "writings that seek to state *the case of the nation*—and to do so in such a way as to alter its case" (6). Chandler examines what the texts could be said positively to "state" or what their "self-representation" makes of the historical moment. In *Modernity's Mist*, sustained attention to the poetic dimensions of Romantic texts enables me to extend Chandler's claim about Romanticism's historical engagement to what I call (following Keats himself) a "negative" poetics. In a world that resists direct representation, jarring, asymmetrical relations between semantic meanings and poetic effects point toward an aspect of human experience that eludes full semantic representation (whether of self or nation or world)—a remainder that cannot be fully grasped and that prevents absolute or even comprehensive knowledge of the present. Shaping an aesthetic experience of time through sensory effects, these texts fashion ways of imagining history that are inextricably tied to their "negative" poetic dimensions—ways of imagining thus unavailable, or available differently, in other kinds of writing. Moreover, if a future anterior perspective on the present prevents self-identity, it would, by implication, also prevent a complete or unified sense of national identity from a historical perspective. Therefore, whereas Chandler contends that Romantic texts construct a national self-representation, *Modernity's Mist* would augment that contention by emphasizing how certain texts, however much concerned they are with historical self-identity or national identity, emphasize the impossibility of perfect or complete representation. Their own constructions of temporality show us the impossibility of identifying either a unified self or a full national representation. Sustained attention to the intersection of concepts of time with the poetics of literature brings this limit to light.

Thinking broadly and theoretically about the relations between literary poetics and history, several Romanticists have recently forged innovative historicist methods that, as Kevis Goodman puts it, "reserve a place at the table for sensation and affect," which cannot be easily or immediately resolved into the conventional categories (or "contexts") of social, cultural, or even intellectual histories.[37] In the spirit of such work by Goodman, Deborah White, and Mary Favret, *Modernity's Mist* reads in gaps and silences—and in the tensions between what a text "says" and what it "does"—evidence of a historical experience that cannot be fully told in semantic terms.[38] This book is distinguished from those accounts, however, first, by its focus on futurity—including on the question of how to conceive the present in the shadows of an unknown futurity—and second, by its method of reading literary temporality. For my readings stress how particularities of form and poetics *enact* concepts of time or history in the "time of reading"—by which I mean the way a reader at least potentially experiences the meanings (and revisions of meaning) of a text across the period of time it takes to read it. Especially because I am working across lyric, epic, and prose fiction genres, each text is certainly singular in the way it brings about, in the time of reading, a sense of uncertainty and multiple possibilities and the idea of a historical process in the future anterior imagination.

The Everyday of Romantic Anticipations: A Rhetoric of Nonprophecy

An anticipatory poetics that gives fullness to the present invites critical discussion about how that temporal mode relates to Romantic modes of the prophetic. Despite overlapping concerns, one might characterize the temporality that Keats's, Austen's, and Byron's works share as non-vatic, eschewing the rhetoric of prophecy. Romantic inheritances and revisions of prophetic traditions were remarkably various, as Ian Balfour has shown in *The Rhetoric of Romantic Prophecy*.[39] Balfour provides the following definition of what characteristics the various modalities of prophetic writing have in common:

> The modalities of the prophetic [in the Romantic period] are complex and varied: All are beset by claims of divine inspiration whose face value is impossible to ascertain, and most are marked by obscure figuration and an unpredictable temporality, even when the temporal parameters seem clearly set out by the prophecy itself. (1)

Following this definition, Balfour discusses extensively the work of Blake, Shelley, Wordsworth, and Coleridge as well as a number of German writers while sidelining, for the most part, the contemporary work of the authors at the center of this study: Keats, Austen, and Byron.

There is a logic to Balfour's selection, for although the anticipatory poetics of Keats, Austen, and Byron invite the unpredictability Balfour describes, they do so while favoring worldly, accessible sources of inspiration rather than longing for an inaccessible "divine" or, finally, aspiring to pure transcendence. Consider even a poem such as Keats's "Ode to Psyche," ostensibly Keats's most prophetic lyric. In it, the speaker practically *stumbles onto* the goddess of the soul, his source of inspiration, during an everyday walk. In Wordsworth's "Intimations of Immortality" ode, by contrast, the soul's distance tends to increase with worldly experience, while remaining the principal source of visionary imagination.

As for Austen, a rhetoric of inspiration may be harder to locate. But Emma Woodhouse's meditation at a Highbury shop doorstep, while Harriet mulls muslins, might be the novelist's most compelling statement about poetic inspiration. As she walks to the shop door, Emma might hope to be stimulated by observing the activity of Highbury's professional gentleman, but when the afternoon traffic yields only the seemingly less consequential figures of an old woman, children, and curs, the narrator affirms that, for a lively mind, the humblest everyday scene will suffice:

> Harriet, tempted by every thing and swayed by half a word, was always very long at a purchase; and while she was still hanging over muslins and changing her mind, Emma went to the door for amusement.—Much could not be hoped from the traffic of even the busiest part of Highbury;—Mr. Perry walking hastily by, Mr. William Cox letting himself in at the office door, Mr. Cole's carriage horses returning from exercise, or a stray letter-boy on an obstinate mule, were the liveliest objects she could presume to expect; and when her eyes fell only on the butcher with his tray, a tidy old woman

traveling homewards from shop with her full basket, two curs quarrelling over a dirty bone, and a string of dawdling children round the baker's little bow window eyeing the gingerbread, she knew she had no reason to complain, and was amused enough; quite enough still to stand at the door. A mind lively and at ease, can do with seeing nothing, and can see nothing that does not answer.[40]

This portrait of a "mind lively and at ease" insists that the resources necessary for inspiration and the work of the imagination are the humblest—the most worldly and everyday. Keats's and Austen's perspectives on the work of the imagination, in this way, contrast sharply with the more elevated elaborations characteristic of their contemporaries who align themselves with the prophetic.

Byron, too, as Jerome McGann has observed, envisions inspiration in the very worldly accessibility of beauty.[41] Beauty is a "real presence" for Byron, claims McGann, whereas for Wordsworth, "The world of Derwentwater, the world of Beauty, lies somewhere else—beyond, in some magical place where we are cradled in our nurse's or our mother's arms, as we are at the outset of *The Prelude*, or play children's games at the edge of the sea, as we do at the end of the 'Intimations' Ode."[42] Like Keats's fascination with the relatively minor goddess Psyche—who was, after all, born human—Byron's imagination in *Don Juan* submits to "the empire of the *Musa Pedestris*. Sublimity is abandoned in order to possess Truth and Beauty in a human register."[43] The sensations of worldly, temporal experience are neither at odds with nor merely a stepping-stone toward the historical vision these poetic works achieve. The "mist" that links these imaginative works together grounds them in the temporal world, the life of sensations and thoughts, as Keats might say (*LJK*, 1:185). The "mist" of modernity at once prevents the perfection of clear sight—figuratively inhibiting full knowledge of the present in its historical dimensions—and offers, in the sensory aspects of poetic experience, engagement with those visual and epistemological limits as productive of imaginative possibilities.

Although I will address concepts of time in Percy Shelley's sonnet "England in 1819" and his *Defence of Poetry* briefly in Chapter 2, to some critics his poetry may appear, overall, conspicuous by its absence from the following pages. I decline to read Shelley here in full not owing to any conviction that his conception of time ought to be sharply and thoroughly differentiated from the other literary works in this study but rather owing to the almost singularly prominent role his poetry has played in deconstructionist criticism, *some* of whose tendencies I want to amend or augment in order to open up a new way of understanding Romantic temporality—a strain of it, perhaps, less visible in Shelley's poetry than in the work of Keats, Austen, and Byron.

Deconstructionist aesthetics associates future anterior thinking with history, and Paul de Man as well as deconstructionist critics writing after him typically understand the "historical" as an effect of language; the historical is that which calls for future retroactive understanding because, by way of the incommensurability of the cognitive and performative dimensions of language, history can be named (only) as what disrupts or dis-figures in the linguistic process. As Marc Redfield puts it,

> History must rather be "true" in the sense of being an *event* that leaves a mark on the tropological systems of truth and falsehood. Such an event must be external to the circulation of meaning, but it must also disrupt, alter, and generate meaning. In other words, the event is historical to the extent that it is linguistic, not empirical.[44]

As my previous discussion of poetics and the readings that follow equally attest, I am deeply committed to reading the "play of the letter that dis-figures the structure of comprehension."[45] However, whereas deconstructionist critics refer this disruption of comprehensive understanding—the disfiguration of easily transmissible knowledge—to the conditions of language through which the historical becomes not transparent (as an identity) but legible (in its "literary" inscription), and indeed comes into being, *Modernity's Mist* augments the deconstructionist account of Romantic historicism by explaining the Romantic poetics of epistemological uncertainties—the silences and gaps, ruptures and disruptions—as a Romantic reckoning with the intellectual history of changing concepts of time and with the contemporary debates and dilemmas in historical writing. The poetics of Romantic anticipation described in this book offer ways of engaging imaginatively with a world in which the present and future could not be understood through patterns of the past and in which the quick succession of seemingly large-scale political and social changes made outcomes and causal logic elusive. The disfiguring play of the letter undoubtedly maintains a crucial role in this book's interest in the poetic grammar of what *might will have been*, with its gift of opening up multiple possibilities that need not fit into a comprehensive whole. To date, however, the Romantic intensity with respect to exposing these aspects of language—which made it the prominent historical literary field for theoretical inquiry during deconstruction's heyday—has not been connected historically to the intellectual history of concepts of time and to historiographical debate of the late eighteenth and early nineteenth centuries.

There is also a negative affect associated with deconstructive readings, which is not characteristic of the poetics I describe, which affirm their creative agency through the representation of teeming possibilities. As Geoffrey Hartman summarized it in the foreword to *Deconstruction and Criticism*, the readings in that seminal volume—in seemingly endless repetition of a fearful drop—"disclos[e] again and again the 'abysm' of words."[46] Percy Shelley is a key figure for the "always already" of deconstructive readings, for the discovery, in the words of J. Hillis Miller, of the "impasse [to meaning], whether this dismantling is performed within the writing of the author himself or in the following of that in repetitive retracing by the critic who comes after, as in my discussion here."[47] Negative affect, as Hillis Miller suggests, is at times derived from the writings themselves—as in Shelley's resonant image of the brain turning to sand—while at other times it is discovered and reinforced by the deconstructive critic, who performs the traumatic repetition.[48]

More recently, Marc Redfield makes explicit how closely tied deconstructive theory is to the temporal logic and negative affect of trauma theory. Redfield explains that, for de Manian deconstruction, "History is the site of resistance: the truth of history, for theory, can only be conveyed as a stutter bearing the unspeakable gravity of a trauma."[49] In Redfield's view, de Man's idea of Romantic temporality links the gesture of historicism to deconstruction's ties to psychoanalytic trauma theory, which so frequently have been advanced with Shelley's poetry at the center. What *Modernity's Mist* endeavors to make visible by highlighting the predicament of a Romantic historiography grappling with a future unmoored from the epistemology of precedents is that Romantic anticipations—imaginings of the "now" as what *might will have been* in all its plural possibilities—make the historical world of the present available as a process. Reading Romantic temporality through this critical lens, the emphasis falls less on the hopeless inaccessibility of the historical world, infinitely deferred to a future never to arrive, than on the teeming sense of possibility afforded by the very imagination capable of foregoing the patterns of the past, which is to say the understanding of history through precedent. At a moment when the present age newly became understood as a distinctive historical period that rendered obsolete the paradigms of the past, the literary work of Keats, Austen, and Byron made legible modernity's grounds of being, always on the move.

Chapter Summaries

Chapter 1 tells a counterintuitive story of how historiographies from the mid-eighteenth to the early nineteenth century understood futurity. This narrative establishes the dilemmas for historiography brought to a peak by the political events of the 1790s and after and in light of which, as the succeeding chapters argue, Keats, Austen, and Byron developed as a response what I call a historiographical poetics. This chapter tracks an increasing sense of the unpredictable in writers from William Robertson, Robert Henry, and David Hume to William Godwin, Helen Maria Williams, and William Hazlitt. The work of eighteenth-century Scottish enlightenment historians, which Keats, Austen, and Byron all were avidly reading, was typically guided by a "four-stage theory" of cultural development, and I show how this structure of development generally meant that the sense of the future could be drawn from patterns of the past and was tied to a linear concept of time. When the 1790s brought the immediacy of war in France and a series of events that exceeded calculation, the question of how to write the history of the present age grew increasingly urgent and difficult, as the narrative reliance on precedents no longer sufficed. Helen Maria Williams, for instance, published assumptions about the course of the French Revolution in 1790 that clearly did not hold up after 1793, when she was still (re-)writing and publishing her eyewitness accounts of France. Having to reconsider previously expressed views about the most recent historical age challenged the explanatory power of the largely linear, progressive narration of history. The chapter concludes with an analysis of William Hazlitt's *The Spirit of the Age; Or, Contemporary Portraits*, which in several ways resists the overall linear temporalities of Enlightenment historiographies in favor of a dilating multiplicity of characterizations of the present. Hazlitt's work, published in 1825, appears as the closest nonfiction analogue to the historiographical poetics of Keats, Austen, and Byron.

Chapters 2 and 3 turn to Keats's sonnets and to his odes, respectively. For most of the last two centuries, Keats has been the poet of aesthetic complexity par excellence. Following the New Historicist critique of his poetry as political escapism, numerous critics recovered his political and historical engagements—in the letters, in affiliations between his poetic language and the political discourse of the period, and in his subversive choices of style (for example, the "Cockney couplet") and subject matter (for instance, a pagan discourse of the soul to displace mechanistic philosophy and Christianity). These chapters read, in the temporal complexities of Keats's poetics, a historiographical critique and engagement. In the readerly anticipation of the sonnet's *volta*, for instance, and in the thwarting of the conventional gesture of closure that follows it, Keats suggests the opening up of historical possibilities and a sense of futurity that resist prediction. The everyday situation of reading often generates the sense of possibility in Keats's poetics, felt in the very visceral sense of breathing in "Chapman's Homer," and it is that insistence on the everyday register that links Keats to Austen and Byron and distinguishes much of his poetry from Percy Shelley's. Keats's odes, allowing for even greater flexibility of form, take that sense of possibility further, making mist and dizziness (two kinds of disorientation) the visceral or sensory components of anticipating an unknowable futurity.

Taking the epistemological uncertainty of Keats's anticipations as a point of departure and focus, Chapter 4 develops a Keatsian-Romantic reading of Austen's novel *Persuasion*. Not typically categorized as "Romantic"—in part because its heroine directly critiques contemporary poets—*Persuasion* nevertheless entails anticipatory imagining, in ways that underscore the kind of epistemological uncertainty about the present that we also encounter in Keats. Moreover, to the Keatsian assessment of modernity's temporality, *Persuasion* brings a provisional, revisionary quality of one's relation to the historical. Because future anterior constructions of the present may turn out to be false or fictional in some actual future moment, Austen's novel tells us that these constructions are more provisional than definitive. However fictional these imaginings may be, Austen scarcely suggests that they are *merely* illusory; her narrative fiction shows their real effects on Anne's experience of the present, including by helping Anne make the decision to act.

This chapter argues, moreover, that Anne's provisional relation to the future—because of its obscurity or unpredictability within the scope of her social relations—is repeated in the novel's manner of evoking Britain's collective historical blindness in 1814 regarding Waterloo. For Austen's situating of the novel in the pre-Waterloo "false peace" of the Napoleonic Wars separates her readers from the perspective of the characters by virtue of the temporal and epistemological gap. Post-Waterloo readers are in a position to imagine the characters' sense of "peace" as that which *will have been* a "false peace." The novel's poetics of anticipation conceive of "self" and "world" as ongoing revisionary constructions. Countering recent claims, I argue that *Persuasion* makes the case that literary fictions and the individual imagination can have creative agency in the world via the temporal imagination.[50] Historicist work over the past decade or so shows how Austen engaged in various ways with historical politics and material culture.[51] I extend this claim to the intellectual history of concepts of time by showing how Austen's literary construction of temporality and of the possibilities of creative agency not only reflects an important strain of modernity but also makes an original contribution to this intellectual history by illustrating the life of future anterior imaginings over time.

Chapter 5 argues that Byron's *Don Juan* takes the logic of future anteriority to its most radical conclusion. The inaccessibility of the future in Byron's comic epic justifies an insistent "presentness" in the narrative discourse; not even the poet-author seems to know where his story is headed. This is not to claim that Byron himself had no plan—even though he famously declared as much to his editor John Murray—but that he depicts his narrator as the writer of the poem who is making it up as he goes along, while highlighting the moment-to-moment writing process in the narrative discourse. This chapter argues that Byron's "presentness" derives from the logic of trying to anticipate how the present *will be remembered*—a perspective the narrator takes on and conspicuously mocks but, I argue, cannot do away with. It is indeed the future anterior logic of frustrated predictions that accounts for Byron's radical "presentness."

Because the narrator cannot predict how his own text will unfold, his sense of what is to come is always roughly equivalent to the reader's. The narrative structure takes the shape not of an arc but of a series of loosely linked episodes, allowing the narrative potentially to veer off at any moment in a number of different directions. The alignment of the reader's perspective with that of the unforeseeing poet-narrator brings the reader, over and again in the time of reading, into a sense of surprise about what happens next. This structure emphasizes the impossibility of anticipating the future based on patterns of the past—or the future based on patterns of the present. As often as not, the strict rhyming demands of the *ottava rima* form are what seem to shape narrative developments. Scarcely derived from the fabric of what has been, these developments exceed and so revise the bounds of what previously seemed possible. Whereas eighteenth- and nineteenth-century notions of progress "closed off the future as a *source* of disruption with the aid of teleological versions of history,"[52] Byron's narrative logic leaves room for the unpredictability of the future. *Don Juan* is neither progressive nor regressive but digressive, imagining a world of multiple possibilities for the present. As in Austen, Byron's "present" appears as an unending revisionary process. But whereas Austen's heroine makes provisional assessments of how the present will appear in memory, Byron's solution to the tensions of modernity is to foreground the materiality of language and rhyme as it bears on the poet-narrator's moment-to-moment writing process. The most radical solution to modernity's mist—the tension between an unpredictable future and the urgency to define the present from a future vantage—is to engage with the present's flux while foregoing anticipations altogether.

1. FROM PRECEDENTS TO THE UNPREDICTABLE: HISTORIOGRAPHICAL FUTURITIES

It is perhaps unsurprising that very little criticism has accrued on the somewhat counterintuitive topic of how historiography conceives futurity. Reinhart Koselleck's *Futures Past: On the Semantics of Historical Time* is a significant exception, perhaps *the* significant book-length exception, which makes the case that an eighteenth-century idea of historical progress ushered in the temporality of modernity. He defines that modernity, in part, as the conception of an unknown and unforeseeable future, which historically displaces other kinds of previously dominant futures—futures shaped by eschatological and rational prediction, for example, as well as those tied to a circular model of time that introduces diagnoses of the past into the future. Describing eighteenth-century philosophical notions of historical progress as introducing a "horizon of expectations" involving an unknown future, Koselleck asserts that it is the idea of progress that divorced the present from patterns of previous experience in the course of the eighteenth century.[1] For historians and philosophers began to imagine in the eighteenth century that a temporal future (i.e., not an eschatological one) could be paradigmatically different from the present; at the same time, what that difference would look like was wholly unforeseeable.

In this chapter, I aim to focus in a nuanced way on concepts of time and progress in historical writing from around 1750 until 1830 in order to show how the idea of a predictable futurity, based on a linear sense of time and causal relations, persisted in many eighteenth-century British historiographies—specifically those historical narratives most powerfully governed by a philosophy of progress. In view of that persistence, I argue that it is the narratives that most overtly sidestep the philosophical assumptions of linear progress and formally stand at odds with linear narration that leave room for an unpredictable futurity. In this way, I revise Koselleck's story about the advent of modernity to suggest that historical narratives that assume alternatives to linear time, both formally and conceptually, better accommodate modernity's unpredictable futurity and its potential to disrupt expectations than do narratives of progress.[2]

Not until the end of the century does predictability become radically questioned in a way that generates altogether alternative temporalities to linear progress, regress, or circularity. In the 1790s, for instance, however much Helen Maria Williams maintains her faith in the principles of equality and liberty and refers to the overall progress of the French Revolution, in the pages of her *Letters Written in France* the present age appears increasingly like an experiment in historical change with an unpredictable outcome. Her epistolary narrative is less progressive than revisionary, as she is compelled by political events to rethink previously stated assumptions. In William Hazlitt's *The Spirit of the Age* with which this chapter concludes, a full-fledged lateral sense of time accommodates a present of proliferating simultaneities.[3] It does so while wholly sidelining the linear chronological development and narratives of cultural progress that crucially organize so much eighteenth-century historical writing. In the majority of eighteenth-century historiography, historians assumed that the patterns established in a historical narrative of past—as in the way a narrative characterized the causal relations between one event and another event that came after it—served also as patterns for understanding the present (and future). In Hazlitt's historiography, however, what I call a lateral temporality unmoors the present from established patterns by not tracing any genealogy whatsoever for the spirit of the age. In *The Spirit of the Age*, the absence of *any* set of past patterns combined with the proliferation of heterogeneous ways in which the spirit of the present age becomes visible, by implication, leaves the imagination relatively free to contemplate wholly new patterns for the future; given the heterogeneity of Hazlitt's present, one can see the future open up in multiple possible ways. In this respect, Hazlitt does not develop but displaces the structures of eighteenth-century philosophical histories: largely unified genealogies that narrate British identity in a chronologically linear fashion from its origins in Greco-Roman culture to modern British commercial society.

Since around the time of J. G. A. Pocock's *Barbarism and Religion*, there has been a critical tendency in eighteenth-century studies to refer not to The Enlightenment but to multiple Enlightenments, suggesting that the period witnessed a number of disparate intellectual movements that do not easily or fully cohere. Pocock wrote, "I have no quarrel with the concept of Enlightenment; I merely contend that it occurred in too many forms to be comprised within a single definition and history, and that we do better to refer to a family of Enlightenments, displaying both family resemblances and family quarrels (some of them bitter and even bloody)."[4] Although that critique evokes a historical sensibility similar to the heterogeneity of multiple spirits of the age we find in Hazlitt's historiography, the rhetoric and formal accommodation of multiplicity are restricted to Pocock's critical lens, appearing largely absent from eighteenth-century historical texts, whose authors, as we shall see, stress the systematic unity of their subject matter and composition. This is not to say that Pocock's historical perspective is at all incorrect but to emphasize that Hazlitt's historiographical sensibility is distinct from that of his eighteenth-century precursors because of his foregoing of the rhetoric of unity for a historical heterogeneity.

In the eighteenth century, with the publication of such historiographical works as *The Age of Louis XIV* and *The Age of Louis XV*, Voltaire (followed by Scottish Enlightenment historiographers, among others) made the present and the very recent past into the stuff of history. This shift to modern historiography intensified the question of how historiographers were to understand the future. As a historical context potentially different from the present and one in relation to which the present would be reevaluated, ideas of the historical future started to affect how writers thought about, and structured, their historical writings. Put another way, the dramatically increased proximity of the future to the historical period that formed the subject of a historical writing put pressure on that relation between historiography and the future. If one were writing about the twelfth century in 1780, the events of the next fifty years would seem relatively inconsequential compared to a situation in which one were writing in 1780 about only a generation or so prior to the present.

This chapter tells a story of how historical writing in the eighteenth and early nineteenth centuries began to encounter and accommodate futurity in order to establish the intellectual context of a historiographical dilemma to which the literary works in the following chapters offer a response. With the historiographical question of how to imagine futurity in view, Keats's, Austen's, and Byron's poetics of anticipation appear more readily, as I shall claim, as historiographical aesthetics in that they address the same question. I begin with the most popular kind of history of the mid- to late eighteenth century: Scottish Enlightenment philosophical history. Despite its pervasive commitment to the idea of linear progress, significant formal tensions with linear temporality persistently mark that historiography, straining or interrupting the idea of progress. These formal tensions with linear narration distinguish Enlightenment philosophical histories from the still highly respected humanist or classical historiographical traditions, which observed a strict sense of linearity both in the chronology of what happened (by which I mean what narrative theorists sometimes call *histoire*) and in the way they presented what happened (the narrative discourse or *récit*).[5] Classical historical narratives move steadily forward in step with the chronology of the stories they tell. As we have seen in the example from Keats with which this study began, the idea of a dark futurity tends to disrupt a linear sense of time. Although mid-eighteenth-century historical writings by and large do not include a sense of the future explicitly in their imagination of history, their disturbances of linear narrative discourse accompany formal innovations in some respects akin to those in Romantic-period writing. Along those lines, this chapter concludes with a comparison of Robert Henry's (mid-eighteenth-century) formal innovations with William Hazlitt's. But whereas Romantic writers explicitly departed from linear conceptions of time, the high sense of decorum guiding eighteenth-century historiography led Enlightenment historians to negotiate—and whenever possible to gloss over—narrative tensions with linear time (at the level of *récit*). This historiographical tension between formal innovations and linear temporality (between *récit* and *histoire*) was brought into new—more glaring and self-conscious—light at the end of the century with the events of the French Revolution.

In my analyses of historical writings, I attend both to the history of ideas, especially ideas related to time and cultural development, and to the formal dimensions of historical narratives. In this double approach to historiographical analysis, I follow the work of Mark Salber Phillips, who observed (about a decade ago) that

> for nearly a generation now students of historiography have effectively divided themselves into two camps. On one side stand those who approach the subject primarily as a problem in intellectual history; on the other we find those for whom historical writing is at bottom an act of imagination to be understood in literary (and especially narratological) terms. Valuable work has been done on both sides of this methodological divide, but it has not proven easy to marry the two approaches.[6]

Beautifully modeling this marriage, Phillips's study *Society and Sentiment: Genres of Historical Writing in Britain, 1740–1820* illuminated how the narrative innovations of eighteenth-century writers helped accommodate a greater range of social experience than historiography hitherto had done in order to appeal to the growing readership of an increasingly literate, commercial society. This chapter aims to bring Phillips's double methodology to questions of temporality, thereby helping us ask more nuanced questions about the relationship between Enlightenment and Romantic historiographies than the comparison typically has received.[7]

While historiography took many new forms and came in an increasing range of genres especially toward the end of the eighteenth century, this first section of this chapter will focus primarily on two philosophical histories, Robert Henry's *History of Great Britain* and William Robertson's *History of the Reign of the Emperor Charles V.* In a fashion exemplary of midcentury philosophical histories, these texts present a range of formal innovations that display, even as they attempt to conceal, significant tensions between, on the one hand, a commitment to linear narration (*récit*) that would formally reinforce the story of forward cultural progress and, on the other, the desire to expand what constitutes history in order to accommodate the new desires and needs of eighteenth-century British readers.[8] I show that eighteenth-century philosophical historiography presented more complex narrative temporalities than critics sometimes acknowledge and suggest that we might see that complexity as a formal destabilization (at the level of *récit*), however subtle, of the philosophy of linear cultural progress (the *histoire*) that these same texts typically espouse.

The subtleties of those destabilizations were largely lost, however, on Romantic-period critics of Enlightenment historiography. In his essay "Of History and Romance," William Godwin reassesses the stakes of historiography when he summarizes the prevailing principles of Enlightenment historiography as offering us only precedents to repeat. He subsequently makes an impassioned call for history, instead, to disclose to us "new and untrodden paths":

> General history will furnish us with precedents in abundance, will show us
> how that which has happened in one country has been repeated in another,
> and may perhaps even instruct us how that which has occurred in the annals
> of mankind, may under similar circumstances be produced again. But, if the
> energy of our minds should lead us to aspire to something more animated and
> noble than dull repetition, if we love the happiness of mankind enough to feel
> ourselves impelled to explore new and untrodden paths, we must then not rest
> contented with considering society in a mass, but must analyse the materials
> of which it is composed. It will be necessary for us to scrutinize the nature of
> man, before we can pronounce what it is of which social man is capable.[9]

Although Godwin expresses dissatisfaction with the aims of Enlightenment historiography, the areas of analysis he identifies appear not altogether different from those we can find in Enlightenment thought: "society in a

mass" and "the nature of man." Godwin emphasizes the relative importance of the latter, but the categories come from his Enlightenment precursors, who circulate in their histories' "dull repetition." Godwin, however,
aspires to draw from historical analysis of the individual "man" a genuinely
new knowledge: to imagine and "to explore new and untrodden paths."
Cultural and social development in the Romantic period need not be a
repetition of predictable behaviors. Rather, at the end of the eighteenth
century, the future Godwin desires for "social man" involves a hitherto
unknown and thus unpredictable future, which nevertheless developed out
of some of the categories and concerns rigorously defined by his Enlightenment precursors.

The idea of cultural progress that dominated eighteenth-century British historiography, sometimes called the "four-stage theory," envisioned a
"culture" (such as English culture) changing and becoming progressively
refined and civilized in four distinct stages. These stages, assumed to occur
in the same order in every culture, were defined above all by the predominant mode of subsistence. Ronald Meek summarizes it thus:

> In its most specific form, the theory was that society "naturally" or "nor-
> mally" progressed over time through four more or less distinct and consec-
> utive stages, each corresponding to a different mode of subsistence, these
> stages being defined as hunting, pasturage, agriculture, and commerce. To
> each of these modes of subsistence, it came to be argued, there corresponded
> different sets of ideas and institutions relating to law, property, and govern-
> ment, and also different sets of customs, manners, and morals.[10]

According to this stadial theory, one could encounter a new society in
another region, such as the Native Americans, and make assumptions
about their degree of cultural development based mostly on observing
their modes of subsistence. Not all societies progressed at the same rate,
and not even all individuals within the same nation did. Hence the focus of
James Chandler's *England in 1819* on the concept of "uneven development"[11]
that came out of the Scottish Enlightenment and the "new conception of
anachronism, now [by the Romantic period] understood as a measurable
form of dislocation."[12] Unevenness refers less commonly to the development within one society or nation than to the comparison, say, between
life in England and in Indonesia. The theory holds that no matter how
undeveloped at present, all societies are progressing in a forward linear
march toward the same end: commercial, civilized society. Certainly, that
was not the only story told. Notably, for instance, Adam Ferguson's *An
Essay on the History of Civil Society* (1767) departed from the assumption

that moral improvement necessarily attends economic progress.[13] Further-more, Ferguson did not trust that the effects of social refinement in civil society were irreversible but worried that the peace secured by legal and military advances would lead to a slackening of civic virtue.[14] However, notwithstanding the antiprogressive threat of moral regression and decline of civil society, Ferguson measured society conceptually in a linear fashion, whether he observed progress, regress, or stagnation.

From the perspective of intellectual and cultural history, the aim of a commercial, polite society defines the Scottish Enlightenment *idea* of time and progress—one model of progress that applies universally. Based on that assumption, Hugh Blair determines the superiority of modern historiography over ancient:

> For instance, in History, there is certainly more political knowledge in
> several European nations at present, than there was in antient Greece and
> Rome. We are better acquainted with the nature of government, because
> we have seen it under a greater variety of forms and revolutions. The world
> is more laid open than it was in former times; commerce is greatly enlarged;
> more countries are civilized; posts are every where established; intercourse
> is become more easy; and the knowledge of facts, by consequence, more
> attainable. All these are great advantages to Historians.[15]

The host of interwoven improvements that Blair lists as characteristic of eighteenth-century British society—commerce, civilization, communication of information and people, and the easy attainment of facts—make historiography better, too. In Jane Austen's novel *Northanger Abbey*, Henry Tilney, who discusses historical writing with the protagonist and is clearly well read in it, channels Blair's stadial theory (and his optimism about British society) when he realizes that Catherine Morland has entertained the idea that his father could have murdered his mother and successfully hidden his crime:

> "Remember the country and the age in which we live. Remember that we
> are English, that we are Christians. Consult your own understanding, your
> own sense of the probable, your own observation of what is passing around
> you—Does our education prepare us for such atrocities? Do our laws connive
> at them? Could they be perpetrated without being known, in a country like
> this, where social and literary intercourse is on such a footing; where every
> man is surrounded by a neighborhood of voluntary spies, and where roads
> and newspapers lay everything open? Dearest Miss Morland, what ideas have
> you been admitting?"[16]

Austen's narrative distances itself from this historical ideology, however, when it turns out that, albeit not a murderer, General Tilney displays a capacity for incivility and real cruelty, suddenly dismissing Catherine from his house without explanation and without even adequate means to be transported to her home. Catherine's suspicions had some hint of truth—a truth that Henry Tilney's logic of historical progress would not admit. The relative skepticism of *Northanger Abbey* aligns its historical thinking more closely with Ferguson than with Blair.

Henry Tilney, of course, is not talking about historical writing, whether here or elsewhere in the novel, as a *form* of mediation—let alone an ideologically charged one. Like Henry Tilney, literary historians and social scientists alike have often abstracted the linear idea of progress from the forms of the historical narratives that develop—and often complicate or distort—its assertion.[17] I turn now to an eighteenth-century historical writing informed by this stadial model of progress to show how, even in its most optimistic expressions, the formal dynamics of eighteenth-century historiography, to a certain extent, come into tension with the abstract idea of progress that the story (*histoire*) tells.

Diverting the Line: Simultaneities in Robert Henry's *History of Great Britain*

Robert Henry's *History of Great Britain: From the First Invasion of It by Julius Caesar. Written on a New Plan* (1771–93) is not now a well-known eighteenth-century philosophical history, but it was widely read in its day.[18] More important, Henry developed one of the most interesting formal solutions to accommodate the widening range of topics considered crucial to the telling of history in the late eighteenth century. Henry's aims in constructing his history on a "new plan" were to maintain middle-class readers' attention with a continuous storyline; to reduce the confusion caused by interweaving multiple narratives (such as ecclesiastical versus military history); and to enable the reader always to have vividly in mind a sense of the "whole." Imagining his audience, Henry explains certain challenges of philosophical historians who typically shared these three aims:

> Writers of the greatest genius find it no easy task to form civil, military, and ecclesiastical affairs into one easy, clear, and unperplexed narration. It is sometimes almost indispensably necessary to break off the thread of one story, before it is brought to a proper period, in order to introduce and bring forward another, of a very different kind. This unavoidably occasions some

confusion. The reader's attention is diverted, the gratification of his curiosity is disagreeably suspended, and it is sometimes so long before he is brought back to his former track, that it is hardly possible for him to recollect the scattered members of the same narration, and to form distinct conceptions of the whole.[19]

In other words, Henry indicates that linear narration, separation of different historical topics into discrete narrations, and clear principles of organization to reduce readers' confusion were at the forefront of his mind when he conceived the innovative structure of his work. Henry *would*, in fact, break his story off at certain points, but it would all be done with predictable regularity and a sense of uniformity.

To reduce confusion, Henry divided his *History*, first of all, into seven separate histories covering the topics of civil and military history; ecclesiastical history; constitution, laws, government, and courts of justice; history of learning and learned men; the arts, useful and ornamental; history of commerce, shipping, coins, and commodities; and manners and customs. But Henry also divided the work chronologically into ten books (each of which contained the seven separate "chapters") running from the beginning to the end of a distinct historical period. The first book, for instance, covers the history of Great Britain from the invasion by the Romans under Julius Caesar until the arrival of the Saxons in 449 AD. That book, as with each of the others, contains seven chapters divided according to topic; chapter 1 covers civil and military history, chapter 2 concerns religious history, and so on.

The purpose of this elaborate plan was to eliminate the sense of the story changing tracks or being interrupted by the introduction of a new topic: that is, to preserve linear thematic regularity. In his preface, Henry explains that the benefits of this design are to provide the reader with great variety without confusion:

The materials belonging to one subject are divided, without violence or injury, from those belonging to another; and each of them are formed into a separate narration, which is conducted, from beginning to end, without interruption, or the intervention of any foreign matter. By this means, every thing appears distinct and clear; and the reader pursues one subject to an end, before he enters upon another.[20]

In a history ordered only by chronology, of course, that kind of "intervention" would have occurred repeatedly. Protected from "the intervention of any foreign matter" as well as "violence or injury"—Henry's war metaphors are remarkable—the reader can enjoy peaceful entertainment. Writing to her friend Martha Lloyd on November 12, 1800, Jane Austen playfully imagined how Henry's "distinct and clear" design might be either undermined or further demarcated in their daily practice:

> I am reading Henry's History of England, which I will repeat to you in any manner you may prefer, either in a loose, disultary, unconnected strain, or dividing my recital as the Historian divides it himself, into seven parts, The Civil & Military—Religion—Constitution—Learning & Learned Men—Arts & Sciences—Commerce Coins & Shipping—& Manners;—so that for every evening of the week there will be a different subject; The Friday's lot, Commerce, Coin & Shipping, You will find the least entertaining; but the next Eveng's portion will make amends.[21]

"[Loose], disultary, unconnected": these are the adjectives of Henry's historiographical nightmare. They are the narrative tendencies that threatened to intrude as the scope of eighteenth-century historical writing expanded. The novelty of Henry's design suggests the lengths to which he would go to try to maintain linear narration, matching the linear idea of cultural progress toward civilization. The challenge came from an equal desire, typical of the eighteenth-century philosophical history, of amplifying the range and kinds of historical knowledge. Henry, like his contemporaries, not only offered readers a broader range of topics than histories typically had ever provided but also attempted to convey a comprehensive understanding of the underlying trends connecting the different threads. That is, Henry's comprehensive historical episteme linked the history of learning in Book V, say, to the same book's history of commerce, and so on.

What Austen's proposed daily program helps highlight is that Henry's expansive *History* proceeds not purely in a linear temporal fashion. At the end of the week, Austen's Sunday reading (or recital) takes her chronologically back to where she began Monday evening. Given Henry's ambition with respect to clarity and order, shifting back and forth between topics to maintain perfect chronological continuity was not an option:

> Examples of some degree of perplexity, proceeding from this cause [shifting between topics or inserting long explanatory digressions], might be produced (if it were not unnecessary and invidious) from the works of our most justly admired historians: and the compilations of so many others are, on this account, little better than a heap of undigested materials. For this reason, it would have been equally absurd and vain, to have attempted to form all the various subjects which compose the following work, into one continued

narration. This could have produced nothing but a perfect chaos of confusion. (xxxvi–xxxvii)

"One continued narration" is the perfect chronological line that Henry sees fit to break, as neatly as possible, in order to accommodate the expansive contents of his historical work as well as to avoid simply compiling "undigested materials." Two competing principles to which Henry was committed come to light in this passage: linear narration and "digestion" or explanation. Both serve the aim of clarity and understanding, but they stand in formal tension with one another. In this respect, the expository challenges Henry faces exemplify Scottish Enlightenment historiography, although historians negotiated those challenges in various ways.

Robertson's *History of the Reign of the Emperor Charles V*: Accommodating a Comprehensive View of Progress

In his remarkably influential *Lectures on Rhetoric and Belles Lettres* (first published in 1783), Hugh Blair set out, among other things, the main principles of historical composition in the Scottish Enlightenment, drawing on classical ideals and adapting them for the emerging audience. Resembling Robert Henry's concern that the events and details not amount to a "heap of undigested materials," Blair's lectures on historiography explain the necessity of the historian's comprehensive view of society, conveyed to the reader so that the various facts and details appear part of a unified "plan or system":

> Whether pleasure or instruction be the end sought by the study of History, either of them is enjoyed to much greater advantage, when the mind has always before it the progress of some one great plan or system of actions; when there is some point or centre, to which we can refer the various facts related by the Historian. . . . We should be able to trace all the secret links of the chain, which binds together remote, and seemingly unconnected events.[22]

The problem for eighteenth-century historians was how to convey the philosophical interrelatedness of events—the "progress of some *one* great plan or system," a unified and comprehensive vision by which we can imagine the "secret links" between events—without compromising the narrative continuity and formal integrity about which, as we have seen, Robert Henry too was so concerned.

For the work that scholars consider his masterpiece, *The History of the Reign of the Emperor Charles V*, William Robertson announced, in his opening words, the narrative primacy and organizing principle of progress: "No period in the history of ones [sic] own country can be considered as altogether uninteresting. Such transactions as tend to illustrate the progress of its constitution, laws, or manners, merit the utmost attention."[23] Robertson deftly negotiated the narrative tension between, on the one hand, the need to make visible an underlying *philosophy* (a unified, comprehensive vision) of cultural "progress" by way of explanations ("disquisitions") and, on the other, the desire for a seamlessly progressive, linear narrative in several ways (xii). Perhaps most notably, he composed a preliminary essay of about one hundred pages, titled "A View of the Progress of Society in Europe, From the Subversion of the Roman Empire to the Beginning of the Sixteenth Century." Rather than occasionally having to stop and fill in the long history of a political institution, manners, a law, or a custom in the midst of telling the story of sixteenth-century Great Britain under Charles V, Robertson offered a sweeping account of that broad European history in his lengthy introductory "View." He explains, "my readers could derive little instruction from such a history of the reign of Charles V. without some information concerning the state of Europe previous to the sixteenth century" (xi–xii). To understand the state of the nation in the sixteenth century, systematic reference to earlier times was necessary. Robertson's prelude, however, deftly defeated the problem of chronological disjuncture that could arise from a reader's need to know the longer history of, for instance, the role of a religious institution or a property law in order to comprehend the significance of its impact or alteration in the sixteenth century.

But even within that preliminary essay on ancient and medieval times, which served to preclude chronological disjuncture in the main body of the work, there lurked the additional formal problem of what to do with scholarly explanations ("critical disquisitions"). Serious scholars would demand the kinds of explanations and verifications of historical claims that, for nonspecialists, would interrupt the entertaining story of what happened and of how past cultures operated. "In this part of my work," Robertson explains,

> I have been led into several critical disquisitions, which belong more properly to the province of the lawyer or antiquary, than to that of the historian. These I have placed at the end of the first volume, under the title of Proofs and Illustrations. Many of my readers will, probably, give little attention to such researches. To some they may, perhaps, appear the most curious and interesting part of my work. (xii–xiii)

Robertson solved the problem with an appendix—for some to ignore, for others to relish. What might have appeared as loose, desultory, or simply non-narrative passages in the midst of the chronologically forward-moving story of Europe prior to 1600 could be, in this way, contained. But the necessity of finding such a solution—what Mark Salber Phillips describes as Robertson's "hierarchy of narrative and non-narrative elements"[24]—points to the tension between maintaining the conventions of classical history while meeting the demands of modern audiences not only to imagine a more capacious view for historical writing but also to satisfy both scholars and laypersons at once. From the perspective of form, Robertson mostly succeeds in maintaining linear narration; that is, potential frictions or mis-alignments between the temporality of the historical "story" and that of the narrative discourse are kept to a minimum, as the main narratives of the history proceed according to a chronological order. However, the different kinds of discourses sealed out in the introductory "View of the Progress of Society in Europe" and its appendix show how much Robertson had to withhold from the main narratives in order to try to preserve the appeal-ingly steady and unbroken line.

Cause and Effect; Or, Mastering the Future with Enlightenment Historiography

In the eighteenth century, historical narratives typically began with the same cultural point of origin from which the narrative line proceeded chronologically forward, tracing cause and effect along the way. In this way, these historiographies elucidated not only what happened but also the underlying *systems* of political and social change. Eighteenth-century British historiographies—such as David Hume's *The History of England* (1754–61) and John Millar's *An Historical View of the English Government* (1787), in addition to the works by Henry and Robertson discussed in the last sections—trace British society from ancient Greek and Roman civilization to the Glorious Revolution of 1688. Hugh Blair famously lec-tured on the importance of the historian's "unfolding of secret causes and springs":

> The first virtue of Historical Narration, is Clearness, Order, and due
> Connection. To attain this, the Historian must be completely master of his
> subject; he must see the whole as at one view; and comprehend the chain and
> dependence of all its parts, that he may introduce everything in its proper
> place; that he may lead us smoothly along the track of affairs which are

recorded, and may always give us the satisfaction of seeing how one event arises out of another.[25]

If, as Blair prescribes that it should, "one event arises out of another" in every case, the "chain and dependence"—that is, the underlying systemic logic of cause and effect connecting event to event—which extends across time, implicitly could include events up to the present and encompass future events as well. A historian who is "completely master of his subject" can "comprehend the chain" that binds events across time, the chain that restricts the possibilities of anything occurring whose relation to events prior would appear to break its logic. Blair notably recognized this narrative quality as specific to the moderns. "Though the antient Historians set before us the particular facts which they relate, in a very distinct and beautiful manner, yet sometimes they do not give us a clear view of all the political causes, which affected the situation of affairs of which they treat."[26] Only in the modern world, according to Hume, does the historian's "mastery of his subject" concern the cause-and-effect relations of events.

Such "mastery" of the subject in David Hume's hands more than implicitly extends into the present and future. In the *Enquiry Concerning Human Understanding*, Hume observes, "all our experimental conclusions proceed upon the supposition, that the future will be conformable to the past."[27] The practical point of understanding the historical "science" of cause-and-effect relationships is for thinking about—and, moreover, helping control and shape—the future. Hume writes, "The only immediate utility of all sciences, is to teach us, *how to control and regulate future events* by their causes" (113, emphasis mine). History teaches us to do so by revealing to us "the regular springs of human action and behavior," which cross all cultures (or at least cross from Greco-Roman culture to French and English):

> Would you know the sentiments, inclinations, and course of life of the Greeks and Romans? Study well the temper and actions of the French and English. You cannot be much mistaken in transferring to the former *most* of the observations, which you have made with regard to the latter. Mankind are so much the same, in all times and places, that history informs us of nothing new or strange in this particular. Its chief use is only to discover the constant and universal principles of human nature, by shewing men in all varieties of circumstances and situations, and furnishing us with materials, from which we may form our observations, and become acquainted with the regular springs of human action and behaviour. These records of wars, intrigues, factions, and revolutions, are so many collections of experiments,

> by which the politician or moral philosopher fixes the principles of his
> science, in the same manner as the physician or natural philosopher becomes
> acquainted with the nature of plants, minerals, and other external objects, by
> the experiments which he forms concerning them. (122–23)

Historical writing—"records of wars, intrigues, factions, and revolutions"—tells us "nothing new or strange" with respect to human behavior. Therefore, "by shewing men in all varieties of circumstances and situations," history can teach the politician or the moral philosopher to predict behavior in a certain possible situation and thereby enable him to manipulate circumstantial "causes" and control future effects.

In this vein, Hume's contemporary Hugh Blair, too, conceived history as "a record of truth for the instruction of humankind."[28] Furthermore, according to Blair, the historian must be well versed in two areas of knowledge in particular: human nature and political situations or systems of government. These are the underlying "springs" and "causes" of what has happened in the world—and, instructively, of what in the future *could* happen:

> I proceed next to observe, that in order to fulfill the end of History, the
> Author must study to trace to their springs the actions and events which he
> records. Two things are especially necessary for his doing this successfully;
> a thorough acquaintance with human nature and political knowledge, or
> acquaintance with government. The former is necessary to account for the
> conduct of individuals, and to give just views of their character; the latter,
> to account for the revolutions of government, and the operation of political
> causes on public affairs. Both must concur, in order to form a completely
> instructive Historian.[29]

Only the historian who wields a comprehensive knowledge of (or, as Blair puts it, "thorough acquaintance" with) both human nature and political science is fit to instruct humankind. Like Blair, Hume imagined the plumbing of the depths of "human nature" as a necessary and realizable goal, achieved through studying not only the "records of wars, intrigues, factions, and revolutions" but also one's own accumulated experience of having seen the "actions, expressions, and even gestures" of men in a variety of professional and social situations:

> Hence likewise [to histories] the benefit of that experience, acquired by
> long life and a variety of business and company, in order to instruct us in
> the principles of human nature, and regulate our future conduct, as well as
> speculation. By means of this guide, we mount up to the knowledge of men's

inclinations and motives, from their actions, expressions, and even gestures; and again, descend to the interpretation of their actions from the knowledge of their motives and inclinations. The general observations treasured up by a course of experience, give us the clue of human nature, and teach us to unravel all its intricacies.[30]

The instructive "end of History" that Hume and Blair envisioned for eighteenth-century historiography demanded of the historian a "thorough" knowledge of human nature in a great variety of political and social situations. Assuming, as Hume overtly does, that the patterns of cause and effect in the future will adhere to those in the past, a person armed with this double knowledge of human nature and political situations can learn from historiography to "control and regulate future events by their causes." It is in this way that eighteenth-century historical writing and its ideas of progress close off the potential for futurity to disrupt patterns of the past.

How William Godwin Imagined the Historiographical Stakes Anew in the 1790s

In *The Social Contract* (1762), Jean-Jacques Rousseau famously aimed to examine things not as they are but as they might be: in other words, to show how the political future might radically disrupt patterns of the past and present. Rousseau's treatise begins by announcing, "I want to inquire whether in the civil order there can be some legitimate and sure rule of administration, taking men as they are, and the laws as they can be."[31] In his essay "Of History and Romance," composed in 1797, Godwin inherited, and interpreted for historiographical purposes, Rousseau's visionary political ambition to imagine a future based not on precedents (how society has taken shape in the past) but on possibilities that exceed experience. For Godwin, the vision of an unprecedented future (whether legal or otherwise) lies in "taking men as they are," while probing the hitherto unexplored depths of their possibilities. Whereas Hume, Blair, and other eighteenth-century historiographers aim to instruct readers how to regulate themselves and manipulate situations according to things as they have been and as they are, Godwin imagines history's purpose as the discovery of human capacities for shaping a world of things as they are not—or, rather, as they have not yet been. Revising the instructive aims of Enlightenment historiography, Godwin's ambition for historiography is to help us envision a world of such "sources and effects, as, though they have never yet occurred, are within the capacities of our nature" (457).

Following the French Revolution, with its abolishing of the ancien régime and surprising bloodshed under Robespierre, the period of the 1790s ushered in a heightened sense that the future could bear little resemblance to the past. As Koselleck has argued of this period in Europe broadly, "the divide between previous experience and coming expectation opened up, and the difference between past and present increased, so that lived time was experienced as a rupture, as a period of transition in which the new and unexpected continually happened."[32] Godwin's essay "Of History and Romance" begins by envisioning that rupture as an opportunity for historiographical thinking actively to shape society based on previously unexplored human capacities. He sees the key to this exploration in the life of the individual.

Although Godwin's eighteenth-century precursors express a sustained historical interest in studying how human nature responds in certain situations, they either focus on a generalized view of human nature or, when focusing on an individual, regard only those individual traits or actions that have some visible influence on matters of public importance. In Godwin's description of prevailing trends in historiography, we easily recognize William Robertson's interest in Native Americans—whom Robertson describes as "ancient inhabitants" of the "new world"[33]—as well as the historiographical rationale of learning causal relations espoused by Blair and Hume:

> It is curious, and it is important, to trace the progress of mankind from the savage to the civilized state; to observe the points of similitude between the savages of America and the savages of ancient Italy or Greece; to investigate the rise of property moveable to immoveable; and thus to operate the causes that operate universally upon masses of men under given circumstances, without being turned aside in the operation by the varying character of individuals.[34]

While these kinds of historical writing study human nature in general, they neglect the singularities of the individual. Godwin observes this distinction in order to assert the value of "being turned aside" by human variations, by precisely the characteristics of the individual that would inhibit generalization. Godwin's provocative expression suggests that the linearity and teleological force of these progress narratives pose a contradistinction to his own conception of a historiography that begins from an interruption—a "turning aside" or digression from the universal "progress of mankind."

As we have seen vividly in Robert Henry's project of writing multiple parallel histories, eighteenth-century historiography expanded its scope to include variety—a variety of material and social histories previously neglected by historical writing. But those innovations, in Godwin's view, still ignore "the knowledge of the individual," which he regards as "that which can alone give energy and utility to the records of our social existence."[35] In contrast to what Godwin sees as the potential for historical writing to "excit[e] our feelings" in a way that would inspire visionary social change, Enlightenment narratives of progress, however formally innovative, only instruct readers in custom and cultural repetition en masse:

> The fundamental article in this branch of historical investigation, is the progress and varieties of civilization. But there are many subordinate channels into which it has formed itself. We may study the history of eloquence or the history of philosophy. We may apply ourselves to the consideration of the arts of life, and the arts of refinement and pleasure. . . . Nay, we may descend still lower; we may have our attention engrossed by the succession of archons and the adjustment of Olympiads; or may apply ourselves entirely to the examination of medals and coins.
>
> There are those who conceive that history, in one or all the kinds here enumerated, is the only species of history deserving a serious attention. They disdain the records of individuals. To interest our passions, or employ our thoughts about personal events, be they of patriots, of authors, of heroes or kings, they regard as a symptom of effeminacy. Their mighty minds cannot descend to be busied about any thing less than the condition of nations, and the collation and comparison of successive ages. Whatever would disturb by exciting our feelings the torpid tranquility of the soul, they have in unspeakable abhorrence.[36]

Even Enlightenment histories about one prominent individual fail to impassion us because they restrict their image to the public self: "I am not contented to observe such a man upon the public stage, I would follow him into his closet."[37] Godwin contends that it is not the visible character but the private selves of great men that interest us; they can excite our passions and provide resources for imagining a different future.

In *The History of the Reign of the Emperor Charles V*, William Robertson resolutely remained on the public stage with the king, explaining in his preface,

> I have endeavored to render my account of [the age of Charles V], an introduction to the history of Europe subsequent to his reign. While his numerous Biographers describe his personal qualities and actions . . . it hath been

my purpose to record only those great transactions in his reign, the effects of which were universal, or continue to be permanent. (xi)

By avoiding "personal qualities and actions," Robertson can write a historical account from the point of view of a comprehensive philosophical eye: an ostensibly all-encompassing view, taking account less of the individual emperor than of "the age." Charles V is the subject only insofar as his qualities are those of the age. In the absence of any peculiarities of the individual, all Britons can find their identity in Robertson's work. Godwin's critique suggests this kind of national identification misses the distinctive characteristics of the individual and thus fails to stir our passions by virtue of personal qualities. The ancient historians fare much better in this respect than do the moderns: "Read on the one hand Thucydides and Livy," Godwin proposes, "and on the other Hume and Voltaire and Robertson. When we admire the personages of the former, we simply enter into the feelings with which these authors recorded them. The latter neither experience such emotions nor excite them."[38] Godwin's point is that a putatively comprehensive historiography that skates over singularities, thus leaving the depth of souls undisturbed, cannot incite visionary insight into admirable qualities, habits, or characteristics that fall outside widely shared cultural norms. Therefore, according to Godwin, Enlightenment historiographers do not impassion us to pursue the "untrodden paths" that these singularities promise to open up. Historiographical insight into the distinctive private lives of great men, Godwin suggests, would serve historiography's legitimate purpose: to inspire a social future based not on the dull repetition of what has defined British culture (customs, shared history) or on a "calculation of probabilities" but on the admirable singularities of great men, promising to create norms anew after their life models. "I should rejoice to have, or to be enabled to make, if that were possible, a journal of [a great historical figure's] ordinary and minutest actions. I believe I should be better employed in thus studying one man, than in perusing the abridgment of Universal History in sixty volumes." With such a course of study both engaging and "mark[ing] the operation of the human passions," Godwin envisions a modern historiography with which "we shall be enabled to add, to the knowledge of the past, a sagacity that can penetrate into the depths of futurity"—a futurity that does not repeat that knowledge but discovers hitherto unknown depths through which the collective society can be advanced.[39]

Godwin's Second Thoughts; Or, the Advent of Unpredictable Futurity

As if turning aside from his own alternative program to philosophical history, Godwin concludes his essay with a revelation that undoes his previously expressed ambitions. Having passionately advanced the idea that a deep "knowledge of the individual" will lead us to "penetrate into the depths of futurity," the essay finally turns upon the inexorable limits of that knowledge, an epistemological uncertainty that would inhibit our exploration of those depths:

> The conjectures of the historian must be built upon a knowledge of the characters of his personages. But we never know any man's character. My most intimate and sagacious friend continually misapprehends my motives. He is in most cases a little worse judge of them than myself and I am perpetually mistaken. The materials are abundant for the history of Alexander, Caesar, Cicero and Queen Elizabeth. Yet how widely do the best informed persons differ respecting them? Perhaps by all their character is misrepresented. The conjectures therefore respecting their motives in each particular transaction must be eternally fallacious.[40]

Here Godwin marks the limits of his own fantasy empiricist account of a historical figure's "ordinary and minutest actions." It is not just the visible world that interests him but also the world of invisible "motives." If historical knowledge involves an understanding of cause-and-effect relations, Godwin reminds us that we need to understand the personal motives behind decisions or actions—that is, the invisible causes of visible effects. In a self-reflexive move, however, he observes how limited our knowledge of historical causes must always be, given how mistaken his closest friends and even he can be about his own motivations. If we assume a degree of self-opacity in everyone, as Godwin clearly does, not even a direct private journal statement of why one made a particular decision can be taken as historical truth. This epistemological limit thus curtails access to the "depths of futurity" that the intimate history of a historical individual had seemed uniquely to promise.

Eliciting simultaneously a preoccupation with an unprecedented futurity and a sense of limited access to it, Godwin's essay is fascinating precisely for its performance of a turning aside to the individual (whether self or other). The individual becomes the focus of historical-epistemological desire, and Godwin extrapolates from this focus the inherent limits of the historiographical enterprise. Individual motivations are always, to some extent, mysterious, so the potential futures that historical individuals might inspire, too, remain out of epistemological reach.

In both the foregrounding of the individual and the attention to an unforeseeable futurity, Godwin's essay, composed in 1797, reflects historiographical concerns that were heightened by the events of the French Revolution. In the 1790s, the individual's experience of revolutionary events often powerfully shaped historical thinking. "I went yesterday to Versailles to satisfy myself what had passed there; for nothing can be believed but what one sees, or has from an eye witness," wrote Thomas Jefferson in a letter to John Jay, secretary of foreign affairs, on July 19, 1789.[41] The verification of the senses is a key episteme at the end of the eighteenth century, and the individual eyewitness is naturally crucial to it. But eyewitness historiography both flourished in the marketplace and faltered as a reliable historical genre during that politically tumultuous decade. It faltered because the revolution kept bringing about events that were unforeseen—and seemingly unforeseeable. While eyewitnesses not only described what they saw and heard but also invariably commented on the significance of the events they witnessed, the sense of an unpredictable futurity made commenting on the historical dimensions of the most recent events at least somewhat precarious, since those dimensions implicitly had to include, in their imagining of the present, the new political world to which these events would lead.

Writing an Eyewitness History in/of Tumultuous Times

Helen Maria Williams's epistolary eyewitness history of the French Revolution, *Letters Written in France, In the Summer 1790, To a Friend in England; Containing Various Anecdotes Relative to the French Revolution*, was published in the same year as the events it describes and was followed by further volumes published in 1792, 1793, 1795, and 1796. Unlike eighteenth-century Scottish Enlightenment historiography, whose modern histories typically stopped their narrations by the end of the previous century, historiography written in the 1790s often concerned the very immediate present, given the major political events in France. Williams's *Letters* aspires to some of the precepts Godwin later in the same decade proposed for historiography—such as employing an eyewitness methodology; foregrounding the individual; eliciting not just reason but emotion and passion; and deriving a sense of futurity and potential universality from the particular/the individual. Williams's *Letters*, as we shall see, both states and performs, as well, Godwin's undoing of that notion that we might foretell the future—let alone control it—by any historiographical means (whether in the form of romance or conventional history), since, as Godwin puts it, "to tell precisely how such a person would act in a given situation, requires a sagacity scarcely less than divine."[42] The ineradicable historical mysteries of human motivation, and thus of cause-and-effect relations, render the future unpredictable. Together with Williams's steady faith in the principles of the revolution, for which her work is most often invoked, we also find in the *Letters Written in France* Godwin's sense of inexorable historical unpredictability. Especially in the volumes after 1790, Williams's historiographical project appears one of careful balancing. The narrative maintains unwaveringly her conviction that the principles with which the French Revolution began are sound, and she never relinquishes her belief that, overall, the revolution is part of a historical narrative of political progress. At the same time, however, her narrative both performs the failure to predict the events that will transpire after 1790 and suggests that no one, not even Edmund Burke in his gloomy outlook, predicted—or could have predicted—the violence of the Reign of Terror by drawing on a historical pattern of cause-and-effect relations.

Williams's epistles to an unnamed correspondent in England give a descriptive account of what she saw in France, but her eyewitness account is also participatory with respect to her insistently impassioned political opinions. Whereas Enlightenment historians were remarkable for their unprecedented focus on modern, as opposed to ancient, history, eyewitness historians brought history into the even more recent past, often recording what they had seen that day. Moreover, added to the sensory and temporal immediacy of Williams's experience of the revolution, speculations of a more distant futurity elevate her fervor. The intensity of immediate experience is heightened, that is, by mediations of futurity—her extended imagining of how the events she has witnessed will be remembered in times to come:

> Future ages will celebrate, with grateful commemoration, the fourteenth of July; and strangers, when they visit France, will hasten with impatience to the Champs de Mars, filled with that enthusiasm which is awakened by the view of a place where any great scene has been acted. I think I hear them exclaim, "Here the Federation was held! here an assembled nation devoted themselves to freedom!" I fancy I see them pointing out the spot on which the altar of the country stood. I see them eagerly searching for the place where they have heard it recorded, that the National Assembly were seated! I think of these things, and then repeat to myself with transport, "*I* was a spectator of the Federation!"[43]

Williams "sees" how future ages will look at the Paris in which she is living as a place where a "great scene has been acted." She claims to inhabit that future perspective enough to hear what those generations will say about the time in which she is living and see how they will regard the places where historical events of her moment took place. It is as if Williams is transported in reverie to the future from which context she looks back at her own role (now in the distant past) of recording contemporary events in the *Letters*. From the future, transported, she can say, "'*I* was a spectator of the Federation!'" Insofar as present and future perspectives merge in this passage, Williams might also have written from the present perspective, *I will have been a spectator of the Federation!* In passages such as this one, however, the speculative future gains a sensory immediacy that, in effect, blurs the relation between present and future even more than the statement in the grammar of future anteriority. Williams goes on to comment, "But these meditations have led me to travel through the space of so many centuries, that it is really difficult to get back again to the present times" (109)—as if future "centuries" could be excluded from the history of "present times." However, the cumulative effect of her stylistic shifts evokes a sense of futurity not *and* but *in* the present—a history of the present as a process of becoming something else. Here, Williams appears confident that the something else will be a political situation in the context of which the revolution will be remembered with international pride as a triumph for humanity.

In the post-1792 volumes, Williams's conjuring of futurity becomes no less definitive of her style, but it comes with a more sophisticated and varied consideration of how to negotiate a belief in the overall "progress" of the revolution together with an increasing sense of its unpredictability. In the 1790 volume, Williams all but assumes that the major violence is over, going so far as to downplay the "popular fury" and "ferocious revenge" of the previous year by recalling the "records of history," which provide so many similarly violent instances: "But, alas! where do the records of history point out a revolution unstained by some actions of barbarity? When do the passions of human nature rise to that pitch which produces great events, without wandering into some irregularities?" (98). From that perspective, the violence of 1789 to 1790 was wholly predictable. In fact, imagining the historical dimensions of the present, Williams concludes in the 1790 volume, however conditionally, that the only unpredictable aspect is how relatively small the amount of violence had been up to that point:

> If the French revolution should cost no farther bloodshed, it must be allowed, notwithstanding a few shocking instances of public vengeance, that the

liberty of twenty-four millions of people will have been purchased at a far cheaper rate than could ever have been expected from the former experience of the world. (98)

One might have expected more. Although Williams's "will have been" scenario hinges on the conditional "If," no other scenario is entertained with which she might have suggested multiple possible outcomes of equal plausibility. Williams thus seems, if not to be predicting "no farther bloodshed," to be placing her bet on the continued relative nonviolence of this period of major political change and celebrating the moment in that light.

Given the often surprisingly violent turns of the revolution to come, Williams had to revise her anticipations. Following the September Massacres of 1792 and their significant bloodshed, for instance, she considers human nature in the particular circumstances of revolution and foresees the possibility of more violence to come:

> [Idle and profligate persons] are, under an established government, checked in their outrages on society, by the terror of punishment; but in the crisis of a revolution they become the dangerous instruments of party rage and faction. They may still commit enormities, of which the bourgeois of Paris . . . may remain pusillanimous witnesses. . . . Hence civil commotions may arise. Upon the whole the French revolution is still in its progress, and who can decide how its last page will finish? (162)

Given such violence, Williams introduces to her narrative a greater sense of uncertainty with respect to how events will unfold on a small-scale (say, daily or monthly) basis. Not quite hazarding a prediction of cause and effect, she nevertheless speculates these persons "*may* still commit enormities" based on the combination of character and situation (emphasis mine). In the face of these relatively small-scale vicissitudes, however, she frames her commentary with repeated defenses of the revolution's principles and assertions of a larger-scale ("Upon the whole") narrative of "progress."

In view of her overall sanguine outlook, Williams not only excoriates Edmund Burke for his pessimism but also denies the accuracy of his predictions. Following the execution of Louis XVI in 1793, Williams writes:

> I cannot give [Burke] all the credit that some do for his predictions respecting the French revolution; for many of them have not been verified, and he that makes a number of bold guesses, will always succeed in some of them. Those that have taken place, have generally arisen from other causes than those supposed by Mr. Burke; and I may add, as to the rest, that the judicious friends of the French revolution foresaw as well as he did, and feared, the

evils he predicted; but as they believed there was a possibility that they might not happen, they were glad to see a trial made for the instruction of the human race. (166)

Williams's critique shows how central questions of predictability—more specifically, predictability based on linear cause-and-effect relations—are to historical debates about the ongoing revolution. Burke had taken issue in 1790 with the proposed constitution: "The effect of liberty to individuals," he cautioned, "is, that they may do what they please: We ought to see what it will please them to do, before we risque congratulations, which may be soon turned into complaints."[44] Based on the planned redistributions of power, moreover, he predicted internal chaos and violence: "The military conspiracies, which are to be remedied by civic confederacies; the rebellious municipalities, which are to be rendered obedient by furnishing them with the means of seducing the very armies of the state that are to keep them in order; all these chimeras of a monstrous and portentous policy, must aggravate the confusions from which they have arisen. There must be blood."[45] Violence indeed followed the institution of Republican policies, but whereas Burke would suggest that such violence was predictable and could have been managed by its causes—that is, ill-conceived new policies—Williams suggests that Burke may not have named the causes correctly. The violence he predicted happened, but not for the reasons he thought it would. That is, she troubles the linear causality that guides Burke's implicit forecast of Revolutionary evils. Friends of the revolution, she adds, "foresaw" what Burke did. But they foresaw other possibilities as well. They conceived the world not based on a historical logic of linear causality, as it is for Burke. Their historical anticipation conceived a world of *multiple* possibilities, not a single inevitable outcome. This explains why someone such as Burke can predict political outcomes based on the historical experience (patterns of cause-and-effect relations) and *sometimes* guess right. But it does not defeat the worldview of those wanting to experiment with the possibilities of human liberty. Although Williams does not develop a full-fledged theory of historical relations to counter Burke's logic of causality, one can see that she does not accept a unified linear approach to imagining the future but rather admires those who foresaw multiple possible futures, perhaps even equally plausible ones. Whereas Burke's historical vision is consistent with Hume's insofar as Burke sees in historical science the capacity to make predictions—"to control and regulate future events by their causes," as Hume puts it—Williams is clearly working out a different historical logic. It is a logic that resists unified, linear thinking, conceiving instead a sense of simultaneous, heterogeneous possibilities for the outcome (and thus historical significance) of the present.

Facets of the Present: Hazlitt's Historical Portraiture

Concluding this discussion of tensions with linear temporality in historical writing, I turn to William Hazlitt's essay collection published in 1825, *The Spirit of the Age; Or, Contemporary Portraits*. I am putting that work in conversation with Scottish Enlightenment thought and Burke's similarly linear causality, as well as with Godwin's and Williams's critiques of those modes, in order to show how Hazlitt creates a model for writing a history of the present that is noncomprehensive or nontotalizing, foregoing the strategy of characterizing the present by tracing its narrative forward from some single origin. In more positive terms, Hazlitt's work presents a heterogeneous collection of different ways of finding or reading (in both senses) the "spirit of the age." He discovers traces of that spirit in the works of various living authors. Suggesting some uncertainty about how to sum it all up, however, these discoveries do not add up to one coherent image of the age but appear as seemingly incompatible possibilities. From the perspective of these proliferating, simultaneous manifestations of the "spirit of the age," moreover, a further kind of possibility opens up: that of individual agency. Indeed, as we shall see, Hazlitt's work suggests the historical agency of authorship—including that of his own essay characterizations. In these ways, Hazlitt's writing shares historiographical ideas with the poetry and prose-fiction that will concern the following chapters—ideas that embrace tensions with linear progression to the degree of developing full-fledged alternatives to linear time. Like Keats's and Byron's poetry and Austen's novel *Persuasion*, Hazlitt's *The Spirit of the Age* imagines history as a dynamic process and the present as a world of equally plausible possibilities.

Let me begin with Hazlitt's provocative title, which already indicates some of the historical work's most significant formal and narratological aspects. Hazlitt does not comment on the choice of title directly, but six years later in a similarly titled essay, "The Spirit of the Age," John Stuart Mill wrote the following: "The 'Spirit of the Age' is in some measure a novel expression. I do not believe that it is to be met with in any work exceeding fifty years in antiquity. The idea of comparing one's own age with former ages, or with our notion of those which are yet to come, had occurred to philosophers; but it never before was itself the dominant idea of any age."[46] If Mill is right that this was the "dominant idea" of turn-of-the-nineteenth-century Britain or Europe, the elusiveness of the age's defining qualities surely contributed to writers' prevailing preoccupation with the topic. The phrase itself points not to an object or any aspect of the material world but to an immaterial force, suggesting that although it lacks a fully identifiable material form itself, the spirit at least potentially touches on all that exists simultaneously.

Hazlitt's subtitle reinforces the notion of simultaneity when it announces a key aspect of the work's formal structure: a series of *contemporary* portraits. Whereas a history by Hume, Robertson, Ferguson, or even Helen Maria Williams ends in a later chronological moment than it begins—whether it moves successively through grand historical periods or in a more personal vein through days, weeks, and only a few years—Hazlitt's final "portrait," his last entry in the collection (on James Sheridan Knowles), is contemporaneous with his first one (on Jeremy Bentham), as well as with those on all the other living authors who feature in the prose portrait collection. In this respect, the narrative moves in time not progressively or regressively but laterally.

What's more, the prose portraits focus primarily on philosophers', poets', and novelists' works in relation to the times—not on their biographies or even on the literary or cultural histories they inherit or revise. Hazlitt's *Spirit of the Age* is an insistently present-focused series of essays based on the oeuvres of a number of poets and thinkers—each assessing how we can perceive the spirit of the age in, or in relation to, their works. For example, Hazlitt writes of William Godwin, "The Spirit of the Age was never more fully shown than in its treatment of this writer—its love of paradox and change, its dastard submission to prejudice and to the fashion of the day" (105). In another entry, Hazlitt describes Wordsworth's genius as "a pure emanation of the Spirit of the Age. Had he lived in any other period of the world, he would never have been heard of" (203). When it comes to Sir James MacKintosh, he announces, "The subject of the present article is one of the ablest and most accomplished men of the age, both as a writer, a speaker, and a converser" (215). In addition to how the portraits are centered on the present, we can see in this selection of excerpts how Hazlitt's collection appears as a group of distinct reflections, without any obvious threads that work to make the title's pluralized "portraits" into one unified, coherent, or comprehensive portrait of the age. How does Godwin's status of most "full[y] show[ing]" the spirit match up—or compete or contrast—with Wordsworth's as the spirit's "pure emanation"? Hazlitt's is a collection of balkanized contemporary histories rather than a unified, grand historical narrative.

In addition to Hazlitt's present-centered selection of authors, within any given "portrait" nothing like a chronologically organized history of a writer's career appears. Hazlitt traces the historical present neither back to the origins of British identity in the culture of Greece and Rome (as Scottish Enlightenment historians overwhelmingly do) nor back to the biographical beginnings and successive development of the individual authors on whom he focuses. Rather, the painting metaphor of Hazlitt's title evokes the way in which Hazlitt seems to assess each writer's work *at the given moment*. However much that image of a moment might suggest a past or future, in the way that a portrait subject's dress or collected objects might suggest a past experience or future ambition, it is the past or future only as embodied in that precise historical moment—of becoming. All of these essays in succession describe Hazlitt's own contemporaries: all living writers, most of whom are still actively writing. That is to say, Hazlitt's critical assessments inevitably forego the ambition of being comprehensive representations even of these individual authors' oeuvres. As a historical narrative of the spirit of the present age, the collection unfolds in a series of simultaneous reflections of that spirit in the character or work or genius or treatment of a writer. The narrative progression thus tells a story that is not so much a linear temporal progress as it is a proliferation of simultaneities, figures living contemporaneously with one another, reflecting the spirit of the age in accumulating heterogeneous ways.

Hazlitt's formal simultaneity recalls the formal structure of Robert Henry's seven chapters in each of *History of Great Britain*'s "books" of history, insofar as those seven successive chapters represent the same historical period, rather than moving chronologically forward from chapter to chapter. However, whereas Henry strove for unity, working to make the underlying systems connecting all the chapters accessible to readers, Hazlitt's heterogeneity works in the opposite direction. Hazlitt's historical perspective therefore appears potentially more inclusive, more socially capacious, than Henry's narration of British identity. Although Hazlitt focuses on only a few dozen individuals, all of whom are British male writers or philosophers of some kind, while Henry creates a history of Britain that is sweeping in its range, Henry does not attend to the individual or even just a few individuals. It is ostensibly a history of all British people. But Henry's history constructs a narrower, more monolithic view of British history and British identity than does Hazlitt's historiography, which courts a sense of its own incompletion and imaginatively offers multiple, simultaneously available points of contact with the spirit of the age (multiple points of entry), rather than signaling one point of origin in Greco-Roman culture. Where British culture originated appears less important to Hazlitt than are the various possibilities for shaping it anew, available in the present.

Hazlitt's critical valuation of a heterogeneous imagination becomes clear in his very first portrait, when he disparages Jeremy Bentham for the uniformity of his accomplished philosophical thought—as completely tidy as it is unarresting. Assuming the principle of utility as the foundation of his moral and political reasoning enables Bentham to constantly refer his argument back to it. Regarding that unifying principle, Hazlitt observes,

> Perhaps the weak side of his conclusions also is, that he has carried this single view of his subject too far, and not made sufficient allowance for the varieties of human nature, and the caprices and irregularities of the human will. . . . Mr. Bentham's method of reasoning, though comprehensive and exact, labours under the defect of most systems—it is too *topical*. It includes every thing; but it includes every thing alike. It is rather like an inventory, than a valuation of different arguments.[47]

Unlike Bentham, the author of *The Spirit of the Age* is less a philosopher than a critic—he is, above all, a sensitive reader. He takes the work of each author on its own terms, discovering its principles and contradictions and considering how those qualities speak to the political, social, and artistic currents of the day. For instance, he describes Wordsworth's setting up of an opposition between the "spirit of humanity" and the "spirit of fashion and of the world" as "one of the innovations of the time. It partakes of, and is carried along with, the revolutionary movement of our age: the political changes of the day were the model on which [Wordsworth] formed and conducted his poetical experiments. His Muse . . . is a levelling one" (203–4). Not only has Wordsworth partaken of the spirit of the age but also his writing has contributed to its innovations. He has read the age well and therefore helped shape it.

Balkanized "Little Histories": From Nonfiction to Fiction

Concluding this discussion of historical nonfiction, I want to suggest how the temporalities of historical writing that I have described help show what is at stake in those of literary fictions as well. For in view of Hazlitt's definitive departure from the claims to unity and comprehensiveness of philosophical history, we can start to see the historiographical significance of the "little histories" that populate Jane's Austen's novel *Persuasion*.[48] Austen's narrator describes, for instance, the "very awkward history of Mr. Elliot" (8); Anne's "little history of sorrowful interest" with Wentworth (28); and the "pathetic piece of family history" recounting the death of Dick Musgrove in war (50).

Counter to the emotionless linear chronology of Sir Walter's *Baronetage*, Austen's own narrative features competing "little" narrative histories full of feeling. In fact, one might find in the different kinds of narratives within her novel the very sense of a variety of ways in which history can be told. But these mini-histories—unlike the form of history told by the *Baronetage* or even that by the Navy List that the Musgrove sisters pore over in search of Wentworth's ship—are not available through print culture. They are a purely experiential form within Austen's novel. Moreover, they are often semiprivate narratives, unknown even to some people involved in the social encounters that they inform. Everyone but Anne seems to have forgotten her "little history" with Wentworth when he returns; it is of "sorrowful interest" only to her. Only after some effort does Wentworth share the Musgroves' pathos regarding their late son. *Persuasion* evokes a social world teeming with "little histories" that often do not cohere with each other and cannot be shared as a means of social cohesion. Austen's aesthetic of "little histories," like that of Hazlitt's contemporary portraits, displaces the unifying episteme of eighteenth-century grand historical narratives. It points, moreover, to a vision of history that is partial—that admits its own noncomprehensiveness, indeed its aversion to totalizing representation. As we shall see in Chapter 3, when the narrator alludes at the novel's end to the "tax of quick alarm" that Anne would have to pay as a naval wife, that sense of incomplete understanding of the historical dimensions of the present rests on an unpredictable futurity. And it calls for a mental disposition that John Keats named "*Negative Capability*."

2

DIZZY ANTICIPATIONS:
SONNETS BY KEATS
(AND SHELLEY)

From mist to dizziness, Keats courts disorientation. From the title of the poem "I stood tip-toe upon a little hill" to the "dizzy pain / That mingles Grecian grandeur with the rude / Wasting of old time" in "On Seeing the Elgin Marbles" and the sonic-semantic play on whirlwind that creates "world-wind" in the "Paolo and Francesca" sonnet, a visceral sense of disorientation permeates Keats's poetry.[1] In December 1818 in a letter to his brother and sister-in-law in America, that sense of dizziness evoked a world of politics and of technological and social change whereby his closest family members lived across the Atlantic: "How are you going on now? The goings on of the world make me dizzy" (*LJK*, 2:5). Spatio-temporal disorientation, such as dizziness, registered Keats's subjective response to a shared historical condition. In Keats's poetry, moreover, a decentered, revisionary subjectivity that pluralizes interpretive possibilities enabled aesthetic engagement with the uncertainty of a historical present in flux, shadowed by an unknown future.

This chapter will explore the historiographical implications of that dizziness as it takes shape in Keats's sonnets and will conclude with a discussion of how Percy Shelley's sonnet "England in 1819" offers a similarly dramatic, anticipatory turn in its final couplet but without the disorientation of selfhood so pronounced in Keats's poems. One of Keats's earliest and most evocative poetic figures for that vertiginous world feeling, and one in which we can begin to perceive the historical specificity of Keats's sensation, is "stout Cortez." "[U]pon a peak," Cortés stands both for individual, subjective astonishment (a reader's first encounter with Chapman's translation of Homer) and for a shift in knowledge of world-historical significance (the European discovery of the Pacific).[2] The blurring of that seeming divide between the particulars of one's experience and the larger, shared circumstances of historical change is the work of Keats's aesthetic in the sonnets and the odes. In view of the historiographical challenges of the post-Waterloo moment and Keats's own reflections on them, therefore, the formal aesthetics of Keats's poetry appear not as a turning away from the dizzying world but as an engagement with it on new terms. The dizzying sense of disorientation is key to an aesthetic of surprise in Keats's poetry that this chapter aims to describe, an aesthetic that, as I shall argue, had a historically specific urgency in early nineteenth-century England. For Keats's aesthetic suggests a registering, however oblique, of the "goings on" of history that were not being accommodated sufficiently by the predominant historical and political discourse.

Countering critical tendencies to associate Romanticism with a turn toward the past and toward the relations between past and present, this chapter shows how centrally anticipation marks the temporal perspective and sense of disorientation in Keats's letters and poems. The philosophical and historical discourses of modernity that have concerned the introduction and Chapter 1 provide an intellectual context for understanding how an anticipatory perspective entails epistemological uncertainty by the end of the eighteenth century—that is, in a world whose future seemed to promise the unforeseen. Another name for that ability to be with uncertainty is "*Negative Capability*," the quality for which Keats's poems are so well-known. Given that modernity came with a sense of the unpredictable and an unknown futurity, an anticipatory perspective invites uncertainty into the very moment of anticipating—the present. In Keats's poetry—and, as we shall see in the following chapters, in Austen's and Byron's literary works—anticipation and uncertainty about the future afford the present a sense of multiple possibilities. The present, that is, appears as an experience of dwelling with possibilities, a dwelling similar to that encouraged by the plurality of "contemporary portraits" that William Hazlitt envisions in *The Spirit of the Age*, discussed in the previous chapter. In the works of these writers, although this dwelling with multiple versions of the present appears, perhaps, as a slowing down of time, it is far from a turning away from the complexities of modernity (often associated with speed); rather, thinking of the present as multiple affords an engagement with its historical dimensions and thus with modernity's problem of self-definition—that is, the problem that arises when recourse to explanatory models of the past no longer can suffice. In all of the literary works in this study, moreover, that dwelling takes place in what William Godwin complained that eighteenth-century historiography had neglected: the individual subject. Whether it is Anne Elliot as the protagonist of *Persuasion*, the poet-narrator of *Don Juan*, or the reader of Chapman's Homer or of *King Lear*, the individual literary subject takes the pulse(s) of the historical age and makes them, at least partly, audible.

Keats's poetry, moreover, shows us something distinctive about this anticipatory sense of possibilities and unpredictable futurity—something that, even if it is not inconsistent with the aesthetic of *Persuasion* or *Don Juan*, the others do not emphasize. For Keats, *disorientation* precedes or contemporaneously accompanies the "self"-altering process of encountering the unprecedented or unpredictable. In other words, disorientation (in the presence of mist, the feeling of dizziness, or the grammar of a decentered subject) and alterings of the self (what Keats calls "Soul-making") constitute experience in the modern world; they crucially inform our best readings of its historical dimensions, in view of modernity's dark, impending futurity.

To describe the work that Keats's aesthetic does in this way is to suggest that what some New Historicist critics observed as a turn away from history—a repression of history that enabled, in its place, a representation of the self in nature—might instead be seen as a turn toward history on these new terms. For many New Historicist critics of Romantic studies, poetry and history appeared dichotomous to the extent that Daniel Watkins could write of Keats's sonnet "On first looking into Chapman's Homer" that it achieves "poetic mastery . . . at the expense of history itself."[3] Jerome McGann most famously launched this critique of Keats's poetry as escapism in his 1979 essay "Keats and the Historical Method."[4] Even in more recent historicist criticism that discovers positive connections between Keats's poetry and the historical "context," there is a persistent assumption that the two categories (poetry and history) are distinct in a way that attributes to poetry a referential status relative to its perceived "context."[5] In other words, poetry can be understood as politically or historically engaged only insofar as direct links can be traced from its language or allusions to the language or ideas then available in contemporary political or historical discourse. What I suggest in the following readings, by contrast, is that we can see in the poetry an original thinking through of the historiographical challenges of the early nineteenth-century moment, challenges that may still be with us today. The readings that follow show this poetic thinking by attending both to the way that Keats's concepts of time pertain to, even if they are not contained by, contemporary historiographical debates and to how formal and aesthetic as well as thematic dimensions of Keats's poetry help shape the poetry's historical engagement. My aim, then, is not so much to trace connections between the language of Keats's poems and the historical discourse of the period as it is to elaborate what we might call the poetry's historiographical aesthetic.

Vertiginous Subjectivity

Keats's sonnet "On first looking into Chapman's Homer" is the poem most often cited as the first evidence of the poet's potential, and the poem itself takes the discovery of previously unknown possibilities as its theme. In the way that an astronomer's discovery of a new planet or Cortés's discovery of the Pacific is depicted to alter their respective cosmic and global senses of what *is*, the poet's reading of Chapman's Homer unleashes a sense of hitherto unforeseen *literary* possibilities. The sonnet's octave sets up the weight of previous experiences—much traveling as a figure for much reading—so as to stage the remarkable contrast of that knowledge with what Chapman's Homer offers. The contrast establishes the surprise of a difference that had not been previously imaginable. As such, the relation of sestet to octave—of Chapman's Homer to previous reading experiences—is not an addition or even a development but a displacement: it amounts to a radical reorientation for (cosmic, global, literary) knowledge itself:

> **On first looking into Chapman's Homer**
> Much have I travell'd in the realms of gold,
> And many goodly states and kingdoms seen;
> Round many western islands have I been
> Which bards in fealty to Apollo hold.
> Oft of one wide expanse had I been told
> That deep-brow'd Homer ruled as his demesne;
> Yet did I never breathe its pure serene[6]
> Till I heard Chapman speak out loud and bold;
> Then felt I like some watcher of the skies
> When a new planet swims into his ken;
> Or like stout Cortez when with eagle eyes
> He star'd at the Pacific—and all his men
> Look'd at each other with a wild surmise—
> Silent, upon a peak in Darien.

As the movement through figurations shows, the significance of the literary discovery the speaker has made is not immediately within imaginative grasp. The conjunction "Or," that is, suggests a world of figurative possibilities. Unlike the careful balancing of multiple possibilities linked by "Or" in "To Autumn," however, here the simile of Cortés seems to improve upon that of the astronomer. For both, the discovery is nothing short of world shifting, but whereas for the astronomer the "new planet swims into his ken," for Cortés the limits of the Pacific, we imagine, exceed what the eyes can see. Cortés finds himself, suddenly and ecstatically, in a world that his visual capacities cannot entirely encompass. The simile of Cortés thus is all the more astonishing for its implication that knowledge of what this obviously transforming discovery will come to signify still, at least partly, eludes him. As Charles Rzepka has observed, this is the speaker's "own sublime 'transport.'"[7] The subjectivity that Keats's poem imagines and elicits thus entails a mobility of perception crucial to inhabiting a world that abounds with possibilities and defies absolute (critical) mastery. Speechless Cortés appears at once triumphant and undone.

"*Negative Capability*" is the name Keats gave to the quality of mind "when man is capable of being in uncertainties, Mysteries, doubts, without any irritable reaching after fact & reason" (*LJK*, 1:193–94). This giving up of sure resting places for thought positively enables the dynamic mobility of perception on display in the Chapman's Homer sonnet, with its movement through multiple figurations, through increasingly closer approximations of the experience the speaker aims to recount and the poet aims to convey. By the time Keats published the sonnet in his 1817 *Poems*, he had significantly revised a line that, in the original version, may have undercut that emphasis on perceptual and figurative play. The line in 1817—"Yet did I never breathe its pure serene"—originally appeared in 1816 as "Yet could I never judge what men could mean" (7). Aside from its obviously greater poetic beauty, the revision is significant in a number of ways. First, it enables critical judgment to be deferred indefinitely, *perhaps* to some future moment of retrospection beyond the lyric moment; the meaning of the reading event is not instantaneous, as the original line suggested, but rather may unfold and alter in time. Second, to "breathe its pure serene" emphasizes a sensory, visceral experience. Receptive to the possibility that the text will change him, the poet takes in the text, intimately absorbing it. As Marjorie Levinson has shown, a host of literary precedents and associations beyond Chapman as translator mediate what then appears a rather paradoxical intimacy with Homer, an impure serene. As the speaker breathes in Homer through Chapman, so the reader who "speak[s] out" the sonnet breathes in the voice of Keats through Milton, Pope, Cary, Dante, and Coleridge.[8] Finally, the revised line relinquishes the claim to a primarily referential status for the text: it is not a question of what "Chapman's Homer" means (to other "men" or to Keats) or of what it represents; it is a question of what it does.

There is a historiographical dimension to what Keats's own formal aesthetic does that has not yet been addressed. Although Keats has been faulted for eliding particular historical realities in ways that may appear incontestable, such an argument, in the example I give here from Daniel Watkins's *Keats's Poetry and the Politics of the Imagination*, rests on an unquestioned privileging of the authority of the eighteenth-century historical narrative considered "the most important historical source for the sonnet" (27): William Robertson's *History of America*. What this argument overlooks are ways in which Keats may have been closer to a certain historiographical predicament of that moment than was his Scottish enlightenment "source." I quote Watkins's conclusion, at some length, which he comes to at the end of a careful comparison of passages from Robertson's history describing Cortés's and Balboa's discoveries:

> The Chapman sonnet is not entirely a moment of triumph for Keats the poet; in fact, the historical details in the poem reveal the extent to which Keats's thought is entrapped in what McGann has called the romantic ideology. The poetic mastery of a historical subject comes at the expense of history itself, creating a tension that Keats's poetry never entirely lays to rest. While the poem displays the poet's interest in historical texts and in the poetic handling of those texts, it establishes at the same time a rigid dichotomy between beauty and history. That is, the inspiration of the poem arises from Keats's sense of imaginative discovery; moreover, the beautifully expressed sense of wonder at this discovery elides much historical reality, and even much of what Robertson chronicles: the savage abuse by European explorers of native Americans; the violence and personal viciousness of Cortez; the imperialist drive for wealth and territory by the European invaders. These matters exist in the extreme margins of the poetic text, becoming visible through Keats's major historical source, and they reveal that the poetic triumph of the Chapman sonnet is in the celebration of the energy associated with discoveries of historical significance, rather than in the articulation or representation of history itself. (31)

The hard, documentable details of what Watkins describes as within Robertson's view and outside Keats's poem seem irrefutable. Watkins, however, not only does not examine the representational assumptions of Robertson (historical narrative as itself a mediation) but also pays little attention to the formal dynamics of the sonnet, specifically to the *volta* and its dramatic turn toward an experience proclaimed as unforeseen because it is completely outside the order of the prior "goodly states and kingdoms seen." It is "Chapman's Homer" that transports the poet *beyond* what prior reading experiences had done. These prior reading experiences include, as many critics have noted, a good number of histories and travels, as well as Pope's translation of Homer. From those other textual representations, Chapman's translation stands out in the poet's experience in a way that discovering a new planet would in an astronomer's and seeing the Pacific would have in Cortés's: it transforms the young poet's horizon of imagining what poetry can do. Although Keats's final image obviously is of Cortés, it should not be paired with the representation in Robertson's *History* in that, clearly, if Keats did have Robertson's text in mind, its representation of Spanish explorers and their discoveries would have to be associated with the much literary traveling Keats had done before looking into Chapman's Homer, here defined against those final similes. Chapman's Homer is not like those earlier voyages (metaphor for reading experiences); it is something else.

Historicist readings tied to a referential model of analysis do not account for these formal dimensions and aesthetic effects. Following Watkins, Nicholas Roe remarks: "In the aspiration to 'goodly states and kingdoms,' Keats's sonnet suggests that political history and poetic imagination coincide."[9] Roe remarks, moreover, that whereas Robertson "describes (and deplores) the Spaniards' vicious exploitation of human beings in the gold mines of Hispaniola . . . Keats's sonnet omits the tragic human cost of Spanish activities in the new world."[10] In a methodologically similar fashion, Greg Kucich countered Watkins: "Keats's opening address to those 'realms of gold' does call attention to the principal aspect of the Spanish colonial institution that Robertson deplores—its murderous greed in the pursuit of commercial gain, overwhelmingly symbolized by its lust for gold."[11] From readings such as this one, Kucich concludes that the poet's "qualifications" to his commitment to progress "frequently assume the form of these models of linear contrariety informing the historical consciousness of Keats's era."[12] In other words, the temporal dimensions of Keats's historical vision derive from the eighteenth-century historiography of which he read so much.

But if political history and imagination coincide for Keats, it is not Keats's sonnet (or Chapman's Homer) and Robertson's *History* that do so, because the formal turn from octave to sestet marks precisely the difference between everything the speaker has read previously and the experience of Chapman's Homer. What I'm suggesting is that in creating an image of Cortés (and his men) to express his experience of wonder in reading

Chapman, Keats implies that the explorer's actual experience of reaching the Pacific (the experience as the sonnet conveys it) may have surpassed any representation of it that Keats had encountered in Robertson or elsewhere.[13] For the formal dynamic of the sonnet's turn and the movement of its figures in the sestet do not develop but rather *displace* previous modes of knowing, narrating, and experiencing.

Moreover, the new mode that displaces former ones is, at the sonnet's end, still somewhat elusive. For the grammatical structure, like the poem's perspective, appears suspended between the image of Cortés both opening and concluding the last clause and the image of his men. Although Cortés clearly holds a place of primacy, the men do not become subordinated grammatically but make the sentence a compound, as if equivalent. Rather than insist that the poet's or poem's perspective is aligned with the one or the many, I want to consider the significance of Keats's including both: the singular and the collective, the silent/frozen and the unfettered/imaginative ("wild surmise"). In doing so, I am building on Marjorie Levinson's insight of Keats's identification with the men from a theoretical perspective of class and of sexual and cultural critique. In *Keats's Life of Allegory*, Levinson claims, "One does not, I think, go too far in associating Keats with those capably disenfranchised men" (13–14). These ostensible opposites are not opposed but become equivalencies; Cortés and his men evoke modes that work in concert to perceive (and create) the new. The poem thus brings about a decentered, disoriented perspective—or a doubly oriented one. Similarly, as we shall see, the reading of "the human heart" in the "vale of Soul-making" letter is the solitary act of a singular subject that makes sociality possible—a turning inward that gives access to the larger, shared world.

In its suggestion about the exhilaration of unknown regions and the possibilities of an experience entirely unforeseen, the force of the sonnet's *volta* thus resonates with the predicament faced by historians, philosophers, and other thinkers especially after the French Revolution and Waterloo. Visible in the proliferation of writing on the topic after Waterloo, the felt urgency to narrate "the spirit of the age" came not from that spirit's self-evidence but from its radical uncertainty. Historian Peter Fritzsche notes of the post–French revolutionary age: "It was the continual production of the new that marked the revolution and left contemporaries disoriented and historians unprepared."[14] Particularly unprepared were precisely those historians who relied on a philosophy of historical progress, such as Robertson and others who were inspired by Hume, Millar, and other Scottish Enlightenment historiographers: "The French Revolution presented a powerful challenge to all those who wrote in the spirit of Scottish philosophical history," observes historian Jane Rendall. "For the relationship between the expanding world of commercial civilization and its individual, social and political dangers still remained to be determined."[15] Keats's vertiginous, disoriented, and ecstatic subjectivity enables his poetic to evoke those historiographical uncertainties that took Europeans and Britons by surprise and in the face of which the philosophy of historical progress was at such a loss for convincing representation.

The notion of (historical) surprise is central to the historical imagination and the critique available in Keats's aesthetic. In philosophical histories of progress, a society was always on a path toward "civilization" and a "goodly state" (Keats) of the nation: "Though the details varied, a common pattern of evolution was of four stages of progress, from savage hunting and gathering communities, to the barbarian pastoral stage, to a settled agricultural cultivation, and finally to the stage of commercial civilization," Rendall summarizes.[16] A commitment to this idea of progress is everywhere in eighteenth-century British histories, including those by Robertson. As Jürgen Habermas has observed, "the notion of progress served not only to render eschatological hopes profane and open up the horizon of expectation in a utopian fashion but also to close off the future as a *source* of disruption with the aid of teleological constructions of history."[17] "Progress" left no room for the disruptive force of something unforeseen. Although eighteenth-century historiographies sometimes experimented with forms that deviated from a smooth chronological or linear progression, the sense of time underpinning their philosophies of progress still did not accommodate the possibility of paradigm-shifting surprise.

Keats's sense of surprise in reading Chapman's Homer is rendered as the personal literary experience of a reorienting—or rather, a disorienting—of comparable systems of knowledge on a grand scale: cosmic and global. The surprise of the sestet leaves the "goodly states" he has seen (or read) behind, implicitly critiquing how the logic of progress forecloses surprise. The experience described and evoked by the sestet exposes the obsolescence of the paradigm of the probable informing the philosophy of historical progress while inviting, in its place, the possible—that is, the surprising force of a not yet conceptualized present that disrupts the formerly predominant ways of knowing. If the "space of experience" circa 1800 appeared distanced from the "horizon of anticipation," in the "Chapman's Homer" sonnet that distance elicits a deferral of articulation.[18] Cortés stands "Silent, upon a peak in Darien." What is *missed* in the rhythmic silence following Keats's evocative comma is the not yet conceptualized present. In this sense, however, the negatively capable aesthetic accommodates a historical uncertainty about narrating the present. Something was happening in England and in Europe that had not found its concept, its language, but to which Keats's rhythmic silence powerfully attests. Articulation probably always has come after, but Keats's historical moment and the nuances of his aesthetic are highly attuned to that phenomenon of deferral.[19]

On the "Preface" to Robertson's *History of America*

Most critics compare Keats's sonnet with Robertson's history by way of the historian's "particular accounts of famous discoveries by Cortez and Balboa, widely recognized as Keats's principal sources for the conception and imagery of the Chapman sonnet."[20] But I find the preface that Robertson wrote for the 1777 edition especially evocative in light of the sonnet's thematic and rhythmic silence:

> In fulfilling the engagement which I had come under to the Public with respect to the History of America, it was my intention not to have published any part of the work until the whole was completed. The present state of the British Colonies has induced me to alter that resolution. While they are engaged in civil war with Great Britain, inquiries and speculations concerning their ancient forms of policy and laws, which exist no longer, cannot be interesting. The attention and expectation of mankind are now turned towards their future condition. In whatever manner this unhappy contest may terminate, a new order of things must arise in North America, and its affairs will assume another aspect. I wait with the solicitude of a good citizen, until the ferment subside, and regular government be re-established, and then I shall return to this part of my work, in which I had made some progress.[21]

Robertson proceeded to write and publish the final two books that he mentions, a history of Virginia to 1688 and of New England to 1652, but it was not until 1796 that they appeared, almost twenty years after he interrupted his writing to publish the first three.

The present as history, or history in the process of becoming, arrests narration. Robertson's history first appears in 1777, therefore, as an incomplete set. Robertson nevertheless insists, in accord with the principles of Enlightenment historiographical composition, that the three volumes alone "form a perfect whole, remarkable for the unity of the subject."[22] Robertson does not imply that the outcome of the "civil war" will alter his sense of America's past, causing him to rewrite it, only that his "inquiries and speculations concerning their ancient forms of policy and laws, which exist no longer, cannot be interesting" at a time of political tumult that promises to give way to "a new order of things" and affairs of "another aspect." Nevertheless the revolutionary events underway in the colonies occasion a gap in his publication, which he cannot imagine filling until the "ferment subsides"—until a perspective on what this "ferment" *will have* led to, the "new order of things," comes into view. While Robertson insists on the "unity" of his historical work of three volumes, Keats's "Chapman's Homer" sonnet registers the moment of surprise and arrested narration that exposes history less as a static object than as a process and a work that is never comprehensive or complete. To this revisionary sense of history, open to the unpredictable, Robertson's preface, however inadvertently, attests.

From the "Chamber of Maiden Thought" to the "Grand March of Intellect"

Keats's epistolary narratives do not consistently critique or thwart the notion of linear progress as vigorously as does the "Chapman's Homer" sonnet. The images of dark passages and mist with which this study began and which, as we have seen, upend the ostensible linearity of the poet's journey appear in a letter that goes on to express an intellectual commitment *to* an idea of progress when the topic turns from individual poetic development to grand-scale historical progress.[23] I quote here a more extended passage from Keats's comparison of "human life to a large Mansion of Many Apartments" than I did for the introduction's epigraph in order to show the full architecture of the poet's imagined life path:

> The first we step into we call the infant or thoughtless Chamber, in which we remain as long as we do not think— . . . we no sooner get into the second Chamber, which I shall call the Chamber of Maiden-Thought, than we become intoxicated with the light and the atmosphere, we see nothing but pleasant wonders, and think of delaying there for ever in delight: However among the effects this breathing is father of is that tremendous one of sharpening one's vision into the heart <head> and nature of Man—of convincing ones [*sic*] nerves that the World is full of Misery and Heartbreak, Pain, Sickness and oppression—whereby This Chamber of Maiden Thought becomes gradually darken'd and at the same time on all sides of it many doors are set open—but all dark—all leading to dark passages—We see not the balance of good and evil. We are in a Mist—*We* are now in that state—We feel the "burden of the Mystery," To this point was Wordsworth come, as far as I can

conceive when he wrote "Tintern Abbey" and it seems to me that his Genius is explorative of those dark Passages. (*LJK*, 1:280–81)

Keats positions himself (and his poet-friend J. H. Reynolds, to whom the letter is addressed) in relation to the first-generation poet he admires perhaps most, Wordsworth, "to show you how tall I stand by the giant," he tells Reynolds in the same letter. To achieve this positioning, he illustrates architecturally a history of individual development: the life of the poet's mind represented as a development in fairly discrete stages or periods—a forward walk or "step[ping] into" room after room.

Keats's mixed imagery of mist and darkening in the "Chamber of Maiden Thought," as discussed in the introduction, renders the poetic self, at this stage in this process of becoming, partly opaque, while it disrupts the ostensibly linear progress that the architectural-peripatetic metaphor had been unfolding. Such an elaborate disturbance of linear progress, however, appears absent when Keats moves from a discussion of individual poetic development (his own, Reynolds's, and Wordsworth's), in an otherwise almost seamless way, into the subject of historical progression: what he calls the "grand march of intellect" through successive historical epochs. The two discussions—individual poetic development and historical progress—are linked by their metaphor of change as a process of walking and by the figure, both "deep" and towering, of Wordsworth:

> [Wordsworth] is a Genius and superior [to] us, in so far as he can, more than we, make discoveries and shed a light in them—Here I must think Wordsworth is deeper than Milton—though I think it has depended more upon the general and gregarious advance of intellect than individual greatness of Mind. . . . In [Milton's] time englishmen were just emancipated from a great superstition and Men had got hold of certain points and resting places in reasoning which were too newly born to be doubted, and too much opposed <oppressed> by the Mass of Europe not to be thought etherial [*sic*] and authentically divine—who could gainsay his ideas on virtue, vice, and Chastity in Comus, just at the time of the dismissal of Cod-pieces and a hundred other disgraces? who would not rest satisfied with his hintings at good and evil in the Paradise Lost, when just free from the inquisition and burning in Smithfield? The Reformation produced such immediate and great<s> benefits, that Protestantism was considered under the immediate eye of heaven, and its own remaining Dogmas and superstitions, then, as it were, regenerated, constituted those resting places and seeming sure points of Reasoning—from that I have mentioned, Milton, whatever he may have thought in the sequel, appears to have been content with these by his writings—He did

not think into the human heart, as Wordsworth has done—Yet Milton as a Philosop\<h>er had sure as great powers as Wordsworth—What is then to be inferr'd? O, many things—It proves there is really a grand march of intellect—, It proves that a mighty providence subdues the mightiest Minds to the service of the time being, whether it be in human Knowledge or Religion.

(*LJK*, 1:281–82)

Keats's analysis suggests, first, that a certain historical "time being," to whose service Milton's mind was necessarily subject, was ushered in by the Reformation. Next, he establishes a distance between his own "time being" and Milton's, in that the superiority of Wordsworth's insight ("into the human heart") to Milton's rests not upon his greater philosophical powers but on "a grand march of intellect." This is not just literary history, which is only starting to form as a separate category around this time, but also a broader history of "human Knowledge or Religion." The historical "grand march" forms a repetition of the individual's path of poetic improvement through the "large Mansion," though here we find no qualifying twist to the linear path of progress. In this respect, Keats's historical theory is approaching the eighteenth-century Scottish Enlightenment historians whose works he apparently absorbed while in school at Enfield and after.[24]

Unsmokeable Shakespeare

In Keats's epistolary historical thinking, his most frequent reference to Shakespeare as his own model poet (because neither has a poetic "identity") poses a persistently troubling figure to such a historical model of overall progress. For Keats's well-known remarks on Shakespeare place the Renaissance poet in an unsurpassable ("unsmokeable," in the Keatsian idiom) position (*LJK*, 2:18). According to Keats, certain epistemological shifts, although ultimately considered as advances, initially present growing pains, and Milton thus appears to him particularly inhibited by the fact that "englishmen were *just* emancipated from a great superstition"; at the same time, Shakespeare's literary works can appear unhindered by the author's historical circumstances (emphasis added). Ronald Sharp concludes:

> By avoiding the more deterministic form of historicism, Keats can confidently and consistently assume that it is possible for Shakespeare to have understood human truth even though he lived at an earlier time. Although Keats's own age may be more enlightened than Shakespeare's, that does not mean that everyone in Keats's age will be free from illusion. Similarly,

though the "grand march of intellect" may have made Keats's age more readily receptive to human truth, that is no reason why Shakespeare could not have perceived it as well.[25]

Sharp presents a Keats whose historicism seems to have it both ways; the apparent contradiction, or absence of systematization, however, Sharp perceives as answering to "the needs of the present," which required a mode of thought capable of achieving "genuine human significance" without positing a metaphysical truth.[26] While Sharp aptly describes the tension between, on the one hand, Keats's usual adoption of Shakespeare as his model (rather than Wordsworth) and, on the other, his notion of the "grand march of intellect," I want to suggest that Keats's lyric subjectivity (modeled on his idea of Shakespeare)—more so than some of his prose meditations such as the "grand march"—proves the more radical response to this problem of how to imagine the present as history, and a response that displaces a linear notion of progress (or regress) in its lyrical dilation of the moment.[27]

Shakespeare, much more so than Milton or Wordsworth, is Keats's abiding model poet because he has no identity, no poetical character; because his poetry and plays produce an unpredictable aesthetic experience; because one cannot "smoke" him. These are three ways of describing the same quality that Keats famously calls "*Negative Capability*" in 1817—the "quality," Keats reflects, "that went to form a Man of Achievement especially in Literature & which Shakespeare possessed so enormously" (*LJK*, 1:193). Writing to Richard Woodhouse in October 1818 to explain the "poetical Character," Keats identifies his Shakespearean model only indirectly, by allusion:

> As to the poetical Character itself, (I mean that sort of which, if I am any
> thing, I am a Member; that sort distinguished from the wordsworthian
> or egotistical sublime; which is a thing per se and stands alone) it is not
> itself—it has no self—it is every thing and nothing—It has no character—it
> enjoys light and shade; it lives in gusto, be it foul or fair, high or low, rich or
> poor, mean or elevated—It has as much delight in conceiving an Iago as an
> Imogen. What shocks the virtuous philosop[h]er, delights the camelion Poet.
> It does no harm from the relish of the dark side of things any more than from
> its taste for the bright one; because they both end in speculation. A Poet is
> the most unpoetical of any thing in existence; because he has no Identity—he
> is continually in for—and filling some other Body—The Sun, the Moon, the
> Sea and Men and Women who are creatures of impulse are poetical and have
> about them an unchangeable attribute—the poet has none; no identity—he is
> certainly the most unpoetical of all God's Creatures. (*LJK*, 1:387)

Even the authorial name as "Identity" has vanished from Keats's prose as the letter conjures Shakespearean creation only through the fictional characters he fills. For Keats, Shakespeare is, as Emily Sun writes, "the impersonal dramatist par excellence, who was 'every thing and nothing,' who could inhabit a variety of characters from Iago to Imogen without appearing in any way as the hero of his work."[28]

Though his admiration for Shakespeare recurs constantly in his letters, Keats forms each of these phrases to describe a Shakespearean quality—most memorably, *"Negative Capability"* and the "camelion Poet"—only once in all the letters that remain, contrary to what their seemingly endless proliferation in literary criticism to this day might suggest. It is as if Keats himself performs, in his constant reformulations, the notion that Shakespeare cannot be "see[n] through"; he writes to George and Georgiana Keats on December 31, 1818:

> Mrs. Tighe and Beattie once delighted me—now I see through them and can find nothing in them—or weakness—and yet how many they still delight!—Perhaps a superior being may look upon Shakspeare [*sic*] in the same light—is it possible? No—This same inadequacy is discovered (forgive me little George you know I don't mean to put you in the mess) in Women with few exceptions—the Dress Maker, the blue Stocking, the most charming sentimentalist differ but in slight degree and are all equally smokeable. (*LJK*, 2:18–19)

This "[un]smokeable" quality of the Shakespearean literary achievement compels Keats to keep finding new epistolary formulations to approximate the poet who cannot be pinned down and thus illustrates as well the potential inexhaustibility of this resource for Keatsian creativity. This Shakespearean effect is the subject of the 1817 sonnet "On sitting down to read *King Lear* once again."

The sonnet on reading *King Lear* anticipates, more than it recounts, a reading of the play. Keats's aim would appear to be creative inspiration and the furthering of Eros through the aesthetic experience of reading. In an illuminating analysis, Forest Pyle has shown how the turn toward the ethics of tragedy is presided over by the "Chief Poet," and thus it is not a turn away from the aesthetic in favor of ethics but an intertwining of the two.[29] The process begins as an interruption of the reading of Romance, a book that must be rendered mute, shut up, for the reading of the tragedy to happen. "Leave melodizing," he commands to the Romance, as he is compelled to sit down with Shakespeare's play instead, anticipating reading as a process he must "burn through"; that is, he will experience it intensely, and the "I" will burn through it in a process of "self"-immolation:

> O golden-tongued Romance, with serene lute!
> Fair plumed siren, queen of far-away!
> Leave melodizing on this wintry day,
> Shut up thine olden pages, and be mute.
> Adieu! For, once again, the fierce dispute
> Betwixt damnation and impassion'd clay
> Must I burn through; once more humbly assay
> The bitter-sweet of this Shakespearian fruit.
> Chief Poet! and ye clouds of Albion,
> Begetters of our deep eternal theme!
> When through the old oak forest I am gone,
> Let me not wander in a barren dream:
> But, when I am consumed in the fire,
> Give me new phoenix wings to fly at my desire.

Neither the "camelion" poet as maker nor the poet as *reader* (particularly in the experience of fruitful dreams or moments of reading that inspire creativity) has identity. The boundaries dissolve. The poem thus ends by extending the figurative burning to an image of self-immolation that leads to an ambiguously located desire of desire: "But, when I am consumed in the fire, / Give me new phoenix wings to fly at my desire." In the double meaning of the preposition "at," these wings are envisioned both to act on his desire or impulse as well as to lead him toward it, an ambiguity that raises the question of possession: is desire one's own, as the first meaning would suggest, or out of one's reach, as the latter would? The ambiguity works to blur the boundaries thus of one-"self," of the individual.[30] It is perhaps this poetics of crossing over the usual boundaries (between self and others or self and world) that leads Keats to go beyond the iambic pentameter line obviously called for by the sonnet conventions and extend it by a metrical foot, making the last line an Alexandrine.

Whereas the sonnet on "Chapman's Homer" is about a first reading, the *King Lear* sonnet is about reading a text for the second (or fifth or sixth) time. What is therefore all the more remarkable about Keats's anticipation of that aesthetic experience is his sense of its unpredictability: "Let me not wander in a barren dream," the speaker pleads, not knowing what the reading experience will bring yet anticipating the potential of Shakespeare's creation to "give me new phoenix wings," to create the reader's subjectivity anew. Not even a previous reading experience of the same text provides a reliable measure for future encounters. Shakespearean unpredictability thus offers the occasion for surprise ruled out by more conventional concepts of time, such as linear progress and development, which inform contemporary historiographies. Even where Shakespeare or his work is not named, Keats's aesthetic of non-identity might be understood as inspired by Shakespeare: an alternative not only to Wordsworth's "egotistical sublime" but also to literary and narrative temporalities that rely on patterns of the past to make sense of the present and future.

Glorious Anticipation in "England in 1819"

Percy Shelley's thought and verse, so often future oriented, tend toward the prophetic in linguistic register and also tend, within individual works, to move progressively toward the abstract in ways that distinguish his aesthetic from the more resolutely everyday and non- (or even anti-) prophetic modes of Keats, Austen, and Byron. Another way of putting this distinction is to say that whereas Shelley's poetics aspire to a comprehensive social picture or a political totality, what we see in the work of Keats, Austen, and Byron is a self-consciously partial poetics—partial in both senses. Shelley's anticipatory poetics nevertheless claim a place within any study of Romantic temporality, especially one such as this, that focuses mainly on second-generation writers.

Like Keats's *King Lear* and "Chapman's Homer" sonnets, Shelley's "England in 1819," which formed the centerpiece of James Chandler's introduction to his magisterial critical study of the same name, is decidedly prospective. It lists the heavy social ills of England in twelve successive lines only to have them reversed from signs of deterioration to potentialities for regrowth by the future illumination of some "glorious Phantom," who appears in the final couplet:

> An old, mad, blind, despised, and dying King;
> Princes, the dregs of their dull race, who flow
> Through public scorn,—mud from a muddy spring;
> Rulers who neither see nor feel nor know,
> But leechlike to their fainting country cling
> Till they drop, blind in blood, without a blow,
> A people starved and stabbed in th'untilled field;
> An army, whom liberticide and prey
> Makes as a two-edged sword to all who wield;

Golden and sanguine laws which tempt and slay;
Religion Christless, Godless—a book sealed;
A senate, Time's worst statute, unrepealed—
Are graves from which a glorious Phantom may
Burst, to illumine our tempestuous day.[31]

The "act of reading the first twelve lines itself becomes the occasion of a resurrection," James Chandler argues, citing the potential optimism available in the many double meanings of words and images that initially suggest only social ill.[32] "Sanguine" is not just bloody but also hopeful; "leeches" not only suck life blood away but also served medicinal purposes; and "muddy springs" suggest not only the corruption of a purity but also a fertilizing stream during years that had witnessed poor harvests. Such a rereading constitutes the fresh political perspective that "may / Burst, to illumine" the present, altering the political situation for the better. Surely this poetic of the present, like that in Keats's two sonnets discussed earlier, elicits the uncertainty and sense of possibility characteristic of the future anterior imagination.

Yet the otherworldly "Phantom" so central to that sense of futurity reaches beyond the everyday and does so along the lines of what leads Ian Balfour to assert that "something 'like prophetic strain' . . . riddles Shelley's poetic production and some of his prose."[33] Shelley's sonnet moves steadily from the precision of Hanoverian bloodline to the abstraction of the "glorious Phantom" that will reverse the total picture of the first twelve lines. By contrast to the political totality of England to which Shelley's sonnet seems to aspire, Keats's two sonnets focus on the everyday, individualized, and bodily experience of reading two specific books. The *King Lear* sonnet emphasizes the physical movement of the experience in the physical movement of "sitting down," while the "Chapman's Homer" sonnet evokes the kinetics of inhaling the air—breathing the "pure serene"—as one reads. By comparison, Shelley's sonnet tends toward the disembodied and the abstract, which one might associate with his "prophetic strain." The scope of society surveyed in the list, moreover, aspires to a sense of social and political comprehensiveness very different from the material, sensuous particularity of Keats's poem.

Shelley's *Defence of Poetry* contains his most overt statements on prophecy. Reflections on futurity pervade his thinking about the future historical realization of the seeds of the present and about the eyes of posterity, which will look back on the moment in which he is living. "[T]he future is contained within the present as the plant within the seed," Shelley writes

(511). Because of such relations he draws between present and future, he quickly distinguishes his notion of poetic prophecy from prediction:

> For he not only beholds intensely the present as it is, and discovers those laws according to which present things ought to be ordered, but he beholds the future in the present, and his thoughts are the germs of the flower and the fruit of latest time. Not that I assert poets to be prophets in the gross sense of the word, or that they can foretell the form surely as they foreknow the spirit of events: such is the pretence of superstition which would make poetry an attribute of prophecy, rather than prophecy an attribute of poetry. (513)

The matter of prediction aside, Shelley nevertheless focuses on the positive capacity of the poet to *capture* the "spirit" of the future, to "foreknow the spirit of events." What I have aimed to show in Hazlitt's *The Spirit of the Age* and in Keats's sonnets, and as we shall see in Keats's odes, Austen's *Persuasion*, and Byron's *Don Juan*, is an emphasis on the *elusive* spirit of the present insofar as the anticipation of a radically unknowable futurity inhabits it.

3

ACCOMMODATING
SURPRISE: KEATS'S ODES

Keats's odes have been contextualized in a variety of sophisticated ways—
from James Chandler's situating of "Ode to Psyche" in relation to the
cultural "scene" of philosophical and religious discourses of the soul at the
end of the eighteenth century to Nicholas Roe's locating of "To Autumn"
in the midst of the 1819 discourse of political conspiracy, by virtue of the
poem's word "Conspiring."[1] This chapter extends the critical practice of
contextualizing Keats's political ideas to the politics of his concepts of
time. This politics is especially salient in Keats's ode forms, which draw
on sonnet conventions while also altering them in the making of the ode
stanzas. As we shall see, Keats's poetic innovations in the ode form engage
with the largely linear notions of progress informing Enlightenment historiography in order to imagine alternative conceptions of time that facilitate
a new way of being in the world attuned to the temporal complexities of
modernity.

Fainting with Surprise

"Ode to Psyche" is a poem about coming to terms with surprise, a surprise
encounter with the Greek goddess and her lover Cupid in the grass. To cele-
brate Psyche in the world of early nineteenth-century England is, as James
Chandler has shown in *England in 1819*, to displace the content of normative
cultural narratives of progress toward civilization. It is to recognize the
historical neglect of Psyche ever since Apuleius composed his narrative at
the end of the second century AD and to decide to make amends for that
neglect against the current of much contemporary thought. In narratives of
cultural progress popular in Keats's moment, even the Christian discourse
of the soul, which had long ago overridden the authority of pagan deities,
had been superseded by mechanistic philosophy. For dissenting intellec-

tuals such as William Godwin, as well as for Scottish Enlightenment philosophers such as William Robertson and David Hume, use of the rational
faculties—rather than an appeal to the soul (which, as William Cowper
memorably puts it, "does not always think")—becomes valued as the high-
est achievement of human progress.[2] The following discussion will build
on Chandler's insight about the ode's historical engagement by attending
to the poem's formal and aesthetic dynamics as themselves making an
intervention in the historical "scene" that Chandler describes; that is, the
temporal logic of displacement by surprise, I shall argue, counters the very
notion of linear progress itself that informs normative cultural narratives
of Keats's moment and that remains in play in Chandler's own alternative
history.[3] Unlike in those narratives, in Keats's ode, time moves laterally—
not by progress or by even or uneven development but by displacement and
dilation. What progressive narratives of human or cultural development
close off is the capacity for historical surprise.[4] And what Keats's encounter
with Psyche shows us is a complex temporal movement from the beginning
to the end of the poem that turns out to be a kind of doubling back—the
slow delay of human knowledge that we know in psychoanalytic terms as
deferred action. It is also the temporality of a present adequate to registering the experience of (historical) surprise.

Keats inherits from Shakespearean drama a principle of non-identity,
a mobility of mind that moves with ease from imagining an Iago to an
Imogen. This principle of imagination, however, serves for Keats primarily
nondramatic purposes.[5] For the lyric subjectivity of "Ode to Psyche," it
means a blurring of the usual boundaries of the "I"—the boundaries, for
instance, between self and other or subject and object, as well as between
waking and dreaming states. The first stanza delivers us into a world of
uncertainties, a world in which the speaker has recovered from fainting
but where the boundaries between dreaming and waking have not been,
perhaps may never be, entirely restored:

O Goddess! hear these tuneless numbers, wrung
  By sweet enforcement and remembrance dear,
And pardon that thy secrets should be sung
  Even into thy own soft-conchèd ear:
Surely I dreamt to-day, or did I see
  The winged Psyche with awaken'd eyes?
I wander'd in a forest thoughtlessly,
  And, on the sudden, fainting with surprise,
Saw two fair creatures, couchèd side by side

In deepest grass, beneath the whisp'ring roof
Of leaves and trembled blossoms, where there ran
      A brooklet, scarce espied:
'Mid hush'd, cool-rooted flowers, fragrant-eyed,
  Blue, silver-white, and budded Tyrian,
They lay calm-breathing on the bedded grass;
  Their arms embraced, and their pinions too;
  Their lips touch'd not, but had not bade adieu,
As if disjoined by soft-handed slumber,
And ready still past kisses to outnumber
At tender eye-dawn of aurorean love:
      The winged boy I knew;
But who wast thou, O happy, happy dove?
      His Psyche true! (1–23)

A blurring of boundaries appears in the poem's originating question—"Surely I dreamt today, or did I see / The winged Psyche with awaken'd eyes?" (5–6)—a question that remains throughout productively unanswerable. That blurring of boundaries, the impossibility it suggests of a distinct, complete self-identity, is enacted as well in the stanza form. The short, almost hidden line of "A brooklet, scarce espied" (12) literally appears "beneath the whisp'ring roof / Of leaves and trembled blossoms" (10–11), a formal canopy (iambic pentameter lines) that hangs over the middle of the stanza (a nestled trimeter line) to suggest the enclosure that is disrupted by the arrival of the speaker who stumbles onto the divine couple. What's more, in developing the ode's stanza, Keats experiments with the sonnet form in a way that thwarts both the English and Italian sonnet's formal tendency toward resolution and closure in the final couplet or sestet, respectively. The ode's rhyme scheme develops patterns that suggest hybrid components of the sonnet: two English quatrains followed by an Italian sestet, followed by the unrhymed ("grass"), two couplets, and an English quatrain.[6] The first fourteen lines make up a mixed sonnet, but the stanza exceeds that limit by nine more lines and, though it incorporates couplets, ends with the less tightly closed English quatrain and the irregularity of an unprecedented dimeter line. That the quatrain comes after the compression of two couplets, moreover, gives the sense of an ending where the perspective opens up.

If the lyric form of the surprise encounter with Psyche is an opening up, its temporal dimension would seem to have to offer some alternative to normative modes of linear progress, since the notion of progress closes off the future's potential to disrupt expectations. The poem's grammar moves from past tense in the first stanza ("I wander'd in a forest" [7]), to present tense in the second and third stanzas ("temple thou hast none" [28] and "I see, and sing" [43]), and to future tense in the fourth ("Yes, I will be thy priest" [50]). This is not to say that the ode's temporal movement is linear, however. For, first of all, that linear movement from past to present to future in the course of the poem is all contained in a present moment by the utterance's scene of invocation: "O Goddess! hear these tuneless numbers" (1). Second, a circularity of the stanza sequence creates tension with the grammatical linear progression from past to future. That is, the stanzas form a structural chiasmus, *ABBA*, insofar as the first and fourth stanzas have clear affiliations, as do the second and third. The result is a tension that is neither temporal progress nor circularity but dilation of the moment and a sense of time that approximates what we know in psychoanalytic terms as deferred action, an *après coup*: the experience of an event the taking place of which appears delayed by one's initial failure to comprehend or under-stand the event.[7] It is the temporality of a present adequate to registering the experience of (historical) surprise.

"Ode to Psyche" tells the story of the process of the mind's coming to awareness; in this respect, it resembles the story Keats tells in his letter on human life as a "large Mansion of Many Apartments" which, as we have seen, forms a prelude to and model for the historical "march of intellect." Moreover, the ode's language and its images recall that letter of 1818, which moves from the infant chamber to the "Chamber of Maiden-Thought" and pauses at the edge of "dark Passages." In the initial encounter in the first stanza, for instance, the speaker's wandering "thoughtlessly," with-out intentional direction, into the natural, protective haven "beneath the whisp'ring roof / Of leaves and trembled blossoms," evokes the Mansion's "infant or thoughtless Chamber, in which we remain as long as we do not think," as the contours of the bower enclose the speaker's world like nature's chamber. The spatial aspect is clear. What the wandering ends in, moreover, is unconsciousness; the speaker here "faint[s] with surprise" (8)—experiences weakness and vulnerability—in a world in which Psyche can be seen, in simple terms, as a "happy, happy dove" (22).

The speaker's very ability to recall the encounter indicates a recov-ery of consciousness, and the middle two stanzas evoke thus his exhil-arated sense of her state, "O brightest!" (36); likewise, Keats writes in the letter that in the "second Chamber, which I shall call the Chamber of Maiden-Thought, . . . we become intoxicated with the light and the atmosphere, we see nothing but pleasant wonders, and think of delaying there for ever in delight." Even in the middle two stanzas charged with intoxicated praise, however, a sense of regret for the historical injustices of Psyche's neglect begins to intrude, sobering the voice. Similarly, in the epistolary middle chamber, "among the effects this breathing [of the light atmosphere] is father of is that tremendous one of . . . convincing ones [*sic*] nerves that the World is full of Misery and Heartbreak, Pain, Sickness and oppression—whereby This Chamber of Maiden Thought becomes gradually darken'd." To that end, thoughtless and passive wandering is replaced in the fourth stanza by the "shadowy thought" (65) of an actively "working brain" (60); the enclosed bower gives way to the speaker's mindscape materially entwined in a landscape of prospective vision, constructed of "branched thoughts, new grown with pleasant pain" (52).

While the resonances between the letter and ode are fairly abundant, an aesthetic shift in the final stanza—a scene of, at once, the anticipation of an unknown future and a doubling back to the first stanza—significantly challenges the notion of linear progression, a progression less substantially challenged in epistolary form. In the ode's final stanza, rather than reconstructing the spatial contours of the original bower scene by envisioning and observing Psyche clearly placed in her temple (as she was clearly positioned, although not immediately recognized, in the opening bower), Keats gives us no distinct spatial orientation. Psyche's "lucent fans" (41) of the third stanza disappear, or merge into the mental "fane" (50); it is as if her identity, her material existence itself that at first had so undone the speaker, has been absorbed into the materials of the poetic construction, into the poetic activity of "feign[ing]" (62) her place. The clear distinction between lyrical subject (poet-speaker) and object (Psyche) breaks down. What this process leads to is the disorientation in the last stanza of the speaker's place and of the poem's point of view:

> Yes, I will be thy priest, and build a fane
>   In some untrodden region of my mind,
> Where branched thoughts, new grown with pleasant pain,
>   Instead of pines shall murmur in the wind:
> Far, far around shall those dark-cluster'd trees
>   Fledge the wild-ridged mountains steep by steep;
> And there by zephyrs, streams, and birds, and bees,
>   The moss-lain Dryads shall be lull'd to sleep;
> And in the midst of this wide quietness
> A rosy sanctuary will I dress
> With the wreath'd trellis of a working brain,

With buds, and bells, and stars without a name,
With all the gardener Fancy e'er could feign,
    Who breeding flowers, will never breed the same:
And there shall be for thee all soft delight
    That shadowy thought can win,
A bright torch, and a casement ope at night,
    To let the warm Love in! (50–67)

There *is* a "casement ope" (66), but unlike in the first stanza's encounter, one is hard-pressed to say from what point of view, inside or outside the frame, the poem's perspective is situated. Where, indeed, is Psyche? In the first stanza, the couple's continued static absorption in one another ushers in the question of how to respond insofar as Psyche and Cupid figure a disturbing psychic otherness to which the speaker's "faint[ing] with surprise" attests—an otherness so profound that even the speaker's recognition of the enigmatic goddess comes only after some delay: "The winged boy I knew; / But who wast thou, O happy, happy dove? / His Psyche true!" (21–23). Although we encounter a beautiful *couple* and the focus is on Psyche rather than Cupid, the scene is reminiscent of a pattern that Karen Swann has observed in *Endymion* of single "abstracted dreamers, all piercingly beautiful": "Adonis," she writes, "is one in a series of boys, boys, boys—mute, self-enclosed, and infinitely seductive."[8] To take account of the speaker's initial encounter, as the ode proceeds purposefully to do, is spatially to open the bower up and aesthetically to open the poem up toward the mute lovers, to what is closed off from the speaker in the bower of the lovers' mutual absorption. Thus the expansive "wild-ridged mountains" (55) in the final stanza would replace, with a sense of unknown possibilities, the first stanza's soft enclosure: its "whisp'ring roof / Of leaves" (10–11) and "bedded grass" (15). The "wild" mountainous region, however, appears not yet conceptualized or envisioned as a clearly defined *scene*. The image is only "*some* untrodden region" as yet only vaguely anticipated (51, emphasis mine). And so, the formal parallel between the first and last stanzas is at least slightly asymmetrical, not a circle enclosed; rather, it is the exposure of a space that might acknowledge a radical otherness but whose parameters are not yet—perhaps cannot finally be—clearly defined.

An Aesthetics of Deferred Action

From the point of view of aesthetics, moreover, what emerges in the final stanza is an aural resonance between the temple the speaker vows to build, "a fane" (50), and the act of imagining as artifice, "all the gardener Fancy e'er could feign" (62). To accommodate Psyche in the present, artifice, fiction, even falsehood appears required. What the aural resonance of "fane" and "feign" then retroactively brings into play is the "faint[ing] with surprise" in the first stanza, the speaker's response to the encounter with Psyche and Cupid that initiated the whole meditation in the first place. My reading of the poem follows the sonic play, pursuing the temporal logic of the encounter through this aural resonance that leads us back to the bout of unconsciousness; what follows the initial encounter and unconsciousness is a process of awakening that calls for fictional construction (feign/fane) and the invention of a new space, a new way of being—the need for which the speaker's initial act of fainting announces. The affiliation of fainting and feigning as the precursors to Psyche's arrival, moreover, suggests unconsciousness (including its linguistic methods of association) as the potential path to a radically new truth; for this new way of seeing the world, the imagination of a place of "buds, and bells, and stars without a name" (61), is anticipated as a potentially retroactive means of accommodating the encounter with "Psyche true!" (23). In this way, the ode's temporal logic appears neither progressive nor circular but otherwise—perhaps by virtue of that very linear-circular tension. It is a logic of deferral in which the final stanza's act of anticipation, of imagination, becomes the necessary prerequisite for thinking the initial encounter, for that encounter's becoming, in this sense, possible. The slow delay of the speaker's recognition of Psyche in the first stanza, then, stands for the time of deferred knowing: "The winged boy I knew; / But who wast thou, O happy, happy dove?" (21–22).

"Ode to Psyche" thus offers us a model of change, of historical change perhaps, that foregrounds the subject's process of coming to terms with an interruption—with the encounter that disorients the speaker and disrupts the apparent laws of what is. In the formal, ostensibly circular chiasmus of the four stanzas, as well as in the aesthetic mode of linguistic affiliation between "fane," "feign," and the surprise of "faint[ing]," unconsciousness and fiction become allied in a complex temporal path to a radically new truth, "Psyche true!" (23); the ode enacts, that is, a temporality of surprise that the spatial stability of the "large Mansion of Many Apartments" letter cannot.

This temporal difference between the formal aesthetics of letter and ode calls for critical reassessment, given the way in which the relationship between the two has been treated. In regard to precisely this issue of relationship, Stuart Sperry's discussion of the pairing, while it suggests that the letter's "tentative conclusions become the subject of reconsideration in Keats's ode," remains nevertheless within the spatial terms of the letter;

Sperry writes, "Indeed the recognition the ode finally intimates is that for the poet of the present day there can be no escape from shadowiness and subjectivity, that the effort to push further into the region of the unknown leads only to the perception of further passages and implications, that it results in a sense of ultimate inconclusiveness that is ironic."[9] Helen Vendler employs the letter even more directly in her reading of "Psyche": "we sense a positive effort, at the close of the ode, to stave off the encroaching dark passages."[10] My effort to more substantially differentiate the two literary productions derives from my sense that a remarkable achievement of the ode's particular aesthetic is to enact what the letter can only begin to describe: a radical change in the experience of time (and space) that takes place in the process of the mind's coming to a new awareness.

Just before copying the poem out in a letter of 1819 to George and Georgiana Keats, Keats writes: "You must recollect that Psyche was not embodied as a goddess before the time of Apuleius the Platonist who lived afteir [sic] the A[u]gustan age, and consequently the Goddess was never worshipped or sacrificed to with any of the ancient fervor—and perhaps never thought of in the old religion"; he adds, "I am more orthodox tha[n] to let a hethen [sic] Goddess be so neglected" (LJK, 2:106). James Chandler's historiographical reading of the poem has brought out Keats's complex engagement with certain tasks of modernity, his self-conscious situating of the poem at the end of the Christian era as well as after the more recent period of enlightened skepticism toward the soul; Chandler accomplishes this reading, in part, through his attention to Keats's acknowledged source for the Psyche myth, Apuleius's prose narrative The Golden Ass, written toward the end of the second century AD. Keats's characterization of Psyche in the letter to George and Georgiana, as well as in the poem itself, displaces the neglect of Apuleius's plot, in which Venus complains of the neglect of her own worship as a result of the very attentions paid to the beauty of the mere mortal Psyche. Outside the narrative embodiment by Apuleius, the neglect in Keats's account is located, instead, in Psyche's (historical) reception, as the speaker addresses her in the second and third stanzas:

> O latest born and loveliest vision far
>   Of all Olympus' faded hierarchy!
> Fairer that Phoebe's sapphire-region'd star,
>   Or Vesper, amorous glow-worm of the sky;
> Fairer than these, though temple thou hast none,
>   Nor altar heap'd with flowers;

Nor virgin-choir to make delicious moan
    Upon the midnight hours;
No voice, no lute, no pipe, no incense sweet
  From chain-swung censer teeming;
No shrine, no grove, no oracle, no heat
  Of pale-mouth'd prophet dreaming.

O brightest! though too late for antique vows,
    Too, too late for the fond believing lyre,
When holy were the haunted forest boughs,
  Holy the air, the water, and the fire; (24–39)

Psyche is "latest born" (24) because, in Apuleius's narrative, she is the youngest sister, but her embodiment in narrative by Apuleius, her textual birth, is also late: as Keats puts it, "afteir [*sic*] the A[u]gustan age, and consequently the Goddess was never worshipped or sacrificed to with any of the ancient fervor." Embodied in narrative at an unfortunate historical moment, she is "too late for antique vows" (36). The character of reception turns upon the historical period, the cultural epoch. Chandler has suggested that Keats attempts thus to pick up where Apuleius left off; this effort involves not "striving to recapture Apuleius's moment" but rather "continuing a process that Apuleius had advanced and that a millennium and a half of Christianity had interrupted." In other words, the neglect has been a consequence of the appropriation of the discourse of the soul by a dominant Christianity, followed by "the mechanist strain in Enlightenment moralist philosophy," which neglected to acknowledge a psyche or soul at all.[11] The poem represents itself thus as the proper—if deferred a millennium and a half—response to the birth of the goddess.

As Keats offers his own historical moment, however difficult, as a potential turn in Psyche's story and his speaker as playing a key role in that turn, the narrative is decentered in these twofold ways (subjective and historical). At the same time that Keats's moment entails an urgency to know—and write—the present as history, neither the self nor the historical present appears fully knowable. Keats's historiographical aesthetic thus involves a self-consciousness of that limit; it enacts a historiography that is provisional and a subject that emerges not as self-identical but in the shifting grounds of being:

Yet even in these days so far retir'd
  From happy pieties, thy lucent fans,
  Fluttering among the faint Olympians,
I see, and sing, by my own eyes inspired. (40–43)

The time of "happy pieties" (41) registers a twofold significance in that not only from a historical point of view is the poet far removed from the ancient world of "fond believing" (37) in Greek and Roman mythology but also in respect to his own poetical career, he has left "the realm . . . / Of Flora, and old Pan" (*Sleep and Poetry*, 101–2). In other words, recapitulated in the shape of his own poetic development, the poet-speaker has experienced, through a dilation of the lyrical moment, historical developments of the Western world since antiquity, while the present task of hastening the world toward a future, redemptive circumstance for Psyche has fallen to the individual subject, suspended grammatically by the floating modifier "Fluttering" (42)—between what Psyche (the psyche) possesses ("*thy* lucent fans" [41]) and the claims of the individual ego, the "I." The space between Psyche and the "I"—the motion of "Fluttering"—bespeaks the poetic play of ambiguity, its destabilizing power, at the same time that it exposes, perhaps as the same thing, the impossibility of perfect self-reflexivity, of complete self-knowledge or identity; this productive destabilization occurs in view of a subjectivity that comes into being through fictions and reveals the boundaries and unity of "selfhood" as themselves a fiction. The "one," for Keats, is not one, which is to say that the subject is never entirely self-identical. It is no accident, or no meaningless one, that in "Ode to a Nightingale" the speaker's return to "my sole self" (72) rhymes with "deceiving elf" (74).

This foregrounding of the lyric subject as revisionary fiction makes possible Keats's subtle, albeit tentative, identification of his present position as seer and singer (composer of lyric) with Psyche as she appeared in Apuleius's narrative in late antiquity. Visible at the ode's turn, near the close of the third stanza, this identification of Psyche and speaker (across the floating modifier "Fluttering") appears to enable the shift toward the future-oriented final stanza. When the speaker announces, "I see, and sing, by my own eyes inspired" (43), one recalls Psyche's most defining characteristic aside from her beauty: Psyche represents "an empiricism that insists on the proof of the senses."[12] In Apuleius's narrative, twice Psyche's curiosity to know *by her own eyes* ostensibly sets her love for Cupid back. This identification is underscored by the next line in the suggested grammatical substitution of "me" for "thy": "So let me be thy choir" (44), which is to suggest the speaker as transmitter (as "thy voice, thy lute" [46])—Ode *from* Psyche—and to acknowledge the otherness of poetic voice and creative inspiration.

The identification also appears earlier, in the second stanza, in an even more forceful suggestion that the poet's own reputation might find a similar temporality, a historically deferred proper reception. Percy Shelley, in any case, perceived a similarity between the poet himself and his representation of Psyche: in Keats's words, "latest born and loveliest vision far" (24). For Shelley's elegy on Keats, *Adonais*, depicts the poet as the "youngest, dearest one" (46), "the loveliest and the last" (51), in an echo of Keats's Psyche.[13] Since the course of Psyche's cultural role in Keats's cultural present (and future) cannot be derived from her role in the past, his poetic embodiment reflects this difficulty, modernity's challenge of apprehending how a present incident will look from the remove of some unknowable future.

James Chandler thus has posed and addressed the following questions about the poem: "But what is the *scene* of this utterance? The scene depicted *in* the utterance is clear enough. . . . How might we understand the scene of the utterance that describes such a scene?"[14] Chandler's assumption that the "scene depicted *in* the utterance is clear enough," however, downplays the difference that the ode's aesthetic makes in both spatial and temporal terms. What this assessment misses is the way in which the ode radically unsettles the very notion of a definable *scene* itself—an unsettling that has historiographical significance especially when we recall the characterization of modernity (in Chapter 1) as a facing of the very difficulty of representing the scene of the present as the most recent historical age. Rather than envisioning a historical scene, Keats's lyric subjectivity in "Ode to Psyche" elicits, more than it semantically conveys, a sense of interruption that calls for a reimagining of the very grounds of being as continually shifting in a world characterized by the unpredictable and enriched by surprise.

Keats's "soul" is a worldly discovery and a human creation; it is earned through "the wreath'd trellis of a working brain," a work that is also the interwoven sonic play crucial to accommodating Psyche. Psyche is both impetus and potential consequence of surprise in a poetic formation that clearly challenges a conventional logic of cause and effect. Surprise, for Keats, comes not through naïve innocence but in a state not unlike William Blake's notion of organized innocence, won in part through worldly experience.

Hornbook as the Threshold to the World

The worldly making of the soul—as opposed to the soul's preexistence or fully formed presence at birth—is the subject of Keats's letter on the world as "vale of Soul-making," and I turn now to it as a way of thinking about the historiographical implications of the "hours by hours" of "To

Autumn." The sense of time in Keats's ode constitutes a dilation of the moment as at once proliferation of possibility and proleptic mourning of that proliferation. Read in light of the "vale of Soul-making" letter as well as in relation to the intellectual predicaments of modern historiography discussed earlier, "To Autumn" appears in its proliferation of possibilities not only as an aesthetic thinking through of the challenges of imagining and writing the present as history in post-Waterloo England but also as itself an event that takes place through reading.

For many in the post-Waterloo period, the whole course of the revolution, as well as its "termination" at Waterloo, appeared radically out of joint with previous history.[15] Unprecedented, astonishing, overwhelming: it is no surprise that the discourse of the sublime provided one way of talking about the felt ineffability of Waterloo's historical significance. The official discourse of the victory abroad as moral splendor appeared to many incompatible with the social, economic, and political duress at home.[16] Philip Shaw has written that in the years immediately following 1815, Waterloo "as a recent event in the history of the English . . . as yet has no 'figure'" through which the event could be assimilated to national consciousness.[17] Thus the sublime—"whose greatness [is] comparable to itself alone," according to Kant—helped indicate the unforeseen quality of recent events that contributed to a pervasive sense of historical astonishment.[18]

What we find particularly in "To Autumn" is not just a way of thinking about the challenges of narrating the present in the post-Waterloo moment but a way of thinking that, while it suggests the unforeseen quality of events that occasions an astonishment like that of the sublime, provides an alternative to the sublime by opening the present to multiple possibilities. Burke wrote of the sublime in nature that "the mind is so entirely filled with its object, that it cannot entertain any other, nor by consequence reason on that object which employs it."[19] Whereas the experience of Burke's sublime is totalizing (to the exclusion of "any other" object but one), the temporality of Keats's post-Waterloo present—though mysterious, and like the sublime not fully comprehensible—is more heterogeneous, accommodating multiple, distinct ways of imagining the time. For Keats, the present appeared as neither progressive nor regressive but digressive, decentered, and decidedly nontotalizing. It suggested a world not of predictability or even probability but of contingency and multiple possibilities—a world not subject to being stabilized by reference either to patterns of the past or to a clear trajectory into the future.

The self-reflexive density of Keats's poems has been cause for historicist concern, most notably in Jerome McGann's much-cited critique of "To

Autumn"; self-reflexivity and the appeal to the visual arts, according to McGann, fostered Keats's "attempt to 'escape' the period which provides the poem with its context."[20] Nicholas Roe, however, has countered McGann's analysis by connecting Keats's verb "conspire" with the political discourse of the moment. Showing that "political debate in August and September 1819 focused on the word 'conspire,'" Roe has established a "credible link between the ongoing discussion of national crisis in the newspapers and conspiracy in 'To Autumn.'" He relates as well the reaping "hook" and "last oozings" to the "dreadful, sanguinary" contemporary responses to Peterloo: "Through such verbal details the apocalyptic harvest of the fields of St. Peter is acknowledged." Finally, Roe traced the goddess Ceres' "symbolic roles" of instituting justice and equal distribution in Keats's schoolboy reading of Lemprière and Ovid to suggest the political implications of evoking her in the highly charged political atmosphere of Peterloo.[21]

In Roe's analysis, however, Keats's ode appears to echo a political position that was already part of the ongoing political debates in 1819. Roe refers suggestively to the poem as Keats's "negatively capable intervention" (in contrast to a Godwinian approach to politics, i.e., perfectibility), but his analysis stops short of reading the poem's aesthetic or formal enactment of negative capability in the service of a political intervention.[22] Ever since the 1986 special issue of *Studies in Romanticism* on the topic of Keats and politics, numerous critics have explored the positive connections between Keats's poetry and its historical or political "contexts."[23] From the outset, though, a certain limit to what political or historical "contexts" can do has been apparent, as when, in his essay on Keats's Cockney couplets, William Keach writes, "We seem to arrive at a point where the explanatory usefulness of the political context for Keats's early couplet style breaks down."[24] Similarly, Roe's analysis of "To Autumn" did not ask what role the poem's form or its self-reflexivity plays relative to its historical and political dimensions.

Paul Fry's subtle reading of "To Autumn" in the 1986 special issue of *Studies in Romanticism* critiques the notion of history that McGann espouses in "Keats and the Historical Method" and that has seemed since to live on in Roe's analysis. "The real challenge for 'the historical method,'" Fry writes, "is to resist arranging a few beads like Peterloo, Pentridge, the Holy Alliance, and the arrest of Major Cartwright along the string of class conflict and calling it history."[25] For Fry, "The question . . . is not whether we all understand that nature was invented by culture—we all do—but whether in interpreting poems like 'To Autumn' we can reserve the conviction that within culture the existential register is still sometimes more appropriate to emphasize than the historical one." In the last stanza, Fry observes the "dry and bracing place . . . of soft dying" that McGann's analysis ignores. Quoting Stanley Cavell, he asserts that Keats's dangerous "'intimacy with existence'" amounted to a "refusal to sublimate mortality as a social conspiracy"; that the poem is not "historical" in McGann's sense, that is, does not make it escapist.[26]

Insofar as subjective and historiographical uncertainties often implicated one another in Keats's letters and poems, however, we need not imagine Keats's appeal to what Fry calls the "existential register" as an automatic opting out of historical engagement to confront existence instead. Although Fry appears to assume the mutual exclusivity of the existential and historical registers, he writes that the "existential register is still *sometimes* more appropriate," implying not the timelessness of Keats's utterance but its timeliness.[27] At the same time that Fry rejects McGann's historical method, Fry's claim for "To Autumn" opened the interpretive possibility that the poem was nevertheless in some way appropriate for the time, for Keats's historical moment. It is in the spirit of pursuing that possibility that I reread the poem as engaging with the kinds of intellectual problems that faced historiographers and others in the early nineteenth century. More specifically, insofar as the uncertainties that Keats's existential register elicits engaged with the kinds of intellectual and practical problems historians themselves faced in Keats's moment when trying to imagine and write the present as history, the ode might be understood to intervene in the historical register by changing its terms. In contrast to conventional historiographies, the ode imagines a present alive to temporal flux, without relying on the past as a model or having access to what is yet to come. Whereas progressive histories had happiness as their goal, Keats's ode, especially in the last stanza, made the possibilities that open up in a dilating present the subject of a proleptic mourning.

My aim, then, is to explore a historical dimension of Keats's ode by way of its self-reflexivity and its formal and aesthetic dimensions and thus to complicate the assumptions about "text" and "context"—the very division between concepts such as "poetry" and "history," the "existential" and the "historical"—that have persisted in approaches to Keats's poetry following McGann's: the assumption, for instance, that historical or political "context" is a set domain to which poetry, if it is to be politically or historically significant, refers. A return to the issues of self-reflexivity and to reconsidering Keats's positive political engagement now can provide a reading of the ode's historical specificity that does not rely on an idea of poetry's referential status to a presupposed object of "political culture."

For Keats, who famously conceived of the poetical character as having "no self," self-reflexivity, I want to suggest, might be imagined not as the self-enclosure and escape that McGann suggests but as a loophole to the ostensibly "exterior" social and historical world in flux. Far from being the unequivocal tool of escape, self-reflexivity, Deborah White theorizes in *Romantic Returns*, can enable poetry's singular access to history. "Reflexivity," she writes, "can never be entirely (self-) reflexive; it always contains the surplus of difference that enables it to re-fer (or bear back) toward itself. . . . A reading that engages not only what a text says or even how it says it, but what it does inevitably opens upon its ostensible, 'historical' exterior. In this specific sense," White continues, "even the most vertiginously reflexive of Romantic texts—or, rather, especially the most vertiginously reflexive of Romantic texts—offer a point of entry into the field of history. They break down the border between different fields of discourse, different genres of 'text,' and different 'contexts' of interpretation."[28]

By implication of White's formulation, a "surplus of difference" that follows from the failure of perfect self-reflexivity ensures the impossibility of perfect textual self-mastery: a limit by virtue of which the text opens onto an "ostensible, 'historical' exterior."[29] A preliminary detour through Keats's letter on the world as a "vale of Soul-making" will help make visible the movement from self-reflexivity to history that takes shape in "To Autumn," for the April 1819 letter to George and Georgiana Keats performs the very displacement of progressive history that I seek to describe in Keats's poetry. It does so, moreover, by virtue of a self-reflexivity that becomes, we might say, simply *reflexivity*, removing from the process the notion of an unalterable consistency in essential "selfhood."

Critics have frequently framed the significance of Keats's notion of the world as a "vale of Soul-making" as an alternative to the Christian consolation for mortality in the afterlife, the world as a "vale of tears."[30] What this exclusive focus overlooks is that Keats's formulation in the letter serves also as an alternative to what he sees as the failures of historical discourse, even though it is precisely the shortcomings of historical narrative that appear to prompt the idea. The 1819 letter to George and Georgiana Keats vividly shifts from a discussion of the problems of trying to understand the world through William Robertson's *History of America* to a proposal for the solution to those problems: the poet's own philosophy of subject-making in the worldly, temporal making of a soul. For Keats, the world is not suited for making progress toward happiness in civilized commercial society; it is a place to learn to read the "human heart" and to be altered by that reading.

Prompted by the shortcomings of Robertson's mode of historical discourse, Keats proposed instead that the world was a "'vale of Soul-making.'"

"I have been reading lately two very different books, Robertson's America and Voltaire's Siecle De Louis xiv," Keats wrote. "It is like walking arm in arm between Pizarro and the great-little Monarch" (*LJK*, 2:100). However different from one another, the books are both histories of the modern period displaying a commitment to the notion of cultural progress. To illustrate the move Keats makes from historical discourse to the "vale of Soul-making," I quote at some length his analysis of Robertson's history, which serves as a critical prelude. Although Keats does not refer again directly to Voltaire's history, the commentary critiques some of its most prominent assumptions about time and progress as well:

> In How lamentabl[e] [*sic*] a case do we see the great body of the people in both instances [Robertson and Voltaire]: in the first,[31] where Men might seem to inherit quiet of Mind from unsophisticated senses; from uncontamination of civilization; and especially from their being as it were estranged from the mutual helps of Society and its mutual injuries—and thereby more immediately under the Protection of Providence—even there they had mortal pains to bear as bad; or even worse than Baliffs [*sic*], Debts and Poverties of civilized Life—The whole appears to resolve into this—that Man is originally "a poor forked creature" subject to the same mischances as the beasts of the forest, destined to hardships and disquietude of some kind or other. If he improves by degrees his bodily accommodations and comforts—at each stage, at each accent there are waiting for him a fresh set of annoyances—he is mortal and there is still a heaven with its Stars abov[e] his head. The most interesting question that can come before us is, How far by the persevering endeavors of a seldom appearing Socrates Mankind may be made happy—I can imagine such happiness carried to an extreme—but what must it end in?—Death—and who could in such a case bear with death—the whole troubles of life which are now frittered away in a series of years, would the[n] be accumulated for the last days of a being who instead of hailing its approach, would leave this world as Eve left Paradise—But in truth I do not at all believe in this sort of perfectibility— the nature of the world will not admit of it—the inhabitants of the world will correspond to itself—Let the fish philosophise the ice away from the Rivers in winter time. . . . The common cognomen of this world among the misguided and superstitious is a "vale of tears" from which we are to be redeemed by a certain arbitrary interposition of God and taken to Heaven—What a little circumscribe[d] straightened notion! Call the world if you Please "The vale of Soul-making." (*LJK*, 2:101–2)

Keats's commentary departs from Voltaire's historiography when he detaches the emergence of genius, in the form of a figure such as Socrates, from the forces of cultural development. "The most interesting question that can come before us is," Keats declares, "How far by the persevering endeavors of a seldom appearing Socrates mankind may be made happy." A "seldom appearing Socrates" comes into view now and then in human history, but there is no assumption that progress promises any greater frequency. Moreover, it is the individual genius who possesses any promise of power to improve social conditions rather than the cultural forces of progress that produce the genius. This logic of cultural change reverses that of Voltaire in *Le Siècle de Louis XIV.* "For Voltaire, the appearance of persons of genius was a consequence of the overall advancement of civilization . . . the superiority of the moderns was beyond dispute. . . . *The Age of Louis XIV,*" Pierre France explains, "was predicated on a refutation of Dubos's theory on the relationship between a *siècle* and its geniuses"; Dubos had contended that "true greatness comes from genius, which is individual and ultimately unrelated to the overall degree of civilization."[32] Aligned with Dubos's theory, Keats's meditation on cultural progress contradicts not only Voltaire's commitment to valorizing modern history and culture but also Keats's own sometimes commitment to cultural progress and its effects on genius. A year earlier, for instance, he had reasoned that Wordsworth was deeper than Milton, for although Milton "had sure as great powers as Wordsworth," "He did not think into the human heart, as Wordsworth has done" (*LJK,* 1:282). From this observation, Keats concluded, "there is really a grand march of intellect" (*LJK,* 1:282). Keats departs from that statement as well as Voltaire's strong historical convictions when he posits the almost random historical appearance of a Socrates, while reflecting on the histories he has been reading. This is not to say that one or the other view should be taken as Keats's official word on historical theory but to show how Keats's engagement with various ways of thinking about history was an ongoing preoccupation because the available discourse appeared to Keats inadequate for imagining the present as history.

In the "vale of Soul-making" letter, the more overt critique centers on Robertson, with the key words "happiness" and "perfectibility." Underlying Robertson's historiography was the assumption of happiness as a perfectible, achievable goal. But this model and its aims—a social and cultural progress toward civilized happiness—struck Keats as false, ill suited to the world as he found it: "In truth I do not at all believe in this sort of perfectibility—the nature of the world will not admit of it." Stadial progress of civilization, even if it were viable, would not reduce overall human discomfort; discomfort would only come in new forms—"at each stage," "a fresh set of annoyances."

Keats finds the guiding notion of Christian redemption even more wanting than he found progress—to a similar extent, perhaps, as we find in Blake's image of Tom Dacre in "The Chimney Sweeper." In place of Robertson's mode of philosophical history and the Christian model of salvation in afterlife, Keats's "vale of Soul-making" offered alternative aims. His vale is not a place to find happiness but "A Place where the heart must feel and suffer in a thousand diverse ways!" (*LJK*, 2:102). An unviable aim according to Keats, happiness might not be the most valuable aim either. In Keats's letter, a process of feeling and suffering that rings changes on one's subjectivity so as to make a soul replaces the telos of happiness. The world, Keats proposed in an extended metaphor, is a "school" for the "reading" of the human heart; this schoolroom reading promises circuitous access to the (temporal) world that Robertson's prose had missed. That access crucially hinges upon the singular subjectivity of what Keats here called "identities": "There may be intelligences or sparks of the divinity in millions—but they are not Souls till they acquire identities, till each one is personally itself" (*LJK*, 2:102). Subject-making, for Keats, is a process of becoming that requires a world in which to feel and suffer, and it is reading that provides access to that world. It is not incidental that images of casements recur throughout Keats's poetry. From the "casement high and triple arch'd" (208) in "The Eve of St. Agnes" to the "Charm'd magic casements" (69) in "Ode to a Nightingale" and the "casement ope at night" (66) in "Ode to Psyche," windows provide ways of seeing the world and are figures for reading that exist on the threshold of interior and exterior, blurring the distinction between schoolroom and world.

The language of "identities," which indicates Keats's notion of the singularity or uniqueness of each soul that is made, should not lead us to think that Keats upheld any static notion of essential selfhood or that this notion of the soul is anything other than a social process, a process that makes sociality—the imagination of the social world and thus social engagement—possible. "That you may judge the more clearly," Keats wrote, "I will put it in the most homely form possible" (*LJK*, 2:102). Here follows the crucial formulation:

> I will call the *world* a School instituted for the purpose of teaching little children to read—I will call the *human heart* the *horn Book* used in that School—and I will call the *Child able to read, the Soul* made from that *school* and its *hornbook.* Do you not see how necessary a world of pains and troubles is to school an intelligence and make it a soul? (*LJK*, 2:102)

The purpose of the world, in Keats's model, is to enable one's reading of "the human heart" and, in turn, one's alteration by that process so as to become a soul, where before there was only an "intelligence." This notion of an identity or soul as earned entirely in a figurative process of reading that occurs in the temporal world marks Keats's break not only from the discourse of Christianity, which Keats called "vulgar superstition," but also from the idea of one's identity as originating in inherited rank or blood. The Keatsian subject is not reducible to the body or to social identity; nor is it an entirely private subject, sealed off from social experience. For Keats does not make the hornbook equivalent to one's own heart (an object that appears individually possessed); rather, it is equivalent to "the human heart." The ambiguity of this phrasing enables the concept to pivot between one's own heart (one's unique circumstances and experiences of feeling and suffering) and a broader notion of "human" suffering in a "world of pains." In the kind of "reading" Keats describes, the separation between "identities"—between one's own heart and the hearts of others—breaks down, dissolving in the capacious notion of "the human heart."[33] Keats imagines his reading as a more adequate means to understand man's present circumstances than what the philosophies of Scottish Enlightenment historiography could provide. What appears ostensibly as a self-reflexive turn inward, in reading the heart, turns out to mark not a separation from the world but a finer model for reading it.

Legibility, however, does not imply what Keats called "smokeability," the notion that a text could be transparently understood once and for all.[34] No all-knowing schoolmaster appears in Keats's model. The soul is figured as what in us learns to read but also, significantly, as what remains always a child reader. In a world that defies perfect mastery, one maintains a sense of wonder and is, as a capable reader, still able to be surprised. Unlike in progressive narrative histories that close off the potential for the unexpected, in Keats's sense of the world, the future cannot be predicted through patterns or lessons of the past ("the nature of the world will not admit of it") or be rationally controlled but is subject to the unpredictable alterations of nature that come through reading the heart. For "what are proovings [sic] of [man's] heart," Keats asks, "but fortifiers or alterers of his nature? and what is his altered nature but his soul?" (*LJK*, 2:103). The plural present participle, "proovings," evokes the incompletion and ongoing process of the Lacanian future anterior: "what I shall have been *for what I am in the process of becoming.*"[35] It is openness to the worldly, unpredictable process of altering one's "nature" that makes a person—that makes a distinctive soul and a capable reader.[36] That openness to encountering the new or the unpredictable—an openness to something so different from previous experience that it revises one's understanding of self and world—is the kind of subjectivity that Keats's poetry so often both describes and elicits. Turning toward "To Autumn" with this notion of "Soul-making" in view, the question I want to pursue is what it would mean not only to take seriously Keats's model of inward/outward turning toward the temporal world, toward history, but also to take literally Keats's figurative language of reading—that is, to read "To Autumn" as hornbook to the world.

A Modernity of Slow Time: Reading "To Autumn"

The formal dynamics of "To Autumn" set it apart from Keats's earlier odes, each of which introduces some explicit occasion for surprise or disillusionment. Dizziness has matured into a diffuse, mobile, protean sensibility invigorated at the minutest turns by the felt proximity of death. Unlike the thoughtlessly wandering speaker in the "Ode to Psyche," the speaker in "To Autumn" is thoughtful from the outset, conscious of inhabiting a world of mysteries and untrodden regions not subject to transparent understanding. With "To Autumn," that is, we have moved from dizzying surprise to what Geoffrey Hartman has called "progressive surmise."[37] In "To Autumn," reflexivity, which obscures the demarcations of individual selfhood as did reading in the "vale of Soul-making," has not simply opened the casement but obscured the boundary between interior and exterior (between the self and the social and natural worlds) to the point of banishing its visible signs.[38] Hartman summarizes this difference:

> Most of the odes are a feverish quest to enter the life of a pictured scene, to be totally where the imagination is. In the Autumn ode, however, there is no effort to cross a magic threshold: though its three stanzas are like a composite picture from some Book of Hours, we are placed so exactly at the bourn of the invisible window picture that the frame is not felt, nor the desperate haunting of imagination to get in.[39]

Instead of constructing a sense of time around an epiphanic encounter (with gods, urn, or bird, for example), "To Autumn" presents a mood that is steadily meditative. Its sense of surprise comes in smaller sensations.

Keats's ode self-consciously alters our sense of time, while it plays with our patterns of breathing. The course of the poem dilates the moment in a way that opens the present to multiple possibilities drawn from obscurities that the season of plural "mists" immediately puts in play (1). In the opening phrase, pluralizing the word "mist" appears an entirely arbitrary

semantic choice. Rhythmically, however, making "mists" plural immediately and insistently slows the pace of reading, expanding the middle of
the line by an extra syllable. Associated phonetically with mystery, "mists"
imply an impediment to clear sight and an epistemological challenge. An
atmosphere of mists suggests that we cannot see what is coming—hence a
further impetus to slacken pace:

> Season of mists and mellow fruitfulness,
>   Close bosom-friend of the maturing sun;
> Conspiring with him how to load and bless
>   With fruit the vines that round the thatch-eves run;
> To bend with apples the moss'd cottage-trees,
>   And fill all fruit with ripeness to the core;
>   To swell the gourd, and plump the hazel shells
>   With a sweet kernel; to set budding more,
> And still more, later flowers for the bees,
> Until they think warm days will never cease,
>   For Summer has o'er-brimm'd their clammy cells. (1–11)

Loaded with monosyllabic words, the ode calls for us to slow down. If
modern time-consciousness entails a sense of acceleration, Keats offers an
engagement with modernity on different terms.[40] The speaker's enjoyment
of lyric delay is knowing, unlike the bees'. The speaker enjoys time's slowness all the more, it seems, in light of its tentative quality, in light of the
knowledge that warm days *will* cease, even if the senses for the moment
suggest otherwise. Geoffrey Hartman has observed in the ode "a westerly
drift like the sun," indicating that although the perspective shifts in the
course of the poem, the time of day does not significantly progress. "'To
Autumn,'" he writes, "does not explicitly evolve from sunrise to sunset
but rather from a rich to a clarified dark. Closely read it starts and ends in
twilight."[41] Keats's lyrical suspension of time's progress thus is both rhythmic and thematic.

As we read, however, the poem's rhythms alter our patterns of breathing
in unpredictable and telling ways, registering aesthetically the speaker's
anticipation of change. Although Keats frequently enjambs lines, eliminat-
ing the room for breath at the line's end, enjambment occurs at different
points in each stanza (lines 3 and 7 in the first stanza; 2, 6, and 8 in the
second; 5, 6, and 9 in the third). Alterations of breathing as one reads thus
occur unpredictably. The use of caesura is equally irregular, suggesting that
the poem self-consciously asks that we breathe with Keats. In anticipation
and delay of the stanza's end, for instance, the notion of endlessly warm

days is interrupted by a pause after "cease," both rhythmically and semantically (even if by negation) bringing the sense of ending into play (10). This interruption momentarily contradicts the continuous sense of enjoyment the line has just suggested, while providing a space to draw life-sustaining breath, however paradoxically, from the anticipatory sense of finitude that joins poet and reader.

A self-reflexive invocation of the poet occurs even earlier. For autumn is, we immediately learn, "Close bosom-friend of the maturing sun; / Conspiring with him how to load and bless / With fruit the vines that round the thatch eves run" (2–4). Hearing a pun of "maturing *son*," one might recall Keats's self-consciousness about his own poetic maturity when he wrote in the preface to *Endymion* that the poem had proceeded from a place somewhere between "the imagination of a boy" and "the mature imagination of a man."[42] His relentless ambitions to become a better, more mature poet, like the Wordsworth he described in 1818 as having explored the "dark Passages," placed him lingering before them. With this association between the "maturing" poet's work and nature's growth processes, the season's work of "load[ing] and bless[ing]" appears self-consciously interwoven with the poet's. Keats famously advised Percy Shelley "that you might curb your magnanimity and be more of an artist, and 'load every rift' of your subject with ore" (*LJK*, 2:323). In "To Autumn," he has semantically loaded the very activity of "load[ing]" with the poetic process of creating rich figuration. Grammatically it is, of course, Autumn who "conspir[es] with" the "maturing sun." The language suggests not just the political plotting of conspiracy to which Roe alerts us but also, in its etymological affiliation (from the Latin *conspirare*, literally to "breathe together"), the process of a reader's breathing together with the "maturing sun," with the poet as maker. That Keats's most memorably recalled reading experience took the form of an extraordinary event of breathing ("Yet did I never breathe its pure serene") suggests how attuned to this physical, sensory aspect of reading he was.[43]

To keep pace in breath, however, is still to be eluded, at least in part, by the poem's ostensible subject, Autumn, whose fruits finally cannot be contained by their overly "plump[ed]" "shells" (7) and "cells" "o'er-brimm'd" (11). This sense of Autumn's intractable excess is heightened in the second stanza, where the personified Autumn is addressed as at once obviously immediate and oddly elusive. "Who hath not seen thee oft amid thy store?" the speaker asks rhetorically, as if to counter Wordsworth's melancholic longing, in the "Intimations" ode, for a past that is lost. Wordsworth's poem begins in search of a lost past: "There was a time" (1). And the mood culminates in the speaker's longing questions: "Whither is fled the vision-ary gleam? / Where is it now, the glory and the dream" (57–58). Whereas Wordsworth's imaginative energy aimed to recover the "visionary gleam" of a gloried past, Keats's poem conjured instead the ongoing season of the present. To breathe with Keats is to sense an elusive yet immediate present and thus to open the interpretive possibility that Autumn is Keats's figure of elusiveness for the "goings on of the world" that seemed to defy narra-tive control.

Breath, spirit, soul-making: If the world is to be understood not as a politically progressive history but as a "vale of soul-making," then Autumn, its prime inhabitant for the time being, might very well be Keats's candidate for the "spirit of the age" in the post-Waterloo period.[44] The second stanza shifts from the present-perfect of "has o'er-brimm'd" (11) to the present tense, as if to underscore Autumn's immediacy, but it is also structured by the repetitions of "Sometimes," "Or," "And sometimes," and "Or," which suggest a certain slipping away in the very abundance of possible locations:

Who hath not seen thee oft amid thy store?
　Sometimes whoever seeks abroad may find
Thee sitting careless on a granary floor,
　Thy hair soft-lifted by the winnowing wind;
Or on a half-reap'd furrow sound asleep,
　Drows'd with the fume of poppies, while thy hook
　　Spares the next swath and all its twined flowers:
And sometimes like a gleaner thou dost keep
　Steady thy laden head across a brook;
　Or by a cider-press, with patient look,
　　Thou watchest the last oozings hours by hours. (12–22, emphasis mine)

These conjunctions conjure the difficulty of pinning autumn down in a world of diverse, evenly balanced possibilities.[45] In "To Autumn," all possibilities appear equally plausible, even if incompatible; the speculations about Autumn, that is, do not improve on earlier ones in the course of the stanza but defy a progressive movement of thought. Along these lines, Helen Vendler has noted the chronologically disordered presentation of processes: "Where we would expect (in this minutely conscious poem) first reaping, then gleaning, then threshing, we find instead first thresh-ing, then reaping, then gleaning, a sequence invented."[46] Not only does this nonchronological sequence suggest a self-consciousness about poetic artifice; it insists on the nonprogressive, lateral movement of time—of "hours by hours."

In her essay "Looking at the Stars Forever," Rei Terada writes of the post-Waterloo era: "The idea that it is no longer possible to tell revolution and restoration apart . . . is more disturbing than any 'failure' of revolution."[47] Whereas Terada observes that for Keats in *Hyperion* "impasse is more of a solution than a problem," in "To Autumn" the personified Autumn, as a figure for the present, gives us a different response to impasse, from the point of view of the speaker. The difficulty of pinning Autumn down, despite the season's visceral immediacy, creates an impasse that leads not so much to stasis as to *lateral movement*—in its proliferation of simultaneous possibilities, side by side. Indeed, this suspension of time's forward movement, enabling the moment to dilate, seems to be a phase in the poem's larger movement of opening up that the slow delay of transforming the plural "mists" into the upward and outward "skies" underscores. No teleological trajectory would seem to close off the generating of yet another possible locale, a different narrative point of departure.

In addition to the way conjunctions grammatically multiply possibilities, the stanza form Keats develops in "To Autumn" reinforces the sense of prolonging the present and opening up. Keats borrows from the sonnet form—a form traditionally marked by the resolution of a sestet or the closure of a rhyming couplet—to achieve something else. If the traditional English or Italian sonnet begins with the larger verse unit to develop a problem that the shorter couplet or sestet often resolves, Keats reverses this pattern, beginning his stanza with one Shakespearean quatrain followed by a modified Italian sestet (extended to seven lines). Not only does the larger verse unit come last so as to counter the traditional closure of the English couplet, but the pattern of the last seven lines is close enough to a sestet to make the (extraneous, added) penultimate line (which forms an internal, though not an ending, couplet) seem to distort the form slightly; insofar as the stanza conveys, however critically, an idea of the present as timelessness, the added line delays the pressure of temporality by putting off the stanza's end.

The aesthetic of "To Autumn" is, however, conscious of the pressures of time, a consciousness audible, as we have seen, in the rhythmic silence following the very notion that "warm days will never cease." In the "vale of Soul-making" letter, that the making of a soul takes the shape of unexpected alterations of the self over time emphasizes the centrality of the temporal imagination to Keats's alternative historiography that I am suggesting the ode brings to bear. To that end, the temporal imagination is precisely what appears to be lacking, ultimately, in the drowsy absorption in the present that Autumn, in the second stanza, both enjoys and elicits. The "hours by hours" of Autumn's "patient look" would seem to go on forever, as could the speaker's speculations of possible places in which to find her, or so it seems, in an endlessly digressing proliferation of possibilities. Formally curtailing the deceptions of a world without temporality, however, the stanza does end.

The tension between what the second stanza says and how it says it, between a present that expands with possibilities and the ending or finitude of this description of timelessness, does something different from what it says or how it says it: it calls on a temporal imagination whose conception of the present would include the possibility of a future different from the present. To that end, the final stanza's anticipatory gestures provide an alternative to the fully absorptive timelessness of the present. The stanza is ushered in, moreover, by the poem's most overtly self-reflexive gesture and in a turn from the visual to the aural, clearly shifting from what might have appeared as the second stanza's endlessly expanding mode: "Where are the songs of Spring? Ay, where are they—," the speaker asks in a poem about writing a poem about autumn:

> Think not of them, thou hast thy music too,—
> While barred clouds bloom the soft-dying day,
>   And touch the stubble-plains with rosy hue;
> Then in a wailful choir the small gnats mourn
>   Among the river sallows, borne aloft
>   Or sinking as the light wind lives or dies;
> And full-grown lambs loud bleat from hilly bourn;
>   Hedge-crickets sing; and now with treble soft
>   The red-breast whistles from a garden-croft;
>   And gathering swallows twitter in the skies. (24–33)

Reflexive questions do not narrow the poem's horizon but usher in its most spatially expansive perspective, whose contours are decidedly aural and whose temporal concerns include hints of impending futurity—of winter and of death—but these remain only hints in that winter is the one season unnamed: the darkness of wintry futurity appears, in this sense, elusive and inaccessible. The subtly impending darkness, however, does not deaden but seems to inspire poetic and temporal movement. For temporal change, which seemed absent in the second stanza, turns out to have been only dormant. In the last stanza, the conjunction expressing simultaneity, "While" (25), gives way to the temporal progression of "Then" (27) and finally to the distinct immediacy of "and now" (31).[48] With the temporality of a narrative, the obscurity of winter gets things moving, as if accelerated time went hand in hand with an impending dark futurity.

Whereas in the second stanza the speaker envisions a number of places to find Autumn, the final stanza focuses on listening to the multiple, distinct songs of Autumn's music, not all of them joyful. Autumn's aural tones are mixed, ranging from plaintive "bleat[ing]" to joyful "sing[ing]" and "whistl[ing]" and sorrowful "mourn[ing]," and the speaker's ear is attuned so finely to each across the landscape and sky as to suggest the acoustics of an astonishingly mobile or diffuse subjectivity.[49] With the suggestion of beginnings in "bloom" and the several homophones of born ("borne," "bourn") together with shadows of winter and death (as in the "wailful choir" and "soft-dying day"), contrasts between alternatives sharpen in the language of this stanza, but they are harmonized by the musicality of the verse and the protean capaciousness of the speaker's perception.[50] There is no Wordsworthian deictic as, for example, when in "Tintern Abbey" the speaker remarks: "I again repose / Here, under this dark sycamore, and view / These plots of cottage-ground" (9–11). James O'Rourke is, I think, right to revise Vendler's notion of an "unmoving center from which all is seen and heard"[51] by observing instead "the stylistic effect of a pendulum-like swing."[52] With no "I" figuring in the poem, the lyric subject appears less an "egotistical sublime" than a "thoroughfare for all thoughts" (*LJK*, 1:386, 2:213).

The landscape, too, appears a thoroughfare for "light wind," leading Fry to see the scene as "a faintly breathing thing . . . like the lungs in an interval of pain."[53] Jonathan Bate's ecocritical reading of the poem extends this attention to the wind by putting the poem in the context of Keats's epistolary discussions of the weather's effects on his health around the time he was writing "To Autumn." "The consumptive has no choice but to gape after the weather," Bate reminds us. "Air quality is of the utmost importance for those whose lungs have been invaded by Mycobacterium tuberculosis. Keats was hurried to his death less by his reviewers, as Byron supposed, than by the weather." In Bate's view, the ode's celebratory tone should be understood in light of the fact that the "good summer and clear autumn of 1819 very literally gave [Keats] a new lease on life."[54] If the "light wind" held personal meaning for a consumptive poet who had seen both his brother and mother die from the disease, however, it also suggested a larger, shared condition of uncertainty about the forces of intellectual and social change, as the heavier-handed "mighty winds" did in *Sleep and Poetry*:

> What though I am not wealthy in the dower
> Of spanning wisdom; though I do not know

The shiftings of the mighty winds that blow
Hither and thither all the changing thoughts
Of man: though no great minist'ring reason sorts
Out the dark mysteries of human souls
To clear conceiving: yet there ever rolls
A vast idea before me (284–91)

Like the "changing thoughts / Of man," the small gnats in "To Autumn" are "borne aloft / Or sinking as the light wind lives or dies" (28–29). Keats's concern with breathing and wind invites an intimation of mortality that alters the second stanza's emphasis on abundance; it also envisions an atmosphere of flux in which the only force against the shifting of the wind is a temporal imagination that sees the present as transient and, without access to a predictable futurity, anticipates the unexpected. This present as surmise lifts the speaker above the helpless delusions of the absorptively present-minded bees and wind-tossed gnats. It is perhaps overly simplistic to say that what separates human nature from Nature is the contrast between the finitude of the life of the singular human subject, who lives in a linear trajectory from birth to death, and the circularity of the seasons that gives Nature an eternal quality whereby no loss need be mourned. For Keats's ode "To Autumn," like his "Ode to Psyche," constructs a literary subjectivity out of the very tension between the sense of timelessness, of merging with the natural world in the experience of listening, and the sense that the present must end, that human finitude cannot be overcome.

Teeming with possibilities and heterogeneous in tone, Keats's conception of the present implicitly makes the onward writing of narrative history—or at least the kinds of histories available in early nineteenth-century England—appear impossible, for the futurity that shadowed the present in "To Autumn" appears indefinite and unknowable. That sense of uncertainty renders Keats's sense of time incompatible with the assured notion of stadial progress informing Enlightenment histories.

Geoffrey Hartman has established the stakes of "To Autumn" in "the ongoing history of poetry." "Keats's poetry," he writes, "is indeed an event in history: not in world-history, however, but simply in the history of fiction, in the history of our awareness of the power and poverty of fiction."[55] From the point of view of temporality, "To Autumn" becomes an event in literary history by revising how our sense of the present might be informed by an imagined dark futurity. In contrast to Keats's ode, in Wordsworth's "Tintern Abbey," the speaker values the present for the way in which it will be remembered in the future by his then matured sister: "When these wild ecstasies shall be matured / Into a sober pleasure" (139–40), he envisions, "with what healing thoughts / Of tender joy wilt thou remember me, / And these my exhortations!" (145–47). The model of the sister's future development clearly comes from the speaker's sense of his past, for he "read[s] / My former pleasures in the shooting lights / of thy wild eyes" (118–20). This sense of the past becomes the basis for predicting a continued place for the self in the future of the sister's memory. By contrast, Keats's "full-grown lambs" (30), alluding to ways in which the past inhabits the present, provide no model for the impending next phase. "To Autumn" delineates a world of possibilities without guarantees.

By introducing my reading of "To Autumn" by way of Keats's "vale of Soul-making" letter, I resituate the poem in the context of Keats's own logic of displacing Enlightenment progress by conceiving the world as not subject to its model of knowing. Keats conceived the world as a "vale of Soul-making" in which the self must be continually remade according to one's unpredictable readings of the heart and encounters with the world, ever a source of the new. The model of cultural stadial progress informing Enlightenment history left no room for the unforeseen and therefore, in Keats's view, missed its mark in a world that called for our ideas of it to be open to revision. "To Autumn" is admittedly short on direct political or historical statements, and that is surely why it became the center of debate with the rise of New Historicism in the early 1980s. What that lack of direct statement enables, however, is a consideration of what the distinctive *poetic* qualities of Keats's verse can say and do, providing a sense of the "altering" self, an ordering of time and the senses, that Keats described as so crucial to approximating the shifting world that political histories did not admit.

In view of the early nineteenth-century contest over the temporality of narrating recent history, Keats's sense of proliferating possibilities in a world of vanishing predictability makes the poem not only an event in literary history, but also an event of historiographical thinking. To live in Keats's time, the poem tells us, was to anticipate an improbable future in the midst of a present whose visceral elusiveness made the narration of its significance in conventional historical forms impossible. If the spirit of the age remained elusive, how could one confidently narrate its significance in a sequential history of before and after? To what might this elusive present lead? The world "would not admit of" the probabilistic narrative practices upon which Enlightenment historians relied. Read allegorically, Keats's "To Autumn" conceptualizes an early nineteenth-century historiographical problem—the urgency and impossibility of comprehending the present as history—as the consequence of a present that does not have recourse to the past for its self-understanding, but that abounds in imagined alternative scenarios and opens toward an unknown futurity. The way of reading offered in "To Autumn" is not epistemological, but ethical in the sense that the world it conceives is not subject to complete understanding. Considered as a historiographical intervention, "To Autumn"—hornbook to the historical world—offers a reading of the present as multiple and de-centering, teeming and mysterious: mists suggesting something missed, or an historical dimension elusive and palpable at once.

4

CONTINGENCIES OF THE FUTURE ANTERIOR: AUSTEN'S *PERSUASION*

Anne Elliot—the pensive protagonist of Austen's last complete novel, *Persuasion*—thinks in patterns of anticipated retrospection. She repeatedly imagines how the present *will have been*, and she appears highly attuned to the contingency of this thinking, which cannot be reduced to straightforward prediction. Both the impulse to imagine the present as a future memory and the apparent tenuousness of such imaginings organize as well the historical mise-en-scène of the novel. In *Persuasion*, the spirit (or character) of the present historical age is not a given but is precisely the question that animates the novel's narrative patterns and dynamics of historical situation, for the sense of the present cannot escape the implications of an unpredictable futurity.

Persuasion is set in the years 1814 and 1815, ending just before Napoleon escaped from Elba in a re-eruption of the wars that were assumed to be over. Insofar as Austen began composing the novel just after Waterloo, the question of how the moment will appear in retrospect, which repeatedly burdens Anne, is one that carries historical weight vis-à-vis the narrator's (and the readers') post-Waterloo perspective on the 1814–15 moment. That is, in the novel's final sentences, the narrator alludes to a historical eventuality that the characters do not foresee, when she describes the "dread of a future war" as "all that could dim [Anne's] sunshine."[1] Characters in the novel generally refer to their historical moment as if it were postwar peace, but Anne is burdened by the possible transience—and consequent reassessment—of that state. Austen and any post-1815 reader would know that, although the British military engagement in the 1815 warfare with Napoleon was relatively brief and the navy not involved, the characters' perception of their moment *will have been* a false sense of peace. The temporality of that suspended knowledge aligns the novel's historical thinking with Anne's anticipations of retrospection. The insistent contingency of anticipated retrospection, moreover, delivers us into a world that is, like Keats's, never fully knowable, for its meanings are constantly unfolding in the shadows of a future that promises the unpredictable, that ushers in the unforeseen. This peculiar sense of anticipation and uncertainty makes Austen's novel both historical (insofar as it is self-consciously situated in relation to contemporary events) and historicizing (in that it develops a transhistorical model for imagining history as an ongoing process in view of an unknown future); specific ways in which the novel is so have yet to be described.

Contemporary reviews do not mention its historical implications, and one might reasonably wonder why such an innovative imagining of history escaped comment for so long. There are, however, a number of ways to explain this omission. One has to do with a widely held assumption in early nineteenth-century British culture that Austen satirizes in *Northanger Abbey* and Anne Elliot addresses in a conversation with Captain Harville near the close of *Persuasion*: that history is written neither by nor about women.[2] Given this predominant cultural assumption, who would have thought to consider Austen's novels from a historical perspective? Another explanation comes from some of Austen's own expressed attitudes toward her work, such as the oft-quoted letter to her nephew James Edward Austen in which she contrasts his "manly, spirited Sketches, full of Variety & Glow" to what she describes (with presumably ironic modesty) as the "little bit (two Inches wide) of Ivory" on which she works.[3] Austen herself hardly theorizes or even mentions the historical and historicizing import of her novels.

Ever since Marilyn Butler's richly historicizing *Jane Austen and the War of Ideas*, published in 1975, however, the question of how Austen's novels engage with history (and politics) has been an increasingly prominent subject of critical debate.[4] Butler has read Austen's novels as unswervingly anti-Jacobin, influenced by sermons and conduct books and the conservative social contexts within which the author moved. Claudia Johnson's *Jane Austen: Women, Politics and the Novel*, published in 1988, built on that sense of Austen's serious engagement with her political and historical contexts but argued powerfully that the novels should be understood as subtle—yet active, imaginative—questionings and critiques of the politics of conservative texts. Johnson's method entailed close readings that focused on the way Austen incorporates and manipulates the lexicon of conservative texts and genres—as she writes of *Mansfield Park*—"so as to oblige [conservative ideologues] to discredit themselves with their own voices."[5] In the literary and social contexts where Butler had found influence, Johnson affirmed Austen's intellectual independence: the novel not as mirror but as critical lamp.

The question of intellectual independence (as authorial agency), which is also the question of the relation between literature and history, continues to animate the most recent studies of *Persuasion* and history—studies by Mary Favret, Anne Frey, William Galperin, and Deidre Lynch, for instance, all of which draw in various ways on the novel's processing of the British response to revolutionary France and the Napoleonic wars.[6] With varying degrees of explicitness, critics seem to be asking, What does it *do*, and what does Austen suggest it can do, for her to write this literary world and for us to read it? Is literature to be understood by our measuring it against its historical "contexts," or can it function as a distinct kind of context itself, giving us access to historical perspectives and aesthetic experiences that texts themselves made possible, aspects of history unavailable in other kinds of writing? Critics who focus on Austen's conceptions of time tend to suggest greater prospects for individual and literary agency, such as when Lynch posits, "*Persuasion* grants memory a role of releasing buried potentiality and not just affirming the inevitability of things as they are."[7] Time, in *Persuasion*, appears to take an astonishing range of forms or shapes, suggesting its very flexibility. As we shall see, time is not a given but a conceptual medium through which a narrator or a character can shape her world in a specific way among multiple possible alternatives. To approach the novel by focusing on concepts of time is to discover a positive sense of agency, of the mind's capacity to alter one's experience of the world by giving it temporal shape. What's more, the novel extends the power of Anne's imaginative agency—with respect to her immediate experiences and individual history—to her, and our, understanding of history in the broad sense. By implication, that is to say that imagining the historical present with an anticipation of retrospection, however tentative such a construction may be, alters—in the very moment—one's relation to, and experience of, that present.

Building on studies such as Johnson's and Lynch's that focus on the novel's sense of the past and its implications for history and individual agency, this chapter explores both how *Persuasion* conceives Anne's anticipatory sense of her own story and how it engages with the idea of a collective or national history. For the novel remarkably imagines the historical present, too, in a turn toward futurity. In neither of these senses is *Persuasion* about prediction. Instead, a sense of inaccessible futurity repeatedly shadows the present in *Persuasion*—Austen's most self-reflexive novel in respect to its sense of individual and shared history and her most complex and pervasive in its aesthetic of anticipation. Although the novel undoubtedly "takes an interest in . . . looking backward: in reviewing and historicizing," as one critic puts it, the "historicizing" work it does should be understood not only as its process of "reviewing" the past but also—and crucially—as its anticipation, its patterns of looking ahead.[8] It is only by attending to the aesthetic of anticipation, I argue, that we can see the novel's most innovative thinking through of the question of how to imagine the present as history—a question, as discussed in the introduction and in Chapter 1, that similarly animates contemporary historiography as well as, more broadly, a strain of philosophical modernity inaugurated around 1800.

The story that Austen's narrative uniquely tells about modernity's anticipations of retrospection is this: while we are compelled to think in these temporal terms (to imagine how a moment will appear in retrospect), situations rarely, if ever, unfold according to the particulars of how one imagines them.[9] In this sense, Austen should be understood as a theorist of philosophical modernity, for *Persuasion* makes a distinctive contribution to the elaboration of modernity's implications. Austen tells—or rather enacts—this story of modernity via *Persuasion*'s narrative *durée*, in that the narrative discourse resists the linear temporal logic that Anne's "future anterior" imaginings ostensibly project.[10] Anne-Lise François has done most to describe a literature of such inconsequence: "One waits, and waits, and then gives up—such a movement yields a temporal sequence set loose from the ordering energies of the quest for possession and freed from the pendulum of anticipation and (non)fulfillment."[11] However misaligned with later events and discourse these anticipations are, Austen also shows us their very real effects on the present. For instance, more than once, thinking in such terms definitively shapes the way Anne comprehends a situation and thus alters her experience of it, regardless of whether what she imagines might happen never actually does. In *Persuasion*, that is, what pronouncements in the form of anticipated retrospection *do*—they alter the sense and experience of the present by offering a new and alternative vantage on it—appears more important than what they *say* about how the moment will look in retrospect.

Attention to this space between what the narrator and characters say and what the narrative does—how the narrative focus shifts, for instance, to produce epistemological gaps and silences—sheds light on Austen's distinctive contribution to philosophical modernity and to the Romantic discourse of anticipation. Although critics have explored aspects of the novel's temporal complexity, the sense of time has not been assessed in this respect. The novel's aesthetic dimensions make profoundly resonant the notion that something eludes direct statement. I argue, moreover, that the aesthetic does so in a way that links silence and incompletion with its sense of anticipation. For the novel's particular treatment of anticipation as a highly tentative conception of the future provides the very logic whereby the epistemological gaps and rhythmic silences appear as part of the author's shaping of a new sense of history that has its eye on an uncertain futurity. This is the logic of "future anteriority" which, in the introduction, I explained with reference to Samuel Weber's book *Return to Freud*; the present can never be complete when our understanding of it is always, at least in part, yet to come. This logic underpins the sense of anticipation in *Persuasion*, which, in turn, shows both its particular effects on the present and its linear-chronological ineffectiveness (or at least indirection) with respect to the future moments (or potential outcomes) to which the narration sometimes alludes. While Keats's letters and lyric poems give us a sense of how anticipation and uncertainty can open the present up as a space of multiple, incompatible possibilities, Austen's prose narrative only reinforces the notion that the temporality of anticipation concerns the moment in which the process of anticipating occurs, not the chronologically distant future to which it alludes.

Persuasion engages with history and with its own historicity in its aesthetic dimensions—in the gaps and silences and the tug between what the narrator and characters say and what the narrative does. The historical dimension that this chapter aims to illuminate entails less what the novel "represents" or "depicts" than how it enacts a sense of time in this tug between saying and doing. I trace this sense of time and the kinds of anticipation it elicits in what I call the novel's double "time of reading"—that is, both in Anne's "story" (her experience and processing of interpretive fluctuations across time) and in the novel's shaping of an aesthetic experience that, without announcing that it does so, changes the significance of events as the narrative discourse unfolds, page by page and chapter by chapter, in the time of reading the novel. In this double "time of reading," the narrative both describes (typically Anne's) anticipations of retrospection and elicits such imaginings and uncertainties for readers, aesthetically enacting a sense of anticipation that is distinctively modern and historicizing.

Anne Elliot's Future Anterior Tense: "An Alloy in Some Momentary Apprehensions"

Unlike the well-known Marxist and Freudian question of how the past is playing out in the present, the question for Anne often appears to be how the present will figure into an imagined future as memory; Anne's is decidedly a *prospective* imagination. The grammar for this thinking about the present is the verb tense of the future anterior—Anne's speculative imagining of what *will have been*. It is also a grammar that invites association—or even alignment—with what we might call the temporality of narrative itself, that is, the time signature of the way narrative engages a reader's imagination, as Peter Brooks so well describes it in *Reading for the Plot*: "Perhaps we would do best to think of the *anticipation of retrospection* as our chief tool in making sense of narrative, the master trope of its strange logic."[12] In the "strange" time of Anne's reading (the temporal shape of her sense-making), anticipatory thought patterns suggest her narrative view of her own life.

The circumstances eliciting this shape of thought appear to be the extremes of either intense pleasure and happiness or their opposite. The imagination of a future memory serves, for instance, as a source of consolation for distressing apprehensions when Anne perceives the threat to her father's marital status posed by the "dangerous attractions"—albeit acerbically qualified—of the widowed Mrs. Clay; she decides to warn Elizabeth, in however futile an effort:

> Mrs. Clay had freckles, and a projecting tooth, and a clumsy wrist, which [Sir Walter] was continually making severe remarks upon, in her absence; but she was young, and certainly altogether well-looking, and possessed, in an acute mind and assiduous pleasing manners, infinitely more dangerous attractions than any merely personal might have been. Anne was so impressed by the degree of their danger, that she could not excuse herself from trying to make it perceptible to her sister. She had little hope of success; but Elizabeth, who in the event of such a reverse would be so much more to be pitied than herself, should never, she thought, have reason to reproach her for giving no warning. (34)

Anne conceives her present effort to advise Elizabeth and is able to act by anticipating a possible future "event of such a reverse," a future in which her fears are realized; in view of such a hypothetical situation, she *will have been* a responsible, irreproachable sister for having warned Elizabeth, regardless of whether Anne's warning succeeds in its immediate aim of making her sister observant. If Mrs. Clay came to usurp Elizabeth's role as mistress of the house, the "warning," Anne thinks, would figure for her as a consoling memory—and that very notion functions to console her in the present. This thinking also mildly counters the sense of social alienation evident in Anne's clear understanding that she has no voice in her family. Although her "word had no weight," as the narrator puts it at the outset, Anne still shares it with Elizabeth, choosing to act based on the notion that, in retrospect, she might be heard (5).

In another instance of Anne's distress, a knowing nostalgia of the present moderates—not by forgetting but by variegating—Anne's relation to her present. Weary of Mary's hypochondria and ill-mannered children at Uppercross and eager to avoid a social encounter between Lady Russell, Captain Wentworth, and herself, Anne anxiously "anticipat[es] her removal" to Bath (93). With pleasing thoughts, however, she imagines that "Her usefulness to little Charles would always give some sweetness to the memory of her two months visit there, but he was gaining strength apace, and she had nothing else to stay for" (93). Anne considers how the visit will appear in her own future remembrance while she is still suffering it. In Anne's anticipatory imagination, the two-month visit yields a "sweetness" to counter the sources of suffering that originally form her "chief solicitude in anticipating her removal." What this peculiar relation to the present afforded by Anne's imagination does, in part, is to alleviate her suffering—not by blinding her to the sources of immediate displeasure but by making her relation to the present take multiple forms. A speculative future orientation offers an alloy to her conscious anguish coming from immediate sensations. In otherwise distressing circumstances, there is some consolation available in thinking that the present will become the past. Put another way, the grammar of future anterior thought affords Anne a multiplicity of presents.

Anne can imagine and predict how her present moment will look as a past one, but the accuracy of that perspective depends very much upon the context of what unfolds—hence Austen's insistence on the hypothetical status of future anterior conceptions. This peculiar source of consolation cannot be complete in that it rests upon an uncertain future state of affairs. To that end, neither of these hypothetical future remembrances is explicitly realized in the narrative discourse that ensues. Austen never shows us an Anne nourished by the specific memory of her past "usefulness" to little Charles at Uppercross, and when Mrs. Clay's plotting becomes apparent, the narrative discourse conspicuously deflects its lens away from Anne's response, as if to suggest that any possible gratification achieved in a chronologically future moment, which Anne was imagining as far off, is beside the point. Rather than give us Anne's thoughts on Mrs. Clay at that later moment, the narrator becomes suddenly circumspect—providing only a general assumption about Sir Walter and Elizabeth's responses and then shifting in a paragraph break to Anne's totally other concerns:

> It cannot be doubted that Sir Walter and Elizabeth were shocked and mortified by the loss of their companion, and the discovery of their deception

in her. They had their great cousins, to be sure, to resort to for comfort; but they must long feel that to flatter and follow others, without being flattered and followed in turn, is but a state of half enjoyment.

Anne, satisfied at a very early period of Lady Russell's meaning to love Captain Wentworth as she ought, had no other alloy to the happiness of her prospects than what arose from the consciousness of having no relations to bestow on him which a man of sense could value. (251)

Whereas Anne had imagined a future moment in which she might be concerned about whether she had acted upon that early insight regarding Mrs. Clay, that imagining actually seems to free Anne, to a degree, not only from having to anticipate possibly being reproached for the past but from having to think much about that particular issue at all. In other words, the kind of temporal imagining Austen employs at the level of narrative discourse, and attributes to Anne's consciousness as well, does not adhere to linear, teleological plotting. A depiction of Anne's feeling of gratification in the last pages that *she had told them so*, for instance, would have resolved the issue in a linear way with respect to Anne's consciousness *and* a reader's process of connecting the two moments in the narrative discourse because they hinge on the same moment in the "story." Instead, what the anticipatory imagination allows Anne to do is disavow those matters of the past, replacing them with other concerns. Anticipations of retrospection become significant less for proving true or untrue in relation to some actual point in the future than for structuring by productive displacement Anne's relation to the present and, in that respect, serving as consolation. The "self" in *Persuasion* is constructed of *narratives of time* (narratives that tell, however provisionally, how the present self will be related to a future self, for instance), which are also *subject to time* (narratives the implications of which are continually under revision)—even the significance of future remembrance alters in the course of *Persuasion*'s novelistic time. That is, what began by appearing as fixed memories that will nourish the mind of a future self—not unlike what the poet-speaker imagines for his sister in Wordsworth's "Tintern Abbey"—turn out to be relatively ephemeral ideas with respect to content. Nevertheless, throughout the novel this temporal structure of imagining plays a part in the process of negotiating the present—a process whereby both self and world are imagined anew.

However fictional Anne's anticipations may prove to be, these auto-narratives provide her real consolation in distressing moments. They express, through her imaginative power, a measure of individual agency by making a certain *sense* of things, which affects the painful and the pleasurable; in other words, her sense-making alters the senses, by adding sweet thoughts and sensations to a moment otherwise gone sour. More difficult to account for is this temporal structure when it counters not times of distress or pain but moments of almost pure happiness. At the climax of the novel, when Anne has just accepted Wentworth's renewed proposal, the narrative discourse reveals the two not embracing their joy straightforwardly but instead anticipating how this "present hour" will figure into their "future lives":

> Soon words enough had passed between them to decide their direction
> towards the comparatively quiet and retired gravel-walk, where the power
> of conversation would make the present hour a blessing indeed; and prepare
> for it all the immortality which the happiest recollections of their own future
> lives could bestow. (240)

A "present hour" is proclaimed, but only insofar as it will figure into their imagined "future lives" as a memory. Although the grammar of this sentence remains somewhat ambiguous with respect to whose "recollections" are in question, it seems to be the couple who anticipate recollecting this moment in the context of "their own future lives," thus "bestow[ing]" on the moment a significantly qualified "immortality." Insofar as Anne and Wentworth imagine this moment in relation to their "future lives," the moment of present joy is not embraced directly; part of its joy, part of how it is understood, comes from imagining how the two of them may recall it in the years ahead.

What is odd about imagining and articulating the significance of the "present hour" on the "gravel-walk" in this way is that Austen uses the vocabulary of Romantic timelessness and transcendence—"immortality"—but inscribes the idea within an ultimately transient scene, apparently limited to their two lives.[13] This hour will not even go down in Sir Walter Elliot's *Baronetage* for future generations to read about; its "immortality" is inscribed within Anne and Captain Wentworth's future memories without any certain appeal to a life beside or beyond. Austen's invoking of "immortality" thus seems ironically to undermine the notion of transcending a world of instability and flux—a world in which even the experience of a memory's "immortality" remains grounded only in the temporal world.

Soon after this scene of reconciliation, Anne returns to the house, and again her disposition restrains her from simply soaring in this "high-wrought felicity," for she suspects its transience: "she re-entered the house so happy as to be obliged to find an alloy in some momentary apprehensions of its being impossible to last" (245). An active temporal imagination alerts her to a peril in such pure—unmixed and unbridled—happiness, and she finds an alloy to the "high-wrought felicity" in the understanding that it cannot be expected to last. In *Persuasion*, falls from high places, such as Louisa's physical one, are indeed seen to be perilous. Anne thus subdues her high felicity by hypothetically inscribing it in an imagined future retrospective context in which it will have been short-lived, mixing the moment of triumph with the anticipatory sadness of its eventual loss or lessening.

Imagining future memories often amounts, then, to a temporal strategy in Anne's intellectual and imaginative efforts to avoid self-delusion. After all, the critical capacity of a temporal imagination is an aspect of human beings that potentially elevates us above, for instance, the helpless delusion of John Keats's bees who "think warm days will never cease" ("To Autumn," line 10). The critical awareness of the "present" offered in Anne's future retrospective temporality, however, is inherently incomplete in that it takes into account what is unaccountable: a future that holds uncertainties. We can see in this temporal structure of self-understanding an inherent source of epistemological uncertainty insofar as the heroine's sense of self appears to come from a position that rests partly upon an unknown future set of affairs.

While Anne's constant effort of critical awareness—her effort to *read* her situation by imagining it in the temporality of a narrative—would seem admirable, Austen's attitude toward it is actually somewhat difficult to register, in that Anne's attempts to know the present can seem to lead her away from it. Anne's embodied experience of the present, that is, largely eludes the narrative discourse, which is preoccupied instead with anticipating events, recollecting them, and anticipating recollecting them. Epistemological gaps and rhythmic silences evoke a present that is hard to pin down or to embrace in any straightforward way.

When residing at Mary's home in Uppercross, for instance, Anne receives only a few moments' notice that Captain Wentworth will be arriving; this will be the first time that Anne will have seen him in the eight years since her refusal of marriage. Her anticipatory feelings are so numerous that they cannot seem to be squared with what happens or resolved coherently into a narration of the encounter: "a thousand feelings rushed on Anne, of which this was the most consoling, that it would soon be over. And it was soon over" (59). Like Keats's Cortés, Anne is too overwhelmed by the experience to organize the multiplicity of its possibilities into narration. The "thousand" reduces to one unnarratable "it," the power of which is evoked by the rhythmic silence between sentences. Shifting abruptly from before to after, the narration of ostensibly significant action in the present seems to have slipped through the space between sentences and been lost. In the most immediate recollection, moreover, the interpretive significance of the event remains elusive—both to character and narrator—and the language of recollection simply repeats that which anticipated "it." In both story and narrative discourse, the "time of reading" entails deferred understanding—a deferred sorting out of all the "thousand feelings," that is, all the multiple, conflicting feelings Anne has about seeing Wentworth again. The significance of the encounter appears too numerous in its possibilities for narration.

In yet another instance of conspicuously arrested narration, Wentworth lifts Anne into the Crofts' carriage: "Captain Wentworth, without saying a word, turned to her, and quietly obliged her to be assisted into the carriage. Yes,—he had done it. She was in the carriage" (91). Anticipation of the event gives way immediately to an afterward—a moment in which the event has already taken place, but its significance is not yet clear. What this temporal structure indicates, then, is Anne's frequently alienated relation to the present. That in the world of *Persuasion* the exigencies of human life, of continuing, appear to necessitate these structures of alienation as the most intelligent response available, the only response with creative potentiality, is the novel's source of its profound sadness, the heart of its narrative desire, the peculiar emotional force of its aesthetic. These gaps and silences, moreover, appear consistent with the logic of future anteriority. The aesthetic of *Persuasion* is "laden with silence, litotes, and negation," as Mary Favret has described it, and I want to suggest that this particular aesthetic load registers the implications of imagining the present as anticipated retrospection.[14] For the present as future anteriority, always in the process of becoming, can never be complete. Aesthetic spaces or gaps in *Persuasion* thus convey, in these interruptions of narrative discourse, the experiential implications of inhabiting a world ruptured by an uncertain futurity.

There is, however, a remarkable exception to this slipping away of the present: it is the scene at Lyme describing the aftermath of Louisa's fall, narrating the state of emergency, and elevating Anne in Wentworth's estimation. It is the only scene in which the narration of events takes much longer to read than the events themselves would take to unfold, as if the "present" has expanded in the rare urgency of these few pages. Consider the narration that immediately follows Louisa's being "taken up lifeless!":

> There was no wound, no blood, no visible bruise; but her eyes were closed, she breathed not, her face was like death.—The horror of that moment to all who stood around!
>
> Captain Wentworth, who had caught her up, knelt with her in his arms, looking on her with a face as pallid as her own, in an agony of silence. "She

is dead! she is dead!" screamed Mary, catching hold of her husband, and contributing with his own horror to make him immoveable; and in another moment, Henrietta, sinking under the conviction, lost her senses too, and would have fallen on the steps, but for Captain Benwick and Anne, who caught and supported her between them. (109–10)

The narrator emphasizes the remarkable difference between the long time of reading and the short clock time of the "story" (*récit*) in the evident need to note parenthetically, "(it was all done [even if not told] in rapid moments)" (110). That these moments of "rapid" action appear at odds with the aesthetic slowness shaped by the narrative discourse at this juncture exposes the continuous, simultaneous workings of two distinguishable "times of reading": Anne's situation (and her thinking about her situation) in a narrative mode and the reader's encounter—sentence by sentence, paragraph by paragraph, chapter by chapter—with the succession of events. Although Austen typically aligns the kinds of imagining she models in Anne with the kinds of imagining her narrative discourse works to elicit in readers, this episode separates the temporality of reading *Persuasion* from that of Anne's consciousness, her reading of self and world. This exceptional disjunction makes us conscious that Austen could have done it differently, that she has multiple modes of narration among which to choose.

What's more, both Anne's experience of time and the temporality of the narrative discourse—now a moment dilating, now a present eluding mental grasp—stand clearly at odds with yet another possible mode: the regulating chronological order of life and death on display in Sir Walter's *Baronetage*. Indeed, the whole novel might appear as an alternative family history to Sir Walter's, reordered by the logic of Anne's exceptional perception.

While shifts in modes of narration reflect Anne's decentered experience of the crisis at Lyme, it is furthermore telling that at the center of the scene is a figure of unconsciousness. That is, an embodied experience of the present and the taking of direct action appear in tension with Anne's conscious thought processes, her habitual subjectivity—as much here as in those moments of elusive present narration mentioned earlier. This is to read the scene as a performance of the subjectivity of the novel.[15] To that end, the parenthetical aside, substantially at odds with the narrative slowness—"(it was all done in rapid moments)" (110)—functions as a kind of stage note. The idea that the novel's subjectivity requires a kind of performance would appear sanctioned by the largely nonlinguistic communication of looks and smirks constantly employed by Wentworth and Anne.[16] What's more, this scene entails a startling shift in the usual relationships—between characters as well as between the position of the reader and the heroine's point of view—in that Anne is suddenly absorbed into the scene so that we no longer see things sifted primarily through her consciousness. Instead, and astonishingly, the thrill of the crisis aligns Austen's audience with—if anyone—the "workmen and boatmen . . . collected near them, to be useful if wanted, *at any rate, to enjoy the sight* of a dead young lady, nay, two dead young ladies, for it proved twice as fine as the first report" (111, emphasis mine). Suddenly the narrative perspective is set loose from Anne's moral point of view; rather than reporting events from a perspective of any of the other principal characters, Austen allows the pleasures of reading *Persuasion* to align readers with the onlookers' "enjoy[ment]" of the spectacle of human crisis that the scene lays bare.

This dynamic offers a hint of what Virginia Woolf foresaw taking center stage in Austen's writing after *Persuasion*, had Austen lived to write more: "She would have devised a method, clear and composed as ever, but deeper and more suggestive, for conveying not only what people say, but what they leave unsaid; not only what they are, but what life is. She would have stood farther away from her characters, and seen them more as a group, less as individuals."[17] The "workmen and boatmen" appear as figures for that distance and for the observation of a group. If they have the potential to implicate Austen's readers in their enjoyment, the scene can appear as an allegory of reading, prompting self-reflexivity on the part of readers. What does it mean to enjoy, from a remove, this scene of distress? Rarely are life-threatening situations the stuff of Austen's fiction. That the implication of reading-as-onlooking arrives at this dramatic juncture makes the question prompted by the novel's self-reflexivity appear to address the kind of "degrading thirst after outrageous stimulation" that, in the preface to *Lyrical Ballads*, Wordsworth accused his contemporaries' "frantic novels" of satisfying.[18] In other words, the self-reflexivity addresses a residual cultural popularity of gothic fiction—extremely fashionable when Austen was overtly drawing on and parodying it in *Northanger Abbey* at the end of the eighteenth century and when Wordsworth was composing his preface of 1800.

Provocative as this brief engagement with the cultural history of the gothic is, I have drawn attention to it primarily in order to establish two claims that will be key for the analysis to follow. First, in certain narrative moments of looking, the process becomes a figure for reading, whereby Austen implicates her audience, her readers as onlookers. Second, such pervasive self-reflexivity does not make the novel self-enclosed; rather, it is precisely in the novel's self-reflexivity that its most dynamic engagement with world-historical events takes shape. For not only the narration of the scene at Lyme but also the way in which the novel is situated historically, vis-à-vis its readers, engenders a kind of staging, particularly in respect to its engagement with British perception of the Napoleonic wars.

Reading *Persuasion*: Historiographical Analogy

Austen's narrative at once reflects familiar historical events and social situations of the Napoleonic era in Britain and creates new ways to imagine (and to theorize) history as a process, by virtue of how Anne imagines herself in time and how that imagining appears analogous to the novel's situation with respect to historical events. Thinking in the "future anterior" tense, as we have seen, shapes the protagonist's relation to her present, and this temporality of the present makes epistemological uncertainty part of Anne's everyday experience insofar as she can speculate about how a decision or act will be remembered in the future, but she cannot know how the future will, in fact, unfold; her sense of the present is always, therefore, partly based on sense-perception and understanding and partly provisional. The temporal logic of Anne's provisional imagination—her speculative anticipation of retrospection and the epistemological uncertainty it necessarily entails—has something to tell us about *Persuasion*'s distinctive inscription of its historical moment, for Austen subtly attributes to the entire narrative a similarly provisional status.

Characters in *Persuasion* repeatedly refer to the peace of their present times, scrupulously marked as running from late summer 1814 to 1815. "'This peace will be turning all our rich Navy Officers ashore,'" Mr. Shepherd observes early on in his domestic concern for the financial affairs of the Kellynch household (17). The novel closes, however, ominously: "[Wentworth's] profession was all that could ever make [Anne's] friends wish that tenderness less; the dread of a future war all that could dim her sunshine. She gloried in being a sailor's wife, but she must pay the tax of quick alarm for belonging to that profession which is, if possible, more distinguished in its domestic virtues than in its national importance" (252). What Austen knew when writing the novel in 1815 and 1816, and what her readers, too, would have known, is that this hypothetical "future war" would almost instantly materialize in Napoleon's return from Elba—that is, in a resurgence of the wars, albeit brief, that were thought to have been quite over.[19] The historical orientation of the novel—at once displayed and concealed—tells us that the supposed peace informing it *will have been* a false peace; this knowledge, however, is oddly suspended in the considerable gap between the characters' perceptions of their historical moment and those of post-Waterloo readers.[20] The force of this temporal and epistemological gap is to suggest how uncertain knowledge of the present is when it includes a future that promises the unforeseen. Austen's suspension of that historical knowledge creates an ironic effect by simultaneously distancing her audience from the characters' perspective of the historical moment and, as I shall explain, implicating them in it.[21]

This impending historical turn, effecting an ironic remove, is obliquely registered in the novel when a painting in a Bath shop window fascinates and amuses Admiral Croft, who describes its apparent absurdity to Anne:

> "I can never get by this window without stopping. But what a thing here is, by way of a boat. Do look at it. Did you ever see the like? What queer fellows your fine painters must be, to think that any body would venture their lives in such a shapeless old cockleshell as that. And yet, here are two gentlemen stuck up in it mightily at their ease, and looking about them at the rocks and mountains, as if they were not to be upset the next moment, which they certainly must be. I wonder where that boat was built!" (laughing heartily) "I would not venture over a horsepond in it. Well," (turning away) "now, where are you bound? Can I go any where for you, or with you? Can I be of any use?"
>
> "None, I thank you, unless you will give me the pleasure of your company the little way our road lies together. I am going home."
>
> "That I will, with all my heart and farther too. Yes, yes, we will have a snug walk together; and I have something to tell you as we go along. There, take my arm; that's right; I do not feel comfortable if I have not a woman there. Lord! What a boat it is!" taking a last look at the picture, as they began to be in motion. (169)

Filling out the captured moment with a linear narrative in time from origins (the boat manufacturer) to outcome (impractical gentlemen overboard), the Admiral's utilitarian commentary on a sublime image stands not in awe or horror but in comically critical disillusionment. The specific temporal framework that he supplies supports his negative critique of the painters' "queer" thinking. It tells us specifically how the Admiral envisions the figures within the image in relation to their future: they proceed unaware, or at least unconcerned, that they are about to be "upset the next moment" *because* they have not prepared for the outing with a well-made vessel. The Admiral's narration, that is, fills out the causal relation to an imminent upset that he predicts with confidence. According to the Admiral, moreover, only he, peering through the print shop window from outside, perceives clearly their futurity.[22]

Outside the painting's frame as well as outside the shop window and grounded on land, the Admiral nevertheless does not escape being implicated by an epistemological upending analogous to that which he foresees for the "two gentlemen." That is, the processes of looking and narrating do not liberate the Admiral, insofar as his commentary implicitly spots something akin to what he misses in his own historical situation. For Austen situates the entire novel within a (pre-Waterloo, 1814 to 1815) time of peace that she knows will turn out, in retrospect, to have been a false sense of peace. However brief Napoleon's spring-to-summer campaign in 1815, it suddenly made the prior calm sense that wartime was over appear unfounded. Admiral Croft's ekphrastic discourse thus not only describes the imminent "upset" of the subjects in the painting but also, unwittingly, suggests Napoleon's imminent threat to the "ease" of the characters of *Persuasion*, a threat to the pervading sense of "peace" which, we imagine, will come to have been unwarranted. In other words, we see the Admiral (and the world of the novel generally) as he sees the "two gentlemen": that is, unaware of the implications of their situations insofar as the future may reveal them to have been. But whereas the upset of the two boatmen is predictable—that is, knowable—according to the Admiral's causal logic, Napoleon's return is not at all predicted. The causal logic so central to Enlightenment historiography and the Admiral's thinking falters by virtue of the novel's historical mise-en-scène.

The Admiral looks at—but does not buy—the painting. This missed or declined opportunity for possession reinforces the idea of a knowledge that is somehow *there* at the same time that it cannot be fully possessed or internalized in a way that might prevent the Admiral or Anne from making the same mistakes. Put another way, knowledge and the capacity to act on that knowledge are out of joint, as the Admiral's ekphrastic causal logic has no effect on what happens in the rest of the novel. If we think of the Admiral's reading of the painting to Anne as an "event," then the moment shares something with Wordsworth's, Dickinson's, and Hardy's lyric speakers for whom, as Anne-Lise François has suggested so insightfully, "the going without inflection was the missed event's way of happening."[23] The Admiral's reading of the painting concludes with his simple "(turning away)" from it, as the parentheses function stylistically to further diminish the act of leave-taking.

The epistemological implication of Admiral Croft's ekphrastic commentary—which, in his turning, escapes him—builds on what Mary Favret has described as the everyday register of war in which "gaps and silences" in *Persuasion* are "symptoms of a history not entirely possessed." Austen's novel "call[s] attention to a negative sort of history, a lost history, a history of what seems unable to be told."[24] Rather than reassure readers of *their* historical authority on the 1814–15 moment, Admiral Croft's unwitting commentary on his own historical situation also implicates Austen's post-Waterloo readers. For the scene of ekphrasis draws attention to an inevitability of those "gaps," those blind spots in one's own unfolding situation—whereby it calls for an interminably revisionary historicism of self and world. The novel's historicizing engagement with its post-Waterloo audience repeats the pattern of future anterior imagining in Anne's thought; in both cases, the revisionary process of knowing the present appears less as a shedding of present light on the past than as a speculative imagining of the present in its shadowy relation to futurity.

Questioning the "Foregone Conclusion"

In *Persuasion*, the idea of history as a revisionary process means keeping in mind the notion that any given moment teems with multiple possible implications and interpretive possibilities not always immediately available—implications and possibilities that perhaps will come to light only in retrospect. Even in retrospect, this sense of multiplicity persists. After Anne Elliot reunites with Captain Wentworth, for instance, she does not assume such an outcome was inevitable but imagines how things might have gone very differently for her. That is, although the novel's weighty prehistory of Anne's broken engagement to Captain Wentworth might seem to suggest that their eventual reunion figures as a more than probable conclusion, the heroine herself appears hardly confident about its inevitability, from beginning to end. For when Lady Russell tried to persuade Anne to marry Mr. Elliot, Anne had not been untempted by the idea of becoming Mrs. Elliot and filling the place of her mother at Kellynch Hall. Upon discovering Mr. Elliot's real motives for reconciling with her family, Anne considers, near the novel's conclusion, the alternate reality that might very well have been hers:

> Anne could just acknowledge within herself such a possibility of having been induced to marry him, as made her shudder at the idea of the misery which must have followed. It was just possible that she might have been persuaded by Lady Russell! And under such a supposition, which would have been most miserable, when time had disclosed all, too late? (211)

William Galperin has dismissed Anne's meditation on this possibility as a narrative flaw, regarding the end of *Persuasion* "no less than the resolution of *Pride and Prejudice*" as "entirely a foregone conclusion. . . . I am inclined," Galperin writes, "to regard [Anne's pliancy where Mr. Elliot is concerned] as a badly executed sidebar to the narrative."[25] But however much this moment may seem inconsistent with Anne's "sensation" upon meeting Mr. Elliot "of there being something more than immediately appeared" (140), it insists on imagining a world in which the "event" of Lady Russell's "good" intentions and advice (first regarding Wentworth, then regarding Mr. Elliot) might have been understood retrospectively in a different light. To read from the perspective of this sidebar is to see not only Anne's insistence on that sense of uncertainty about outcomes, persistent even in retrospect, but also Austen's flickering insistence on making her audience aware that her story has alternate narrative possibilities not to be simply dismissed.[26]

In the narrative unfolding of *Persuasion*, Austen alerts us—at the level of narrative discourse—to the shifting over time of perspectives on the past in a way that calls for the judgment about a moment's significance to be never other than provisional. In this way, the novel conceives the present as historical surmise. As the novel opens, Anne Elliot at age twenty-seven thinks differently from how she did at nineteen, now believing that "she should yet have been a happier woman in maintaining the engagement, than she had been in the sacrifice of it" (29). By the novel's end, however, she asserts to Captain Wentworth, to whom she is engaged anew, a sharply contrasting view: "I should have suffered more in continuing the engagement," she explains, "than I did even in giving it up, because I should have suffered in my conscience" (246). Neither Anne nor the narrator comments directly on this discrepancy between whether she would have been happier in the engagement or suffered more; nevertheless, it is there for readers to notice and to contemplate as a performance of reinterpreted significance in altered circumstances. The difference does not signal that the "event" has now decided, that the last view is the "right" one; rather, it makes the ethical understanding of a moment appear as an interminably unfolding process whereby the interpretive possibilities of the moment become, at different points in time, variously illuminated. At the end of the novel, Anne takes into account "conscience" when she says to Wentworth that her early refusal was the decision that would cause the least suffering, and yet she seems conscious of how contingent that view is upon the happiness she finally enjoys: hence the significant tentativeness when she says in the same speech to Wentworth, "It was, *perhaps*, one of those cases in which advice is good or bad only as the event decides" (246, emphasis mine). Although neither the narrator nor Anne explicitly recalls that she earlier emphasized her unhappiness due to taking Lady Russell's advice, one could still wonder whether Anne's late emphasis on the "event" of their reunion and her feelings of filial allegiance to Lady Russell should trump the suffering of long delay. That Anne describes the relation of the novel's prehistory to the late "event" as only "perhaps" one in which the "event decides" suggests a tentativeness about decisive sense-making from a single retrospective view. In the discrepancy described, the narrative discourse invites a reader, too, to exercise such tentativeness, the upshot of which is to imagine more than one possible implication or outcome for the early advice even after later events may have seemed to narrow its possible significance.

Resisting the narrative teleology implicit in a "foregone conclusion," Harry Shaw emphasizes that when Anne reflects on the decisions she made eight years earlier not to marry Wentworth, she identifies and preserves a difference between her past and present perspectives: "She refuses to allow a love-story capped with the acquisition of Wentworth to exhaust the possibilities of her former self and to silence her earlier voice, the voice that said 'no' to him."[27] I take from the dynamics of that refusal not only the implication of an inability to see, at any given moment, how one will come to remember that moment but also the sense that no single or unified perspective, even in retrospect, has the authority to cancel all others. The historical process has no conclusion, much less a foregone one.

Whereas the novel's shifting social circumstances call for the protagonist's ongoing process of moral reconsideration and imagining of multiple possibilities (a *mental* mobility), *Persuasion* has been studied as a novel of *physical* and cultural departures, too—departures contingent upon changing economic and social situations (the leaving of Kellynch for Uppercross, the leaving of Uppercross for Bath, for instance, as well as a shift from the old aristocratic order to the new world of the navy). It is, moreover, the only novel by Austen that does not specify where the couple will live at the novel's end. Evoking a concept of revisionary history and selfhood in the literally and figuratively shifting grounds of Anne's being, body and mind in *Persuasion* appear equally on the move.

Austen's History of the Unpredictable: Displacing the Scottish Enlightenment Historiography of Scott's *Waverly*

In light of how the poetics of anticipation in *Persuasion* make available to us the concept of history as provisional and as an ongoing process, one might ask what place this prose fiction occupies with respect to the genre of the historical novel. Literary history since the early nineteenth century, for the most part, has drawn on a model derived from the works of Sir Walter Scott to define the genre. In the New Critical Idiom book series from Routledge, Jerome de Groot's contribution on *The Historical Novel* (published in 2010) invokes Jane Austen's novels primarily as examples against which to define the genre. De Groot explains in his introduction: "History is other, and the present familiar. The historian's job is often to explain the transition between these states. The historical novelist similarly explores the dissonance and displacement between then and now, making the past recognizable but simultaneously authentically unfamiliar."[28] Austen's novels focus not on a past age overtly distinguishable in manners and psychology from those of the present but rather on a moment in the *very* recent past that is part of the present age. That is perhaps why Austen so often is left out of studies like de Groot's, which construe the historical imagination as that which negotiates the relation between a remote past and the present. But such omissions of Austen's novels overlook how *Persuasion* in particular—in its very focus not on a remote past but on the present age—conceptualizes a historical process of estrangement different from Walter Scott's and contemporaneous to it. As we have seen, instead of estranging the past from the present (as Scott's novels so often do), *Persuasion* estranges the present epoch by "looking ahead." Attending to this dynamic of anticipation in Austen's novel opens new possibilities for our sense of how the novel (as genre) can make available to us distinct ways of imagining history. The historical past "is other," as de Groot puts it; so too is the present, as Austen does.

For *Persuasion*, published posthumously in 1818, revised the relations between literature, character, and history announced by Sir Walter Scott with the publication of *Waverley* in 1814. According to Georg Lukács's famous analysis in *The Historical Novel*, Scott invented the novel in which the psychology and manners of individual characters reflect the peculiarity of the historical period they inhabited. "What is lacking in the so-called historical novel before Sir Walter Scott," Lukács explained, "is precisely the specifically historical, that is, derivation of the individuality of characters from the historical peculiarity of their age."[29] In Lukács's formulation, the historical peculiarity of an age is assumed to be a given quality, or set of qualities, that the historical novelist draws on in order to construct historical characters.

In *Persuasion*, the defining peculiarity of the historical age is less the source of the protagonist's individual character than the question around which the novel frames its mode of historical engagement. Anne's individuality sets her apart from her contemporaries ("—she was only Anne"), and her own persistent questioning and recalibrating of her experiences of the world—a historical world that appears anything but given—perhaps most significantly defines her (5). That questioning and recalibrating of the present is also, as we have seen, a historicizing impulse and a process that the narrative discourse encourages, all the while resisting the totalizing retroactive explanation or conclusiveness. The insistent contingency of Austen's narrative temporality delivers us into a world that is never fully knowable, as its meanings are interminably unfolding in light of a future that surprises with the unforeseen. Whereas protagonists "provide," according to Lukács, "a perfect instrument for Scott's way of presenting the totality of certain transitional stages of history,"[30] Austen's novel historiography appears, by contrast, decidedly nontotalizing because of the prominent roles anticipation and futurity play in figural, narrative, and historical understanding. In any given moment, Austen seems to insist, there is always something significant that exceeds our comprehension.

The sense of anticipation to which Austen's historical imagination so rigorously attends in *Persuasion* is precisely what William Hazlitt announced as regrettably lacking in Sir Walter Scott's overwhelmingly popular novels. In *The Spirit of the Age; Or, Contemporary Portraits* (1825), Hazlitt begins his entry on Scott with an extended critique of the most popular contemporary writer who—with a "speculative understanding [that was] empty, flaccid, poor, and dead"—also appeared to Hazlitt as the contemporary writer least interested in the historical age he inhabited:

> Sir Walter Scott is undoubtedly the most popular writer of the age—the "lord of the ascendent" for the time being. He is just half what the human intellect is capable of being: if you take the universe, and divide it into two parts, he knows all that it *has been*; all that it *is to be* is nothing to him. His is a mind brooding over antiquity—scorning "the present ignorant time." He is *laudatory temporis acti*—"prophesier of things past." The old world is to him a crowded map; the new one a dull, hateful blank. He dotes on all well-authenticated superstitions; he shudders at the shadow of innovation. His retentiveness of memory, his accumulated weight of interested prejudice or romantic association have overlaid his other faculties. The cells of his memory are vast, various, full even to bursting with life and motion; his speculative understanding is empty, flaccid, poor, and dead. His mind receives and treasures up every thing brought to it by tradition or custom—it does not project itself beyond this into the world unknown, but mechanically shrinks back as from the edge of a precipice . . . though every thing changes and will change from what it was three hundred years ago to what it is

now—from what it is now to all that the bigoted admirer of the good old times most dreads and hates! (161)

Although Hazlitt's claim that all that the world "*is to be* is nothing to [Scott]" appears perhaps overstated, his observation about Scott's lack of speculative imagination, especially in view of the wonder that *Persuasion* provokes, offers insight to a significant difference between the temporality of historical imagination shaping *Persuasion* and that informing Scott's *Waverley*.

Unlike Austen's novel, which concerns very recent history—or the present age as history—and does so without overt reference to past historical ages, Scott's novels focus primarily on moments in history significantly more distant from the present. *Waverley; Or, 'Tis Sixty Years Since*, one of Scott's least remote historical settings for a novel, concerns the narrative imagining primarily of the events of the Jacobite rebellion of 1745; while 1745 is the subject of the novel, the narrator self-consciously situates himself in 1805 and addresses his narrative commentary to his early nineteenth-century contemporaries. In this way, the novelistic eye is on the past and the present and the relations between them. The nature of those relations, as we shall see, indicate how much Scott drew from the Scottish Enlightenment's four-stage theory of cultural development for his sense of history as progressive stages.

The concluding chapter to *Waverley*, which, the narrator admits, "should have been a prefatory" one, compares Scottish social change of the previous sixty years to patterns of social change across Europe:

> There is no European nation, which, within the course of half a century, or little more, has undergone so complete a change as this kingdom of Scotland. The effects of the insurrection of 1745,—the destruction of the patriarchal power of the Highland chiefs,—the abolition of the heritable jurisdictions of the Lowland nobility and barons,—the total eradication of the Jacobite party, which, averse to intermingle with the English, or adopt their customs,—commenced this innovation.[31]

This "destruction of the patriarchal power of the Highland chiefs," which Scott's narrative blending of fact and fiction recounts, shifted the Scottish people from a feudal to a commercial, civilized society and, in so doing, brought them up to speed with the cultural progress of the English. For the "gradual influx of wealth, and extension of commerce, have since [1745] united to render the present people of Scotland a class of beings as different from their grandfathers, as the existing English are from those of

Queen Elizabeth's time" (450). This form of comparative analysis implies an uneven speed of progress, but it also assumes the same path (and goal) of progress everywhere (in England and Scotland)—a progress of social and cultural change facilitated by the "extension of commerce," which eradicated the Highlanders' feudal, patriarchal form of society.

The onward march of progress underlying Scott's historical imagination appears, moreover, naturalized—a process treated as basically inevitable. It has happened, the narrator observes, without our even noticing it, which is to suggest without significant conscious effort:

> The political and economical effects of these changes have been traced by Lord Selkirk with great precision and accuracy. But the change, though steadily and rapidly progressive, has, nevertheless, been gradual; and, like those who drift down the stream of a deep and smooth river, we are not aware of the progress we have made until we fix our eye on the distant point from which we have drifted. (450)

History's course is as guided by nature as the path of "a deep and smooth river." Change, moreover, is so gradual as to be almost imperceptible, until one looks back. The model of gradual progress upon which Scott's vision relies appears to be the four-stage theory of progress popularized by the Scottish Enlightenment philosophers in the second half of the eighteenth century, including those whose historical writings formed the focus of Chapter 1. This stadial theory of progressive history upon which Scott's vision and his language draw so heavily appears incompatible with the sense of history to which this chapter has attended in *Persuasion*. For Austen's novel implicitly challenges, by displacing, the four-stage theory so remarkably influential to Scott's popular historical novels.

The four-stage theory of progress took shape in the work of Sir John Dalrymple, Lord Kames, and Adam Smith, among others, in the latter half of the eighteenth century. As discussed in Chapter 1, the stadial theory explained cultural development as progress over time through four distinct stages of subsistence: hunting and gathering, pastoral, feudal, and commercial societies. At any given time, all aspects of society could be understood as tied to an underlying system that unified all its parts and that was defined primarily by its most prevalent form of subsistence. The linear quality of Scott's "deep and smooth river" readily illustrates such a view of progress that insists on these stages as successive, unifying, and directed. According to the four-stage theory, although different states of society could exist simultaneously insofar as the native "Americans" in the eighteenth century, for instance, often hunted for their subsistence, by the second half of the eighteenth century the stages were normally considered distinct and successive insofar as these different states could not coexist, or not for long, in the same place.[32] Accordingly, in Scott's historical vision the swift influx of commerce had rendered the Scottish Highlanders' feudal system obsolete, bringing Scotland quickly up to speed with the rest of Britain and completing the course of progress by bringing the nation to the final stage of commercial society.

A significant influence on the development of the four-stage theory came from contemporary literature about the American Indians, which the majority of eighteenth-century social scientists felt could shed light on "the condition of man in the 'first' or 'earliest' period of its development."[33] America provided a window to ancient European society. In *Waverley*, Scott appears to draw on these assumptions about human progress. For instance, one model of progress through stages fits every society, though societies are not all in the same state at once. Such temporal dissonance across space underlies the British and European sociocultural fascination with the American Indians in the eighteenth century, and it accounts for Scott's portrayal of the Lowlanders' response to the patriarchal-feudal Scottish Highlanders, who move south in what Scott depicts as a materially doomed plot to "change the fate, and alter the dynasty, of the British kingdoms":

> Here was a pole-axe, there a sword without a scabbard; here a gun without a lock, there a scythe set straight upon a pole; and some had only their dirks, and bludgeons or stakes pulled out of hedges. The grim, uncombed, and wild appearance of these men, most of whom gazed with all the admiration of ignorance upon the most ordinary production of domestic art, created surprise in the Lowlands, but it also created terror. So little was the condition of the Highlands known at that late period, that the character and appearance of their population, while thus sallying forth as military adventurers, conveyed to the south-country Lowlanders as much surprise as if an invasion of African Negroes, or Esquimaux Indians, had issued forth from the northern mountains of their own native country. (310)

Scott's comparison of the Highlanders to the "Esquimaux" or "African Negroes" rests on the assumption that the earlier stage of Scottish society represented in the Highlanders brings those people culturally closer to the foreign primitive societies. All societies tend toward commercial organization, and with change in the form of subsistence comes change in character and manner. As the narrator notes in the novel's final chapter, his goal has been that of "preserving some idea of the ancient manners of which

I have witnessed the almost total extinction" (451). With the four-stage theory as a model for cultural progress that applies to any society, from the "Esquimaux Indians" to the "African Negroes" and the Scottish people, the succeeding stage of development of any society appears inevitable. The influx of commerce to Scotland brings it, in Scott's chapter, to the final plateau of cultural development with no view to a further one.

What this model of historical and cultural progress does for Scott's historical novel with respect to temporality is to help inure the imagination against the unexpected or the unpredictable. He can envision for sure that the Highlanders will have been barbarians in the process of becoming part of a civilized commercial society, however long that takes. Austen's historical imagination offers remarkably less assurance about what the historical world is becoming. As we have seen in Admiral Croft's ekphrastic discourse and in Anne's persistently provisional relation to the present, Austen's novel insists on historical unpredictability in a way that opens the present up to multiple possibilities, and it does so by virtue of the future's (paradoxical) promise of the unforeseen (the upset of Napoleon's escape). If we consider *Persuasion* as another "historical novel"—as it seems reasonable to think one should—Austen's insistently provisional historicizing thus displaces the predominant notion of "progress" as the temporal mode through which the genre blends historical fact and fiction in the early nineteenth century.

Anne's profoundly self-reflexive thinking, in patterns of anticipation of retrospection, as well as the novel's self-reflexive anticipations of its own historicization process, does not turn the historical focus strictly inward in a way that closes the self or the text off from the historical world (so that we might claim the text is so much about itself that it cannot be about anything outside the world it creates). Rather, self-reflexivity in Austen's novel dynamically enacts the specific kind of provisional historical thinking I've attempted to describe—teasing out of the historical dynamics of the pre- and post-Waterloo moments a transhistorical theoretical perspective on the temporal process of historical epistemology. History does not appear in the form of an object or as a *period* or *epoch* that can be contained in the past. Rather, it is intertwined with the temporality of narrative as an interminable process of unfolding and shifting meanings, as much created or actively imagined as perceived.

In the way that Austen's *Persuasion* both describes and elicits future memories, the novel conceptualizes the limitations of the kinds of historicism that literary critics looking back on different historical periods often practice today. That is to say, *Persuasion* conceives knowledge of the historical present as deeply elusive because that knowledge crucially depends upon a sense of future retrospection; it depends on how one imagines in the moment that the present might appear as a future memory. In a world of unpredictable change, one can never really have access to the future perspective upon which one's understanding of the present, in part, depends; one can never fully know a present whose grammar is the future anterior of what *will have been*. Enacting this logic, Austen's anticipations throw shadows on the present, rendering one's conception of it persistently provisional. The point of imagining future memories therefore seems to be less a chronicling of the present for a chronologically distant posterity than it is a structuring of one's knowledge of the present as provisional and contingent. In this sense, Austen's novel embeds any reader *in the mist* of the uncertain anticipations that preoccupied John Keats as well. To focus on these temporal aspects thus might be to read Austen from a Keatsian-Romantic perspective. Although Anne Elliot recommends the moral virtues of prose to Captain Benwick, the temporality of her thought and of Austen's narrative discourse introduces—both to the world of the novel and to the reader's imagination—qualities of mind and imagination recognizably close to the poetics of Keatsian *"Negative Capability."*

Austen's apparent reluctance to affirm a positive knowledge of the present—and her insistence on an interminably unfolding understanding of the moment—seem to come into tension, then, with literary historicism's frequent *aim* of recovering a discrete past "as it was"—a past coherent context in which to place the novel, or in relation to which one could understand some aspect of it. Austen's novel tells us, that is, that the historical age never was fully known or even theoretically knowable and that any epistemological gap could radically shift our understanding of its many parts. Rather than promising transparent access to the historical moment from a privileged later vantage, *Persuasion* makes available to us a temporal logic that renders the goal of recovering a discrete past finally untenable. The historical imagination in *Persuasion* is less about what we know than about the complex temporal dynamics and effects of what we cannot fully know.

Unlike in a novel by Walter Scott, the character of the protagonist in Austen's work is not derived passively from the given peculiarity of a discrete historical age. Anne, after all, is precisely notable for her *singularity* in her social world, her frequent sense of alienation from others. Rather than channeling the distinctive characteristics of a sharply defined historical epoch, the shape of Anne's thought brings into play a temporal framework and a process of creating historical understanding that align the figural, narrative, and historical dimensions of temporality in the novel. Through this alignment, the novel's self-reflexivity not only facilitates its distinctive historical engagement with its own moment but also makes available for readers a historicizing logic that takes into account an unknown futurity characteristic of modernity. Calling for an understanding of history not as static knowledge or as an object but as an ongoing revisionary process, *Persuasion* does not merely reflect modernity's dilemma of how to narrate the present as history but, in view of that dilemma, envisions the possibility of historical engagement in future anterior imaginings, however provisionally formed, that afford the experience of multiple presents and of a world malleable enough to be shaped by the imagination.

Although the present in *Persuasion* teems with possibilities, there is also the sense that its perspective is resolutely partial or nontotalizing. It is not a Marxist totality. The imagined historical possibilities are multiple but never exhaustive or comprehensive. Limiting the use of an omniscient narrator, Austen's almost ubiquitous use of free indirect discourse in this novel reinforces that nontotalizing historical perspective. One of the novel's most intriguing examples of the way Anne's perspective can seem so right and yet so partial at once arrives when Lady Russell, from inside a moving carriage and accompanied by Anne, seems to spot Captain Wentworth for the first time in Bath:

> When the moment approached which must point him out, though not daring to look again (for her own countenance she knew was unfit to be seen), she was yet perfectly conscious of Lady Russell's eyes being turned exactly in the direction for him—of her being in short intently observing him. She could thoroughly comprehend the sort of fascination he must possess over Lady Russell's mind, the difficulty it must be for her to withdraw her eyes, the astonishment she must be feeling that eight or nine years should have passed over him, and in foreign climes and in active service too, without robbing him of one personal grace! (179)

The wholly admiring "sort of fascination" Anne describes is clearly her own. Checking Anne's assumption of "thoroughly comprehend[ing]" her friend, Lady Russell turns to Anne to explain that she has been "'looking after some window-curtains,'" with no mention at all of Wentworth. Lady Russell very well may be avoiding the topic of Wentworth with this explanation. Austen provides nothing to confirm or deny absolutely what Lady Russell has seen, but the way Lady Russell contradicts Anne's extensive assumptions shows that the "thorough comprehen[sion]" of everything running through Lady Russell's mind is all Anne's own enthusiasm, her momentary fantasy.

As a historical perspective, moreover, this partial nature distinguishes the novel's historicizing perspective from the eighteenth-century historiographical tendency toward the general or toward society en masse; that is, it resists the totalizing impulse apparent in so many philosophical histories. It also marks Austen's difference from a nineteenth-century critique of those comprehensive histories, represented, for instance, in J. S. Mill's comment on David Hume:

> Does Hume throw his own mind into the mind of an Anglo-Saxon, or an Anglo-Norman? . . . Would not the sight, if it could be had, of a single table or pair of shoes made by an Anglo-Saxon, tell us, directly and by inference, more of his whole way of life, more of how men thought and acted among the Anglo-Saxons, than Hume, with all his narrative skill, has contrived to tell us from all his materials?[34]

For Mill, the universal is to be looked for in the particular: a "single" material object can tell us about "how *men* thought and acted" (emphasis mine). As Mark Salber Phillips has remarked, "Carlyle, Macauley, and others made much the same point," identifying an evocative historical perspective with "the freshness of primary documents, the vividness of Herodotus, or the fictional imagination of Walter Scott."[35] In the particularity of a primary historical document or of the typical nature of the protagonist Waverley we can find general characteristics of a historical age. *Persuasion* is remarkably different, insisting on a narrative perspective that is irrevocably partial (in both senses) in its particularity and inexorably contingent upon an individual subject's limited view. That partiality aligns Austen's historical and historicizing insights less with the vision of her contemporary Walter Scott than with the concepts of history alive in the contemporary work of John Keats, Lord Byron, and William Hazlitt.

5

THE "DOUBLE NATURE" OF PRESENTNESS: BYRON'S *DON JUAN*

Lord Byron's comic epic *Don Juan* takes the insights about temporality of Keats's poetry and Austen's *Persuasion* to a more extreme conclusion by developing a temporality perhaps best described as a narrative "presentness"—a heightened attention to the moment-to-moment writing and imagining process. Like Keats's poetry, *Don Juan* presents a world in which inclinations to anticipate the future lead not to knowledge or a single visionary path into the future (or even a knowledge of the present); anticipations of an uncertain futurity produce, rather, a rich multiplicity of present possibilities. Like Austen's *Persuasion*, *Don Juan* unsettles the notion that some future moment—some future event or so-called outcome of the present—could, or even should, resolve once and for all the significance of the present. Rather than conceiving a protagonist who thinks in anticipatory terms about her present and then exposing in the narrative *durée* how unaligned with events to come those anticipations are, *Don Juan* largely foregoes that tracking of such misalignments, instead directing the reader's attention to the moment-to-moment fluctuations, digressions, and interruptions that characterize the poet-narrator's relation to the story, to his work in progress. I argue that Byron's text makes available to the imagination a temporality that should be understood as historiographical insofar as the poem directly refers to and engages with eighteenth- and nineteenth-century debates about historical writing, debates that often centered on questions of narrative temporality. To leave off anticipating futurity in a world of possibilities, improbabilities, and even unpredictability is, in *Don Juan*, to make the historical dimensions of the present include not only what happens but what does not happen (what *might will have* happened); it is to forego hierarchizing the former at the expense of the latter. This historical imagining necessitates an alternative thinking to the linear chronological principles espoused by Enlightenment historians because events proliferate not just sequentially in chronological time but, more important, laterally: less in a progressive fashion, or even in a progressive-regressive one, than in digressions and other narrative expressions of simultaneity. The digressive mode of *Don Juan*, in other words, should be understood as making available a way of imagining history that entails a rough equivalency between what does or did happen and what might have happened (even if it didn't); these two dimensions appear equally significant to the historiographical imagination of the present.

In light of the Lacanian notion of subjectivity with which this study began as a point of departure—the subject as the "future anterior of what I shall have been for what I am in the process of becoming"—*Don Juan*'s temporality resists the tendency to imagine the present, even hypothetically or provisionally, as part of a narrative that leads into the future. Instead, Byron's poem emphasizes the last part of Lacan's formulation, presenting an immersion in the very "*process* of becoming" as a solution to the problem of modernity's largely inaccessible and unpredictable yet fast-approaching futurity, which destabilizes knowledge of the present. I call that temporal immersion in the moment Byron's "presentness." Its "double"—or multiple—"nature" names the way the poem insists on narrating the experience of the present as a process of holding in the mind more than one possibility or more than one way of imagining the present, whether with regard to its interpretive significance, to its potential outcome(s), or both. This "double nature" of the present appears at odds, in Byron's poem, with an anticipatory thinking that would prioritize a single narrative thread, and as such it constitutes a more radical solution to the problem of dark futurity than we have seen, suggesting that if one inhabits a world in which the future is unknowable, the most adequate response is to immerse oneself in the moment-to-moment, sensory experience of the present. *Don Juan* tends to resist, for instance, the manner in which Austen's Anne Elliot often shapes her experience by anticipating how the moment will be remembered in the future. Austen's narrative develops alternative lines to Anne's anticipatory constructions, undermining her authority on the future and the notion of its predictability, but perhaps because Austen's narrator is less domineering than Byron's, the sense of multiple possibilities (in present and future) appears more subdued in *Persuasion* than in *Don Juan*. The tendency to imagine the future of "what will have been"—to at least try to foresee it—also appears more frequently necessary and even more constructive in Austen's text than in Byron's. Although Anne Elliot's imaginings do not successfully predict what is to come, they nevertheless serve emotional ends by altering Anne's relation to the present. In Byron's poem, such imaginings, however few they are, afford no such benefit; instead, the narrator immediately and overtly critiques or mocks how such memories work to reduce the possibilities of what could have happened in the past to the single notion of what did. Whereas for Austen's protagonist imagining future memories of the present appears to console her by opening up an alternative experience of it, for Byron's narrator, imagining the present in concrete terms from a future perspective produces a reductive form of historical knowledge.

Resisting that reductive tendency of historical memory, the most predominant temporality in *Don Juan* is its radical presentness. For the narrative perspective in *Don Juan* focuses alternately on the moment-to-moment writing process of the poet-narrator and on the unfolding events in the life of the largely unforeseeing, and equally unremembering, protagonist. The poet-narrator, in fact, tends to undermine the notion that he has any more access to the future of his narrative than the reader or Juan does. Such an emphasis on the immediate present affords various means for the opening up of multiple interpretive and narrative possibilities. These features of the poem will strike many as familiar peculiarities of Byron's comic epic— familiar at least since Jerome McGann's *"Don Juan" in Context* (1976).[1] I revisit them here in order to emphasize the temporal implications of the poem's most salient stylistic and narrative features; doing so will make the necessary step toward arguing that these features—which elicit the "double nature" of Byron's presentness—constitute the poem's most innovative engagement with debates about historiography in the late eighteenth and early nineteenth centuries.

McGann has written beautifully and extensively about the prevailing stylistic features and peculiarities of Byron's comic epic and has at times commented on their temporal implications, while others such as James Chandler and Jerome Christensen have written extensively about the poem's reimagining of certain historical circumstances and even its ideas of historical time, commenting that the present appears in *Don Juan* as a moment of decline.[2] Rarely have these two critical tendencies been joined. The analysis that follows attempts to put them in conversation in order to suggest that the "time of reading" elicited by the poetic and narrative features of Byron's verse constitutes an intervention in the late eighteenth- and early nineteenth-century historiographical debates about how to narrate the historical dimensions of the present age.

This chapter begins, therefore, with an analysis of the poem's most prominent poetic and narrative strategies, showing how they elicit for the reader a remarkable experience of temporality in the "time of reading," that is, in the experience that an attentive reader most plausibly has as she makes her way through the poem, from stanza to stanza, and canto to canto. The distinctiveness of this temporal experience when one reads *Don Juan* is what I call the double nature of presentness. The second section brings those temporal dynamics into conversation with historiographical debates, not only those described in Chapter 1 but also another element of those debates, which focuses on digressions. The third and final section brings these analyses to bear on a reading of the English cantos, showing how the issues of Byron's temporal poetics and his frustration with the predominant forms of contemporary historiography become overtly intertwined. In that rhetorical intertwining, the poem not only offers a critique of contemporary forms of historiography but also makes available to the reader a way of imagining the double nature dimensions of the present, which cannot be found in most other forms of historical writing.

Characterizing Byron's "Presentness"

Multiple narrative strategies and poetic effects throughout the sixteen cantos of Byron's *Don Juan* elicit a relation between reader and text that amplifies the sense of the unpredictable future and thus the imagination of multiple possibilities. In *Reading for the Plot*, Peter Brooks theorizes that we read narratives in a spirit of confidence that there is "a future we know to be already in place, already in wait for us to reach it."[3] Byron's poet-narrator does much to undermine our confidence in the idea that he is in control of how (or whether) the narrative unfolds. That Byron published his cantos separately significantly shapes his relationship to his audience, who cannot even be confident that more cantos will come. Building on his contemporary audience's uncertainty about ensuing cantos, the poet insistently disturbs the foundations of the kind of knowledge and "spirit of confidence" in narrative futurity that Brooks describes. At the close of Canto 1, for instance, the narrator suggests he will not continue to write if this canto is not warmly received by the reading public:

> We meet again, if we should understand
>   Each other; and if not, I shall not try
> Your patience further than by this short sample.
> 'Twere well if others followed my example. (1.221)

In other words, Juan's fate is decidedly not yet in place, not yet in textual form, and not even certain to make it there. The textual futurity is largely unpredictable, contingent upon factors beyond the narrator's knowledge or control. The project could die; it could be beloved and successful; it could have some other relation to the audience the poet has not yet even imagined. The multiple possibilities the poet-narrator conceives—the poem itself has a double nature in the marketplace—suggests that what the future brings might be one among those named possibilities or may not be; it might be some other situation entirely. The perspective, in this way, is not complete or comprehensive but admittedly partial, incomplete. Emphasized by the fact that it was originally published without the author's or publisher's name, it is a poem, as Jerome Christensen has argued, without a master.[4] Indeed, the poet suggests Juan's story itself is not even governed by the author's fixed and overarching design; it has, the poet-narrator often claims, no master plan. Poetic design and intention appear as subject to a variety of unpredictable vicissitudes, including those of the literary marketplace, as are the circumstances and fate of the hero. The effect is to align the reader's knowledge of—and relation to—the unfolding narrative with the poet-narrator's, as if both had the same knowledge, the same sense of mystery, about what was to come.

Further undermining readers' assurance that an overarching plan is in place, the narrator announces near the close of the first canto, "My poem's epic and is meant to be / Divided in twelve books" (1.200). By the end of Canto 2, he adds, "I've finished now / Two hundred and odd stanzas as before, / That being about the number I'll allow / Each canto of the twelve, or twenty-four" (2.216). The comma interrupts the rhythm, revises the thought. Audible in that pause is the poet's changeful, improvisational "presentness" and the sense of multiple possibilities—the double nature—that such a relation to the moment entails. It is as if the end word "before" suddenly makes an extension of the poem to twenty-four cantos thinkable. Byron did not write that many cantos, of course, but he did exceed twelve. In Canto 12, the poet-narrator feels compelled to revise, once again, the poem's imagined end point, pushing it yet further into the distance:

> I thought, at setting off, about two dozen
>   Cantos would do; but at Apollo's pleading,
> If that my Pegasus should not be foundered,
> I think to canter gently through a hundred. (12.55)

When Byron's publisher, John Murray, wrote to ask what his intentions exactly were with respect to the larger structure for *Don Juan*, Byron famously responded: "You ask me for the plan of my Donny Johnny—I *have* no plan—I *had* no plan—but I had or have materials—."[5]

Byron's epistolary claim to write without an overarching plan appears in the poem as well: "the fact is that I have nothing planned," the poet-narrator writes, "Unless it were to be a moment merry" (4.5.38–39). The nature of the transition from this digression back to the ostensible action is not incidental: "Meantime Apollo plucks me in the ear / And tells me to resume my story here" (4.7.55–56). The digression is cut short "here" by an image of the god of poetry plucking the narrator's rhymed "ear." Put another way, the poem's logic of what happens next comes as much from the nonsemantic materiality of language in a tight rhyme scheme—figured here as the sensory force on the ear of Apollo's pluck (the tactile and aural senses)—as it comes from the meanings the narrator describes as beyond his own comprehension when he would be "very fine" (the sense). Characteristically, the logic of the narrative transition between the hero's story and the narrator's digression appears less plot oriented and less intentional than driven by the materiality of language and the nature of the senses. Paradoxically, the perfect predictability of the rhyme scheme and stanza form seems to elicit unpredictability in so many other senses—from topic and tone to the high or low linguistic register.

The particular succession of distinct episodes, moreover, never seems to amount to any kind of narrative arc. Hence Jerome McGann's characterization of the overall structure of events as a "bizarre series of coincidental linkages."[6] In slightly less extreme terms, Peter W. Graham describes the "the international and intellectual voyage of *Don Juan*" as "more errant than mapped and charted."[7] Within episodes there may be elements of predictability and the narrator's routine misogyny is certainly clichéd. However, Juan's adventures on the island with Haidée in Cantos 2 through 4, for example, do not help us understand, nor are they retrospectively illuminated by, Juan's experiences with the Sultana and Dudù in Canto 5. That is, on the larger scale, unlike a narrative in which one episode may be illuminated by reference to an earlier or later one, *Don Juan* derives significance from its transitions and the surprise of its adaptability within *ottava rima* stanza form, while over time Juan learns nothing.[8] The poem deliberately, and ostensibly with a light heart, avoids precisely "the principle of interconnectedness and intention which," according to Brooks, "we cannot do without in moving through the discrete elements—incidents, episodes, actions—of a narrative . . . devices of interconnectedness, structural repetitions that allow us to construct a whole."[9] What Byron's strategy of departure and transition creates for the poem is not a horizon of probability, that is, the conventional domain of fiction in which the parameters for what can happen in the story are at least faintly outlined at the start; rather, it is a present sense of simultaneous possibilities and temporal flux that yields increasingly improbable circumstances in no way foreshadowed by early parts of the narrative—as Juan survives a time lost at sea in which the crew eats his tutor and his dog; is sold in a slave market and forced to cross dress and join a harem; fights alongside an Englishman in the battle of Ismail; and becomes Catherine the Great's envoy for a secret mission in England.[10] Narrative developments within the hero's story—most notably, perhaps, those that propel him from one geographical locale to the next—again and again revise the bounds of the possible, eliciting in both the dramatized poet-narrator and the reader a sense of surprise. It is not the sense of surprise one has when reading, say, a novel such as Austen's *Emma* at the moment one discovers that Frank Churchill and Jane Fairfax are engaged. The seeds for that revelation, however well disguised, had been strategically planted early on and the attentive reader recalls them at that moment. Rather, in *Don Juan*, it is the sense of surprise that leads one to wonder in anticipation about what event, what digression, or what improbable scenario could happen next.

Byron was clearly aware of the prevailing narrative principles to which Peter Brooks refers when he explains nineteenth-century narrative temporality. "[W]e read in a spirit of confidence," Brooks observes, "and also a state of dependence, that what remains to be read will restructure the provisional meanings of the already read."[11] The first canto of *Don Juan* overtly entertains such conventional anticipations, but it is as if to do so once and get them out of the way, clearing a space for "presentness"—that is, for the reader's attunement to the notion that the story could turn into a digression (or vice versa) or could veer off in a new geographical direction, while the narrative discourse could take up a new tone; and all of that could happen at any moment, without warning. At the beginning of the second canto, the narrator reflects for a moment on the predictable narrative strategies and readerly expectations that nevertheless shaped the first canto. Its highly predictable succession of events ostensibly contradicts the poem's otherwise prevailing commitment to transition, interruption, and encounters with the improbable. Regarding Juan and Julia's affair, the narrator reasons in retrospect:

> I can't say that it puzzles me at all,
>   If all things be considered: first, there was
> His lady mother, mathematical,
>   A—never mind; his tutor, an old ass;
> A pretty woman (that's quite natural,
>   Or else the thing had hardly come to pass);

> A husband rather old, not much in unity
> With his young wife; a time and opportunity. (2.3)

The narrator gives us, in hindsight, the more-than-probable outcome of his own episode: if an author pairs a young, beautiful woman with an old man, time will certainly make him a cuckold. His fate is sealed from the outset. Given these circumstances, this "context," the narrator recalls the events as more than a coincidental linkage, as something like "the operation of necessary order" contrary to which Jerome McGann has described the poem's form: "And after the event," McGann writes, "in the apparent security of retrospective understanding, the chains of causation and relationship which one perceives represent themselves not as the operation of necessary order but as a bizarre series of coincidental linkages. The result of a Byronic narrative in *Don Juan* is not even retrospectively a sense of probabilities but of achieved possibilities."[12] But the poet-narrator here points to the almost inevitable infidelity, given his setup. Anyone should have seen it coming. That is to say, Byron flirts with the probabilities of "necessary order" in the first canto but seemingly in order to get that narrative mode largely out of the way. For this retrospective stanza at the outset of Canto 2 simultaneously signals a disturbance of the very structural principle it describes. In the midst of the editorial explanation a thought of the moment erupts, breaking the rhythm with its censoring dash: "A—never mind." In the language of the narrator, something unpredictably—*im*probably—stumbles into the line and yet is adeptly accommodated by the poem's improvisational style, which, with its openness to the unexpected and to abrupt shifts, defies the sleek comfort of the foregone conclusions that the very same stanza ostensibly describes.

Expectations that a sleek conclusion would tie up loose ends were obviously alive and well in the early nineteenth century, as evidenced by Jane Austen's ability to play openly with them toward the end of *Northanger Abbey*. Readers broadly assumed, and trusted, that the author had in store an ending with a tidy resolution. Austen addresses this generic expectation a few pages before her novel's end: "The anxiety, which in this state of their attachment must be the portion of Henry and Catherine, and of all who loved either, as to its final event, can hardly extend, I fear, to the bosom of my readers, who will see in the tell-tale compression of the pages before them, that we are all hastening together to perfect felicity" (250). Austen's narrator plays on a gap between what her readers would imagine as the characters' anxiety and her readers' own expectations formed by the genre, which promises to resolve all tensions in a "perfect felicity" achieved by the last page.

Although *Don Juan* ultimately affords its readers no such reassurance, these expectations and the narrative's belying of them deepen the sense of uncertainty; in the terms of this book, one might say they thicken the temporal mist as the reader becomes aware of how little she can foresee, how futile the attempt. Brooks's theory of reading regards the "anticipation of retrospection" as the temporal disposition elicited by the reading process; it is a narrative's "master trope" for the unfolding of meaning according to intention and design. This theory provides a useful resource for thinking about the structure of events in Byron's first canto, even if it does so only there. Byron begins "with the beginning" (1.7), and so we have, among other details, an extended account of the "charming child['s]" education (1.49):

> But that which Donna Inez most desired
>   And saw into herself each day before all
> The learned tutors whom for him she hired
>   Was that his breeding should be strictly moral.
> Much into all his studies she inquired,
>   And so they were submitted first to her, all
> Arts, sciences; no branch was made a mystery
> To Juan's eyes, excepting natural history. (1.39)

Juan thus reads deeply in youth: "But not a page of anything that's loose / Or hints continuation of the species / Was ever suffered, lest he grow vicious" (1.40). We know at this point, Brooks would say, that Juan's curiously expurgated education will figure significantly in some successive development in the plot. We know that the author has placed this detail there in order to make use of it in some later development, which will retroactively throw light on its significance. Juan's oblivion about his sexual attraction to Donna Julia enables an otherwise innocent and not specifically motivated boy to wind up at the center of a sexual scandal, which gets him sent off to sea. Of his own feelings, Juan "had no more notion / Than he who never saw the sea of ocean" (1.70). No feelings of guilt or self-questionings, therefore, inhibit Juan's attraction to Julia. This is also to say that Juan is not responsible for the act of deception. His mother is, whose pedagogical tactics of censorship have blinded Juan to his sexual nature. In retrospect, we see how Juan's peculiar education (his mother as cause) planted the seeds of sexual confusion and how Julia's willing self-deceptions present the opportunity. Anticipating retrospection—that is, moving through the narrative discourse in the mode employed in the first canto—always requires some doubling back in the reader's imagination and construction of narrative meanings.

The climax of the canto's "story" (*histoire*) in Don Alfonso's discovery of Juan vividly enacts the point of doubling back. A midnight intrusion in Julia's bedroom produces nothing of Don Alfonso's suspicions, initially; and the fact of Juan's presence at this point has been kept as much from the reader (though there are clues to tease our suspicions) as Donna Julia has kept it from Don Alfonso. But as the lawyer, Don Alfonso, and his posse depart, closing the door behind them:

> No sooner was it bolted than—oh shame,
>> Oh sin, oh sorrow, and oh womankind!
> How can you do such things and keep your fame,
>> Unless this world and t'other too be blind?
> Nothing so dear as an unfilched good name.
>> *But to proceed, for there is more behind.*
> With much heartfelt reluctance be it said,
>> That Juan slipped, half-smothered, from the bed. (1.165, emphasis mine)

What is "behind" the bedsheets is the young lover of Donna Julia. The narrator who is "proceeding" here, moving forward in the narrative discourse, is also having to backtrack some in the "story," literalizing the process of "anticipation of retrospection" that Brooks claims for the reader's imaginative activity; "for there is more behind"—more, that is, that was not divulged at the moment of original narration but that will be available in retrospect. Narrative temporality is suddenly tied in knots. Don Juan himself becomes a figure for the meaning that was always (potentially) there, but that meaning (and figure) we only perceive as always having been there at the conclusion or climax when, "half- smothered," he emerges. What's more, the earlier suppression of Juan's (sexual) presence in the room with Julia and Antonia repeats at the level of narrative discourse the suppression of sexuality in the story of his early education, at the center of this canto. All, however, appears—or returns—in the end. And a resolution of a sort comes as Donna Julia enters a convent, Donna Inez starts a school for boys, and Juan is shipped off to sea. Narrative ends, in these respects, appear neatly tied. When Juan leaves Spain, however, the poem leaves this narrative mode of probability behind—like Juan, never to return. Canto 1 establishes that the poet knows well the narrative conventions that the succeeding narrative then proceeds to flout. The narrator's metaphor for foregoing the structural satisfaction of an ending that ties things together in a whole is the pleasure of travel for its own sake: "For the less cause there is in all this flurry, / The greater is the pleasure in arriving / At the great *end* of travel—which is driving" (10.72). It is what I call the double nature of presentness in which the imagination of double or multiple possibilities tends to be sustained rather than retroactively reduced to one.

The poem appears constructed so as to remind us, even retrospectively, that this narrative could, at any moment, have taken a number of other directions instead. Consider, for instance, the troupe of Italian opera singers elaborately described that Juan encounters on a boat as they are all being shipped off to the slave market in Constantinople. This description introduces dramatic material Byron might have developed but didn't.[13] Its presence, however, creates an aesthetic not of inevitability or even probability but of multiple potential narrative trajectories, a plurality of possibilities that lie in wait within every historical as well as narrative moment. In the English cantos (11–16), Longbow and Strongbow in Canto 13 and the poachers in Canto 16 similarly appear as richly described narrative seeds that may or may not bear dramatic fruit. If the "future is contained within the present as the plant within the seed," as Shelley says in *A Defence of Poetry*, *Don Juan*'s seeds are multiple and not all bear fruit.[14] Those dormant dramatic potentialities help one keep in mind, even once one knows how the narrative has unfolded, that Don Juan's story might easily have turned out differently.

The Historiographical Intervention of Don Juan's "Presentness"

Whereas the poem's improvisational, spontaneous style and the rhetoric of inhabiting the moment-to-moment writing process may be familiar characteristics, I want to suggest that the sense of the present they create—opening up multiple possibilities without the promise of looking to the past for causal relations and a sense of predictability—has serious implications for historiographical debates about how to narrate the historical dimensions of the present age. Contributing to the poem's present focus, *Don Juan* depicts very recent historical figures (such as Catherine the Great) and contemporary circumstances (such as British commercial society), bringing its story matter even closer to the present age than Walter Scott's *Waverley; Or, 'Tis Sixty Years Since* does. The encounters between the fictional hero and the world historical figure suggest that the poem's investment in modern historiography nevertheless rivals Scott's. Historians of historical writing typically give credit to Voltaire for "withdrawing the historical world from the relatively peaceful atmosphere [of the distant past] in which it had hitherto existed and plunging it into the stream of the present."[15] However, Byron's letters and journals more consistently place the Scottish historians at the forefront of the poet's consciousness: "Robertson—& Hume—you know without my telling you are the best 'modern Historians'—and Gibbon is well worth a hundred perusals," Byron wrote to John Murray in 1814 (*BLJ*, 4:161).

As admiring of the Scottish Enlightenment historians as Byron is, *Don Juan* definitively breaks with a number of their rhetorical principles and philosophical assumptions in ways that have yet to be described. To do so calls for an attention to the temporal complexities of Byron's narrative poetics. Consider, for instance, the instructive purpose those historians saw in narrating historical causal relations so as to anticipate and shape future effects by influencing their present causes. Hugh Blair specifically advised:

> it is not every record of facts, however true, that is entitled to the name of History; but such a record as enables us to apply the transactions of former ages for our own instruction. The facts ought to be momentous and important; represented in connections with their causes; traced to their effects; and unfolded in clear and distinct order.[16]

While Byron's narrator appears obsessed with the topic of linear causality, not only his explicit statements but also the narrative patterns of digression that do very little to explain the story overtly contradict what Blair presents as so central to History's capacity to instruct. The inconsequence of one of the narrator's non-explanations illustrates this point. When Don Juan is introduced to English society ("proper placemen"), the narrator plays with the notion that future narration (the effect) might be explained by present causes but implies the falsehood of such causal explanations. Assuming from Juan's looks that he was an unseasoned, vulnerable youth, the English men "erred, as aged men will do; but by / And by we'll talk of that; and if we don't, / 'Twill be because our notion is not high / Of politicians," the narrator explains (11.36). Except that he explains nothing. The cause is only a cause "if" the narrator does not return to the topic; the fact that he believes he might well "talk of that" later undermines the legitimacy of the explanation, the linear, causal relation. The question of what causes him to talk of it or not would have to hinge, if on anything, on something else. This instance illustrates what James Chandler has described, in his chapter titled "Byron's Causes," as "an anxiety about the uncertain state of Byron's and his poem's own forms of self-intelligibility."[17] Perhaps more than an "anxiety" it is skepticism of an intelligibility built on linear, causal explanations—that is, skepticism of the kind of intelligibility Enlightenment historians worked so hard to achieve.

Don Juan does not simply critique the temporal epistemology of linear causality or the narrative structure of a "clear and distinct order," proposed by Blair; through its temporality of presentness, it makes available for the reader a literary and conceptual alternative to linear time, and to the logic of linear causality, through which the historical dimensions of the present might be more adequately imagined and explored. One of the poem's most remarkable stylistic features, enhancing the double nature of its presentness, is its frequent, unmistakable digressions. Through Byron's use of digression, the poem both engages with historiographical debate on the topic and provides an alternative temporality to the strict linearity that Enlightenment historians were working to preserve.[18] For as we saw in Chapter 1, Enlightenment historians and rhetoricians went to great lengths attempting to avoid lengthy explanations, philosophical digressions, and other detractions from the chronological retelling of events. In his *Lectures on Rhetoric and Belles Lettres*, Hugh Blair allows digressions when they are pertinent enough to the main interest of the history. Blair says of Herodotus: "With digressions and episodes he abounds; but when these have any connection with the main subject, and are inserted professedly as episodes, the unity of the whole is less violated by them, than by a broken and scattered narration of the principal story" (399). Blair pointedly instructs historians to take care with this technique, however:

> But when we demand from the historian profound and instructive views of his subject, it is not meant that he should be frequently interrupting the course of his History, with his own reflections and speculations. . . . On some occasions, when doubtful points require to be scrutinized, or when some great event is in agitation, *concerning the causes or circumstances* of which mankind has been much divided, the narrative may be allowed to stand still for a little. . . . But [the historian] must take care not to cloy his Readers with such discussions, by repeating them too often. (403–4, emphasis mine)

Blair uses the term "digression" (as I will), but "dissertation," "demonstration," "description," "reflection," and "speculation" appear nearly interchangeably in eighteenth-century texts, all referring to the idea of a narrative lapse from the telling of the main action or "story." Digressions appear for Blair as occasionally essential disturbances to which the historian should resort sparingly when the "causes or circumstances" of some event or action require explanation. Digressions are acceptable, for instance, when they make a situation intelligible through an explanation of its causal relations. But "cloy[ing]" explanations will lose an audience.[19]

In his own *Lectures on Rhetoric and Belles Lettres*, Adam Smith weighed in even more austerely on the question of whether digressions were appropriate to historical writing, largely ruling them out as uninteresting interruptions of the important facts and actions:

> As the historian is not to make use of the oratorical style, so neither has he any occasion for the didactic. It is not his business to bring in proofs for propositions, but to narrate facts. . . . Long demonstrations, as they are no part of the historian's province, are seldom made use of by the ancients. The modern authors have often brought them in. . . . These proofs [of facts] however besides that they are inconsistent with the historical style, are likewise of bad consequence as they interrupt the thread of the narration, and that most commonly in the parts that are most interesting.

Historians, according to Smith, do not need digressions, and they typically break the narrative thread, the sense of unity, just when the story is getting good. Moreover, Smith remarks definitively that the appeal of modern history suffers by comparison to ancient history specifically on this point: "The dissertations which are everywhere interwoven into modern histories contribute, among other things, and that not a little, to render them less interesting than those wrote by the antients."[20] Digressions appear to Smith as a symptom of historical writing's modern decline.

Part of the modern impetus for incorporating digressions was the expanded ken of modern history. As historian Mark Salber Phillips explains, in the eighteenth century "politics as it had been conceived by classical histories—the *vita activa* as narrative subject—could no longer be thought of as an autonomous field of activity."[21] Aspects of social life, such as manners and learning, as well as human interiority played a role in modern historical understanding, and at times digressions helped historians weave these threads of historical experience together conceptually by explaining the underlying systems of society. To Smith, however, this rhetorical technique to accommodate that expansion unequivocally detracted from the force of the writing; it was a habit of modern writers to be resisted. Byron's poet-narrator refers, in a digression, to the nonlinear, nonteleological "wandering" of digressive tendencies as "the worst of sinning"—evidently as conscious of the Enlightenment censure as the poem's style appears undeterred by it (1.7). There is no mistaking that *Don Juan* is a poem that relishes digression; in the context of Smith's and Blair's rhetorical advice, therefore, the poem overtly defies the principles of Byron's Enlightenment predecessors.

The temporal dynamics of *Don Juan*'s digressions and their relation to the story revise even more radically the principles of Blair's and Smith's assumptions about historical rhetoric. When Hugh Blair concedes that for the sake of a brief digression "the narrative may be allowed to stand still for a little," his figurative language reveals an assumption about the distribution of motion and (physical and temporal) stasis in narration that *Don Juan* upends. For Blair and others in the eighteenth century, the story (*histoire*) is the place of action and motion, and it is where the primary interest of a historical narration lies. Commentaries from the author, such as digressions, which are pure narrative discourse (*récit*), stop motion. They bring all significant movement to a "stand still," while the authorial voice intrudes to substantiate a fact or explain a systematic relation between things. Byron's aesthetic reverses this distribution of motion and stasis in ways that foreground the very transitions between story and digression and the subjectivity of the poet-narrator.

In *Don Juan*, narrative discourse becomes the place for motion whereas the story appears relatively static. For digressions contain the lion's share of movement: the poet-narrator's mind in the midst of the creative process. The events of Juan's story, by contrast, oddly indicate a sense of stasis. Byron's hero is remarkably passive, for instance, in comparison with the literary tradition of this figure. He is typically propelled by his changing circumstances (seduced, subjugated, or enslaved by various women). He does not shape his own circumstances and he remains oddly unshaped by them. Circumstances simply propel him. In Canto 4, for instance, Haidée defends Juan's innocence to Lambro: "'This fatal shore,'" she says, "'He found, but sought not,'" carried on by waves of circumstance, not by an expression of his will (4.42). However much Juan moves geographically, his character appears fairly unmoved. In his psychoanalytic study *Byron and His Fictions*, Peter Manning observes Don Juan's repeated pairing with a dominant older woman. Drawing on biographical materials as well as on Byron's early letters and journals, he argues that "Byron enshrines his [childhood] trauma in Juan, whose arrest is permanent." The "story" thus is one of fixity, of repetition. Action lies elsewhere, in that movement and surprise occur predominantly in the narrative discourse: "If man's own mutability and mortality are the villains of *Childe Harold*," writes Manning, "they are the heroes of *Don Juan*, which warns against the dangers of fixity and paradoxically suggests that the way to conquer time is not to seek the stillness of the Apollo Belvedere but to give oneself to motion."[22] Once the poet-narrator has described Haidée's near madness, then stasis, and finally death in the face of her father's return in Canto 4, we witness the poetic machinery shifting gears in the mind of the poet-narrator. Dramatized authorial reflexivity moves the narrative focus away from the scene and sentimental strain of Haidée's situation, back to Juan:

But let me change this theme, which grows too sad,
    And lay this sheet of sorrows on the shelf.
I don't much like describing people mad,
    For fear of seeming rather touched myself.
Besides I've no more on this head to add;
    And as my Muse is a capricious elf,
We'll put about and try another tack
With Juan, left half-killed some stanzas back. (4.74)

The vast emotional swing from the sorrowful situation to the exhilaration of fight scenes comes to comic conclusion with the image of "Juan, left"—suspended in time, as if waiting to be narrated out of his situation. As readers, we are reminded at this moment always to hold both narrative modes (digression and "story"-telling) in our minds, however incompatible or unrelated they may seem. The mobility of the narrator's mind appears in the swift and frequent movement between various moods (sorrowful to adventurous) and modes (narrating story, digressing), and it contrasts with the hero's suspension in time, emblematic of his general condition of stasis. Byron's distribution of motion and stasis thus reverses that of Scottish Enlightenment history (locating the action in the very act of digression), while foregrounding the mobility of the writing subject in the creative process.

This reversal is key to Byron's presentness insofar as the temporality of the "story" is almost inevitably, as narrative theory has taught us, one of catching up with the always already having been. As H. Porter Abbott explains, "Story *seems* to pre-exist its rendering (note how often stories are narrated in the past tense)."[23] Byron's shifting of motion and action from the story to the narrative discourse, to the event of writing, emphasizes not the preexistent but the present and the process—a wonder that is oriented more purely toward the future of what is to come. The poet-narrator has begun his narrative discourse at the beginning of the story; with the exception of Don Juan's body as hidden meaning in Canto I, meanings do not come about through a retroactive reflection.

The "present" in Byron's presentness looks neither forward nor back for fulfillment, as if the mystery of one moment might be fully solved in a later one; thus the poetics of presentness never appears to aspire to a complete or comprehensive understanding. This sense of incompletion recalls Samuel Weber's explication of Lacanian future anteriority. The present entails, in Weber's terms, an "irreducible remainder or remnant"—the remainder of the "inconclusive futurity"—"that will continually prevent the subject from ever becoming entirely self-identical."[24] That inhibition to the subject's self-identification is another way of saying that one can never completely know oneself; the subject and the "I" never quite match up, and it is the irresolvable remainder of futurity that accounts for the slippage. Jerome McGann observed the poem's attention to epistemological uncertainty on the world-historical front when he summarized its position thus: "*Don Juan* argues that while the world is the subject *of* our understanding, it is not subject *to* our understanding."[25] Building on McGann's insight, I would suggest that this limit "*to* our understanding" appears to extend to the poem's writing subject, the poet-narrator himself. The fact that Byron's narrator professes never to grasp a coherent poetic (let alone historical) picture leaves doubt not only about Juan's possibilities of self-knowledge (Juan is deeply dopey in this respect) but also about the narrator-poet's—indeed, perhaps even Byron's—knowledge of his own project. In this respect, *Don Juan* may be a literary work in love with its own limitations; it is a poem interested in the idea of what its writer (himself a historical subject, embedded in the world he attempts to describe) does not know:

> I don't pretend that I quite understand
> My own meaning when I would be very fine;
>   But the fact is that I have nothing planned,
> Unless it were to be a moment merry,
> A novel word in my vocabulary. (4.5)

What we might think of as an authorial "mist" of understanding yields poetic fruits; in lieu of an intentional plan, the poem appears guided by the materiality of language and the verse form. These afford, as in the lines just given, a spark to spontaneity and novel forms of expression. At any given moment, the narrative could veer off in one direction or another because of, at times, the demands of language.

That plurality of potential narrative directions is there from the beginning, or rather from the multiple times that the narrator attempts to begin telling the story of Juan's first romance. When the narrator cannot get past the date of Juan and Julia's romantic encounter in Canto 1, and Juan and Julia are left to stand still as the narrator begins and begins again, we see not exact repetitions but repetitions with stylistic variations: "It was upon a day, a summer's day— / Summer's indeed a very dangerous season" (1.102); "'Twas on a summer's day, the sixth of June— / I like to be particular in dates" (1.103); "'Twas on the sixth of June about the hour / Of half-past six, perhaps still nearer seven, / When Julia sate within as pretty a bower / As e'er" (1.104). A digression diverts the storytelling intention each time. The narrator would seem to want to oblige the Enlightenment historical precept of narrating facts, but he cannot get past this single fact. Neither progressive nor regressive, the lateral movement of digression is the very narrative device to arrest linear development, while making a range of potential narrative directions visible.

Outlining a trajectory from the barbarism of the early shipwreck to the commercial society of the late English cantos, Don Juan's shifting locales may begin to suggest a Scottish Enlightenment notion of cultural development, but Don Juan's arrested mental development, as well as the relentlessly digressive tactics, counteracts that developmental idea. The narrative moves but does so more laterally than forward or back. As discussed in Chapter 1, the Scots' four-stage theory espoused a model of development through the four stages of barbarism, nomadic life, feudalism, and commercial civilization. Byron uses a familiar Scottish Enlightenment phrase in describing the poem in a letter to a friend: "D Juan will be known by and bye for what it is intended a satire on abuses of the present *states* of Society—and not a eulogy of vice" (*BLJ*, 10.68, emphasis added). To that end, James Chandler has aptly observed of this comment that "Byron's echo of the Scottish Enlightenment idiom—states of society—clearly establishes Byron's assimilation of the cultural historical model and identifies his resistances to it." Chandler identifies Byron's resistance in the poem's consciousness of different societies being in different "states" of development at the same time. In the plurality of "states," that is, "Byron emphasizes the simultaneity of such states with each other in his scheme of things"; this is "the way in which the poem offers an implicit critique of the very idea of the 'commercial' phase of society or of a 'period' like 1789–1824, even as it so crucially deploys such conceptions."[26] For Chandler, this co-presence of multiple states, through which the hero will pass in a matter of only a few years, resists the Scottish explanatory model of cultural development, which typically informs the historical narrative of a single place over a long period of time, with one stage, or "state," giving way to another.

Chandler argues that "Byron's satirical emphasis on the 'abuses' . . . suggests a stronger emphasis on decline and decay in the course of history than we have seen in the Scottish Enlightenment accounts of the 'progress' and (albeit uneven) development of societies."[27] Byron's depiction of English civil society in many ways undermines the celebration of the progress of civilization that predominates in eighteenth-century Scottish historiographies, and Chandler echoes many scholars' depictions of the Scottish Enlightenment in suggesting that Byron's skepticism about progress in England runs against its grain. For instance, historian David

Spadafora concurs, "on the whole the Scots *did* consider the pattern of development that they discerned in history to be broadly progressive."[28] Byron's depictions of commercial society are hardly celebratory, and yet, as discussed in Chapter 1, already in the Scottish Enlightenment that critique of progressive assumptions had been voiced—for instance, by Adam Ferguson's *Essay on the History of Civil Society*, first published in 1767. By disrupting the very linearity of narrative time in the use of digressions and the proliferation of simultaneous possibilities, Byron's revision of Enlightenment views goes even further than Chandler suggests, by not just reversing the dominant paradigm of progress with suggestions of decline like Ferguson's but also offering the double nature of presentness as an alternative model for imagining history. Byron's model fosters the imagination of multiple possibilities rather than reducing historical epistemology to a narrative of what happened, to what we might call a narrative of the victors.

History and Fiction in the English Cantos

Byron's engagement with Enlightenment historiography becomes most lively when Juan arrives in England in Canto 11; the directness of the engagement is equaled only by the digressions of earlier cantos in which the narrator invokes British culture and politics explicitly. Although British historiographers certainly wrote histories of the world outside England, even when they did so, their motivation often appeared tied up with their anxieties about, and interests in, British national identity. Perhaps most notably, Edmund Burke's *Reflections on the Revolution in France* sought to distinguish the progress of English liberty from what he saw as a very different variety of French innovation; Burke's *Reflections* were responding to the Revolution Society in England whose published proceedings had associated the affairs of France with England's Glorious Revolution.[29] For English and Scottish historians broadly, what was typically at stake when applying theories of cultural and political development to the relations between past and present, regardless of what nation's history they were telling, was British identity.

Just before Don Juan sets off for England, Byron's narrator muses on the question of how the present age in Britain will be remembered, suggesting how distorted the retrospective historical lens can be. He produces a single historical image altogether opposed to the sense of spontaneity and teeming possibilities that characterizes *Don Juan*'s aesthetic. In Canto 9, following a description of Georges Cuvier's theory of periodic upheavals of the earth, the narrator imagines the body of George IV surfacing alongside "other relics of a former world, / When this world shall be former, underground, / Thrown topsy-turvy, twisted, crisped, and curled" (9.37). With both seriousness and great laughter, he continues, "Think if then George the Fourth should be dug up!" (9.39):

> How will—to these young people, just thrust out
>   From some fresh paradise and set to plough
> And dig and sweat and turn themselves about
>   And plant and reap and spin and grind and sow
> Till all the arts at length are brought about,
>   Especially of war and taxing—how,
> I say, will these great relics when they see 'em,
> Look like the monsters of a new museum? (9.40)

With the futuristic image of George IV's body exhumed some generations (or a periodic upheaval) hence, the political history of Byron's present appears as a question. How will the future world construct its retrospective understanding of the Regency past? It is a question resting on a single political figure. Some "new museum" will be part of a fresh historical framework that makes its own (inevitably distorted) sense of the past, by reducing the political picture to this one body, which becomes a synecdoche for Regency England.[30] The future historical representation he imagines is as unintelligible as it is narrow, because the "great relics" will appear as inexplicable and foreign to historical understanding, as deeply out of context, as do "monsters" at any time. The logic assumes a future perspective that is unpredictable in that the narrator can only wonder and question what future generations will remember, but he suspects that future frameworks and modes of understanding the past (Byron's present) will be "new," that is, significantly unlike those current in the first quarter of the nineteenth century. In effect, the narrator's anticipatory move estranges his own historical present. With this image of a future "new museum," the poem underlines the problems of trying to recover early nineteenth-century historical knowledge when contemporaries themselves saw the historical dimensions of their moment as elusive, its meanings as multiple and incoherent.

In the stanza immediately following the pondering of George IV's monstrous future body, the poet-narrator counteracts this historicist logic of recovery by shifting back to the most predominant theme of the poem: the process of writing it. In so doing, he marks the difference between that mode of archaeological recovery and *Don Juan*'s prevailing presentness:[31]

But I am apt to grow too metaphysical:
　"The time is out of joint,"—and so am I;
I quite forget this poem's merely quizzical,
　And deviate into matters rather dry.
I ne'er decide what I shall say, and this I call
　Much too poetical. Men should know why
They write, and for what end; but, note or text,
I never know the word which will come next. (9.41)

The shift from the metaphysical to the material "text" does not rule out anticipation but specifies the kind of anticipations this aesthetic experience entails: anticipation and uncertainty about what will happen next not in a way that narrates the present as a future memory of political power but in a way that leaves open the range of possibilities, even those that go unrealized. The narrator's claim that he has no cause in writing—no intentions or sense of his own motivation, no controlling ideas for the plot, no "end"—raises the question of what driving force he recognizes. By the narrator-poet's account, the creative push comes less from (Wordsworthian) powers of recollection, feeling, or divine inspiration than from the arbitrary materiality of language (its aural affiliations) subjected to the rhyming and rhythmic demands of the strict *ottava rima* form. "[S]ometimes / Monarchs are less imperative than rhymes," the narrator gripes (5.77). The exigencies of the strict verse form thus elicit the narrator-poet's changeful spirit of improvisation and adaptation of ideas to the "ever varying rhyme, / A versified aurora borealis," the poetic project at hand (7.2). Immediately following the comic image of political power in George IV's excavated body, the poet-narrator's concerns about what word comes "next" in a tight rhyme scheme suggest an affiliation. Both monarchs and verse form have a power over their subjects (citizen subjects and the writing subject). They are more or less equally "imperative," and the arbitrary nature of language's aural dimension thus suggests how arbitrary is the inherited power of a figure such as George IV, which may ultimately single him out in historical accounts of the age.

　The problem of historical memory and its narrowing effect becomes all the more explicit and the rhetoric heats up when the narrator turns to historical writing in the midst of the English cantos. British identity was typically traced back to Greco-Roman cultural origins, so British historians maintained an abiding interest in ancient history as the barbarism from which to trace their own progress to commercial, civilized society. The narrator thus notes with regret how selective—how partial or noncomprehensive—the nineteenth-century understanding of Greek culture must be, given the limited number of lives that even one of its best historians, Plutarch, recorded for "Posterity":

> Why, I'm Posterity—and so are you;
>   And whom do we remember? Not a hundred.
> Were every memory written down all true,
>   The tenth or twentieth name would be but blundered:
> Even Plutarch's lives have but picked out a few,
>   And 'gainst those few our annalists have thundered;
> And Mitford in the nineteenth century
> Gives, with Greek truth, the good old Greek the lie. (12.19)

The problem of the ancient Plutarch's dearth of "lives" gives way to the problems that the poet-narrator has with Byron's contemporary historiographer, William Mitford. Byron included the following note to this stanza:

> See Mitford's Greece. "Greciae *Verax*." His great pleasure consists in praising tyrants, abusing Plutarch, spelling oddly, and writing quaintly; and what is strange after all, *his* is the best Modern History of Greece in any language, and he is perhaps the best modern historian whatsoever. Having named his sins, it is but fair to state his virtues—learning, labour, research, wrath, and partiality. I call the latter virtues in a writer, because they make him write in earnest.

That Byron could be so critical of the historian he considers "perhaps the best modern historian whatsoever" suggests his frustration with the state of modern historiography and explains his impetus for engaging with the world through *Don Juan* in a way that would counteract modern historiography's failures or blindnesses. *Don Juan* itself cannot, of course, cover *everything*, but it can expose its own partiality—its bias, in the obviously opinionated narrator, and its self-conscious incompleteness, as the poet-narrator bemoans how even Plutarch had to *select* lives.

   Don Juan's engagement with British historiographers reaches a fever pitch when Juan's circumstances lead him, at last, onto British soil. Recently appointed as the ambassador of Russia by Catherine the Great, Juan arrives in the commercial society of England "wrapt in contemplation," "'And here,' he cried, 'is freedom's chosen station,'" as he trails along behind his carriage, and "'Here'—he was interrupted by a knife, / With 'Damn your eyes! your money or your life!'" (11.9–10). Fed himself, it would seem, by Scottish Enlightenment notions of British progress, Juan arrives with misguided expectations of the political and social landscape. Those notions of linear progress, however, are dramatically interrupted both in the story (*histoire*) with a knife and in the narrative discourse (*récit*) with the space of a dash. A multivalent aesthetic of surprise disrupts the line: the path Juan takes along the road, the writing of historical narrative as cultural progress, and the poetic line with the typographical one of the dash. Juan's description of his present situation bears in that dash, that rhythmic pause, the disruptive force of an encounter with the unforeseen—a cursing criminal. Moreover, the repetition and the revised perspective on England give us two possible, though not exactly compatible, narrative points of departure, since the formal repetition of "here," in effect, opens up an alternative narrative trajectory to that which associates commercial society with the progress of social freedom. The assumption that commercial society leads to greater freedom is displaced by the suggestion that, in fact, it breeds corruption. And so, the narrator summarily reflects, one "May find himself within that isle of riches / Exposed to lose his life as well as breeches" (11.11). The poem does not merely displace progressive assumptions with its claims of regressive corruption. More important, with every interruption, repetition, transition, and, indeed, digression, *Don Juan* pointedly resists the smooth linear conception of time inherent in both progressive and regressive historical narratives— that is, even in the exceptional Scottish examples such as Ferguson's, which conveys an overtly critical view of commercial society. More conspicuously digressive than progressive or regressive, *Don Juan* reimagines time in a proliferation of simultaneous, yet incompatible, narrative and interpretive possibilities. This sense of simultaneities upends Enlightenment assumptions about time and progress by encouraging the reader, for instance, to hold the sometimes irresolvably unrelated strands of the Don Juan story and the narrator's digressions both in mind. Unlike in Enlightenment historiography, *Don Juan* appeals to no underlying system that unifies these disparate strands or seemingly incompatible interpretive possibilities.

In the midst of the English cantos, Byron's narrator contemplates Don Juan's "impressions" on Lady Adeline, her inclinations to become acquainted with the hero, and the anticipatory prospect of a retrospective moral judgment about Lady Adeline's character, should she fall. Is she firm in her character, knowing her intentions clearly as virtuous, or is she obstinate, insisting on her own good intentions in order to allow herself to flirt with the handsome young guest? The question remains, because the common assumption, the narrator suggests, is that decisive judgment must be deferred to a moment when a person's intentions have resulted in action, when they have had phenomenal effect. The later "event" or outcome, more often than not, decides.

The narrator's contemplation of this temporal process leads to an analogy of Lady Adeline's dramatic situation with the historical—and, indeed, the historiographical—situation of the character of Napoleon. By way of this analogy, the narrator suggests that the "event" acquires undue importance in historical and fictional narration, as well as in the cultural imagination. In what the narrator imagines as their potentially plural ("double") nature, Lady Adeline's romantic intentions resemble Napoleon's military ones:

> Now when she once had ta'en an interest
>   In any thing, however she might flatter
> Herself that her intentions were the best—
>   Intense intentions are a dangerous matter:
> Impressions were much stronger than she guess'd,
>   And gather'd as they run like growing water
> Upon her mind; the more so, as her breast
> Was not at first too readily impress'd.
>
> But when it was, she had that lurking demon
>   Of double nature, and thus doubly named—
> Firmness yclept in heroes, kings, and seamen,
>   That is, when they succeed; but greatly blamed
> As *obstinacy*, both in men and women,
>   Whene'er their triumph pales, or star is tamed:—
> And 'twill perplex the casuists in morality
> To fix the due bounds of this dangerous quality.
>
> Had Buonaparte won at Waterloo,
>   It had been firmness; now 'tis pertinacity:
> Must the event decide between the two?
>   I leave it to your people of sagacity
> To draw the line between the false and true,
>   If such can e'er be drawn by man's capacity:
> My business is with Lady Adeline,
> Who in her way too was a heroine. (14.88–90)

The narrator's "Must the event decide?" expresses an almost desperate protest against a temporal operation through which consequences, ends, or phenomenal outcomes retroactively become decisive interpretive factors, narrowing what is here the double nature of interpretive possibility to one view.[32] In this question about Waterloo, Byron insists on a gap between what we might call the experience of a historical moment, flush with the sense of uncertainty and possibilities, and the cultural memory of it, in which victory for Napoleon no longer figures as something that—*even though it didn't happen*—still might have happened.[33] The narrative structure and style of *Don Juan* work to elicit—not only in the present but also in the memory of the very recent past (whether Napoleon's, the narrator-poet's, or Don Juan's)—an ongoing imagining of multiple possibilities; that is, the narrative works assiduously against the cultural tendency for retrospective judgment to obscure this sense of multiplicity.

The temporality of *Don Juan*—with its anticipation and wonder of what could happen next, as well as the sense that what does or did happen was in no way inevitable—presents a world of teeming possibilities, not all of which are realized. Prompting the reader to imagine those multiple, incompatible possibilities—even those that go unrealized—*all* as important, the poem elicits a historical imagination that cannot be narrated in a coherently linear way. Hence the two tracks of story and digression, both of which the reader holds in the mind at once, even when they seem hardly related; hence the population of characters in the poem, not all of whom get taken up as dramatic agents. Unlike the Enlightenment four-stage model of progress and the "clear and distinct order" of causal relations that Hugh Blair advised, Byron's double nature of presentness sends the imagination in lateral directions as one follows the poem's multifaceted movements. Significantly with respect to the "time of reading," the reader is made to wait a very long time before knowing whether Lady Adeline seduces the hero or not, thus holding those two possibilities in view for dozens of pages. The narrator raises the question in Canto 14 but leaves the reader to hold in the mind this specific uncertainty for all of Cantos 15 and 16. In fact, Byron died having only just begun Canto 17, at which point the dramatic action has raised several romantic possibilities but no decisive action has transpired. The "event" that might lead one to see Lady Adeline as either firm or obstinate, therefore, remains forever suspended. That double nature of the heroine, sustained for more than two long cantos, stretches the imagination in a way similar to how so many other aspects of the narrative convey a multidirectional simultaneity that resists linearity: there are digressions/story (throughout); rhythmic/historiographical/peripatetic interruptions (when Juan is held up, entering England); and the firmness/obstinacy of Lady Adeline/Napoleon. With every "double" (or multiple) aspect, Byron's narration challenges the readerly imagination to think, see, or experience time not as a series of past to present to future but as an experience of what I have called presentness—the abounding simultaneity of possibilities. Byron's presentness also makes possible a relation to the historical present that might be conceived in this way, resisting in effect the strict chronological order and the wisdom of hindsight that dominate historical writing.

Coda

William Hazlitt's portrait of Byron in *The Spirit of the Age* captures how *Don Juan* invites a co-presence of multiple tones and subject matters typically kept apart by their culturally strict assignment to different genres. *Don Juan* does it all:

> The *Don Juan* indeed has great power; but its power is owing to the force of the serious writing, and to the contrast between that and the flashy passages with which it is interlarded. From the sublime to the ridiculous there is but one step. You laugh and are surprised that any one should turn round and *travestie* himself: the drollery is in the utter discontinuity of ideas and feelings. . . . A classical intoxication is followed by the splashing of soda-water, by frothy effusions of ordinary bile. After the lightning and the hurricane, we are introduced to the interior of the cabin and the contents of the wash-hand basins. (183–84)

Determining that the low in his style debases the high—"He hallows in order to desecrate"—Hazlitt's ostensibly admiring tone becomes severely critical toward the poet, whom he calls "the spoiled child of fame as well as fortune" (184).

In a surprise turn at its close, Hazlitt's own essay—despite its increasingly negative critical attitude toward Byron that reaches an almost feverish pitch—turns into not only an epitaph but also a stylistically mixed essay itself. In the last sense, it becomes a tribute to the poet's capacity and willingness (Hazlitt might have said willfulness) to let starkly contrasting subject matters and styles sit side by side. Having just referred to Byron's "preposterous *liberalism*" in offering money and horses to the Greeks in their war for independence, the essay breaks off as its author learns mid-composition of Byron's death. One paragraph follows, which is solemn but unsentimental in tone: "We had written thus far when the news came of the death of Lord Byron, and put an end at once to a strain of somewhat peevish invective, which was intended to meet his eye, not to insult his memory" (186). Hazlitt could have rewritten or suppressed the essay, but he leaves it, the critique interrupted by the occasion of the poet's death, concluded by a paragraph on that occasion that reflects also on this editorial choice: "As it is," Hazlitt writes, "we think it better and more like himself, to let what we had written stand, than to take up our leaden shafts, and try to melt them into 'tears of sensibility,' or mould them into dull praise and an affected show of candour" (186). The essay concludes nevertheless respectfully: "Lord Byron is dead: he also died a martyr to his zeal in the cause of freedom, for the last, best hopes of man. Let that be his excuse and his epitaph!" (187). As we saw in Chapter 1, Hazlitt's heterogeneous essay collection puts different facets and various versions of the "spirit of the age" next to one another without appealing to an underlying system that unites them. Similarly, within his essay on Byron, we have, in effect, two Byrons. Although the potentially transformable, living poet (and preposterous liberal) that Hazlitt candidly critiques no longer can be shaped by that criticism, the image—its very lively sense of potentiality—stands next to the knowledge of his death and the respectful image of a political martyr to the cause of freedom. Hazlitt's style offers an aesthetic of sharp contrast, figuring the spirit of "Byron," among the writers living in the present, as these multiple sides, this plurality of interpretive and creative possibilities.

Reflecting on critical methods and approaches, literary scholars today can draw much from the temporal and epistemological implications of Byron's presentness—and, indeed, from the sense of mystery that the poetics of multiple possibilities elicits in the work of Austen, Keats, and Hazlitt. The double nature of Byron's presentness implies for us the importance of considering, along with our claims about what Romantic writers would have known, how deeply the writers in this study felt, and how movingly they recorded, their inability fully to know the historical dimensions of their age. Scarcely an inhibiting factor to creative production, that mist of historical uncertainty ushered forth in some of the most searching meditations and literary conceptions of time of the period, the works at the center of this study. While surely works by Wordsworth, Percy Shelley, and others make temporality equally central to their poetic expression, the works of Keats, Austen, and Byron stand apart for their nonprophetic qualities, their poetics of the everyday, and the self-conscious partiality or noncomprehensiveness of their visions. This study, therefore, addresses a cluster of response to the intellectual problems of modernity that a whole host of writers faced circa 1800, not aspiring to present a comprehensive picture of "Romanticism" but rather presenting these works as one strain, perhaps one Romanticism, and a Romanticism traced across highly distinct formal procedures. Following these writers' own conceptions of a contemporaneous multiplicity of incompatible ideas or interpretations, we might forego the project of attempting intellectually to unify the works we study into a coherent picture. As discussed in Chapter 1, J. G. A. Pocock has emphasized a new kind of historical approach with respect to the Enlightenment, suggesting that "we do better to think of a family of Enlightenments."[34] As *Modernity's Mist* has shown, such a critical approach appears as a legacy of the poetic thinking at work in Hazlitt's *Spirit of the Age,* Keats's poetry, Austen's *Persuasion,* and Byron's *Don Juan.* Attuned to the historiographical challenges of modernity's speed and unpredictability and to the insufficiencies of historiographies that attempted to unify and totalize the historical dimensions of the present age, this distinct strain of Romanticism, across a variety of formal innovations, provided the means of encountering the temporal complexities of the age as its most salient features.

Notes

Introduction: On Being in a Mist

John Keats, *The Letters of John Keats*, ed. Hyder E. Rollins (Cambridge, MA: Harvard University Press, 1958), 1:280–81, emphasis original. Hereafter abbreviated *LJK* and cited parenthetically by volume and page number.

1. I propose the phrase "what *might* will have been" rather than "what *could* will have been" because the auxiliary *could* suggests a clearer vision of the boundaries of possibility, whereas the texts in this study tend to disavow the kind of knowledge that would make even those boundaries visible. The idea for this awkward and gloriously fitting phrase came from Peter Rabinowitz, who organized a panel at the 2012 ISSN (Narrative) conference on "anticipations of retrospection," which he proposed, at one point, to rename "On What Might Will Have Been." He didn't, but I'm happy to borrow his coinage here.

2. William Wordsworth, *The Thirteen-Book Prelude*, ed. Mark L. Reed (Ithaca, NY: Cornell University Press, 1991), 314.

3. Jacques Rancière, "The Politics of the Spider," *Studies in Romanticism* 50.2 (Summer 2011): 245.

4. Wordsworth is, of course, many things—even to Keats, who variously admires and distances himself from the first-generation poet. My point about this letter, however, is that although Keats expresses a desire to move forward so that he, too, can "make discoveries, and shed a light in them," I see in Keats's poetic practice something more consistently close to a hovering at the threshold, where one cannot see into the passages clearly but might instead—in the language of "Ode to a Nightingale"—"guess each sweet."

5. This problem, I am suggesting, constitutes a strain of modernity that persists long after what we now call the Romantic period. In Virginia Woolf's modernist novel *To the Lighthouse* (New York: Harcourt, 1981), for instance, Lily Briscoe, as she stands in front of her painting, struggles with the same multiplicity of a teeming yet elusive present that eludes expressive grasp and makes one always "miss" the compositional target: "And she wanted to say not one thing, but everything. Little words that broke up the thought and dismembered it said nothing. 'About life, about death; about Mrs. Ramsay'—no, she thought, one could say nothing to nobody. *The urgency of the moment always missed its mark*. Words fluttered sideways and struck the object inches too low" (178, emphasis mine).

6. Samuel Weber, *Return to Freud: Jacques Lacan's Dislocation of Psychoanalysis* (Cambridge: Cambridge University Press, 1991), 7.

7. Ibid.

8. Percy Shelley, *A Defence of Poetry*, in *Shelley's Poetry and Prose*, ed. Donald Reiman and Neil Fraistat (New York: Norton, 2002), 514.

9. Giorgio Agamben, *The End of the Poem*, trans. Daniel Heller-Roazen (Stanford: Stanford University Press, 1999), 110.

10. Focusing on the lyric poem, Mutlu Blasing, for instance, observes the challenge to reference (or straightforward "sense") that these distinct yet overlapping patterns pose: "If sounds dominate, sense is compromised; if sense is too fixed, sounds are not free to do their kind of affective signifying work. In lyric poetry, the distinct operations of both the formal system organizing the material properties of the signifier for the voice and the ear and the symbolic system of referential language must be perceivable in their *difference*, their noncoincidence. Neither system can be transparent. The excessiveness of each system to the other necessitates a constant negotiation, a constant choosing and intentionalizing not only of sounds as words but also—and herein lies the difference of poetry—of words as sounds" (Mutlu Blasing, *Lyric Poetry: The Pain and the Pleasure of Words* [Princeton: Princeton University Press, 2007], 29).

11. Forest Pyle, *Art's Undoing: In the Wake of a Radical Aestheticism* (New York: Fordham University Press, 2014), 5.

12. Reinhart Koselleck, *Futures Past: On the Semantics of Historical Time*, trans. Keith Tribe (New York: Columbia University Press, 2004), 42.

13. Ibid., 243.

14. Anna Barbauld, "On the Uses of History," in vol. 2 of *The Works of Anna Laetitia Barbauld, with Memoir by Lucy Aikin*, 1st ed. (Boston: David Reed, 1826), 287.

15. See Koselleck, *Futures Past*, 263–75.

16. See George Nadel, "The Philosophy of History before Historicism," *History and Theory* 3.3 (1963): 291–315. See also Mark Salber Phillips, *Society and Sentiment: Genres of Historical Writing in Britain, 1740–1820* (Princeton: Princeton University Press, 2000), 21–24. Phillips writes: "[T]he Romans ... gave most weight to the instructive value of history. The Renaissance was heavily indebted to Roman rhetorical traditions, and most writers continued to value history primarily for its persuasiveness and didactic power" (22).

17. See Phillips, *Society and Sentiment*. Phillips writes, for instance, of the mid-eighteenth-century British historian: "[David] Hume signals the tension emerging in his day between two historiographical conventions: the exemplary narrative of humanist or neoclassical historiography and the newer, more systematic arguments of philosophical history" (47).

18. See James Chandler, *England in 1819: The Politics of Literary Culture and the Case of Romantic Historicism* (Chicago: University of Chicago Press, 1998), 105–14.

19. Jürgen Habermas, *The Philosophical Discourse of Modernity* (Cambridge, MA: MIT Press, 1990), 7.

20. Fredric Jameson, *A Singular Modernity: Essay on the Ontology of the Present* (New York: Verso, 2002), 26.

21. See ibid., 23–41. Jameson describes the Renaissance, in contrast to Romantic-period modernity, as "still turned towards the re-creation of a past beyond its own immediate past, and intent on ideal emulation and imitation rather than on historically new creativities of its own" (25).

22. See, for instance, Patrick Collinson, "Truth, Lies, and Fiction in Six-teenth-Century Protestant Historiography," in *The Historical Imagination in Early Modern Britain: History, Rhetoric, and Fiction, 1500–1800*, ed. Donald R. Kelley and David Harris Sacks (Cambridge: Cambridge University Press, 1997), 37–68. Collinson argues that the "truth" recorded in historical writing was less significant than its usefulness, "for only fiction is free to favor virtue" (39). That is to say that one looked to historical writing, even that concerning times long before the present, as a guide for moral behavior, without worrying about the potential anachronism of doing so. Such a concern was distinctly modern and also Romantic.

23. See *The Historical Imagination in Early Modern Britain*, ed. Kelley and Sacks.

24. Jameson, *A Singular Modernity*, 25–26.

25. On the "acceleration" of historical events, see Chandler, *England in 1819*, 22. The seminal work on this topic in recent studies of historical temporality is Kosel-leck, *Futures Past*.

26. Habermas, *The Philosophical Discourse of Modernity*, 6.

27. Cited in Helen Maria Williams, *Letters Written in France, In the Summer 1790, To a Friend in England; Containing Various Anecdotes Relative to the French Revolution* (Peterborough, ON: Broadview, 2001), appendix F, 253.

28. William Wordsworth, "Preface to *Lyrical Ballads, 1800*," in *Lyrical Ballads, and Other Poems, 1797–1800*, ed. James Butler and Karen Green (Ithaca, NY: Cornell University Press, 1992), 746.

29. Koselleck, *Futures Past*, 41.

30. I scarcely mean to suggest that the historiographical crisis was caused simply or exclusively by the events of the French Revolution; nevertheless, those political events and their international ramifications made the problem of how to write a contemporary history suddenly more urgent and more visible. As early as the mid-eighteenth century, Hume conceived the difficulty of understanding one's present as a historical age when he reflected on England's turbulent seventeenth century: "we are always aware of Hume's view of the seventeenth century as a time when England was undergoing a political and social transformation whose dimensions none of the participants could be expected to grasp" (Phillips, *Society and Sentiment*, 74). The idea of imagining the historical dimensions of the present and the potential challenges to that imagining without access to a distinctly different future vantage were concepts available to Hume before the French Revolution. In respect to the acceleration toward futurity and its unknown quality, Koselleck concurs: "This began to be apparent well before the French Revolution" (*Futures Past*, 22). At the same time, the "process of technicalization" and the French Revolution gave the earlier sense of anticipation "an unexpectedly solid reality," he claims (41). Moreover, Romantic writers make Hume's perspective self-reflexive, applying that sense of uncertainty to their own age.

31. Habermas, *The Philosophical Discourse of Modernity*, 12.

32. One might think here of Walter Benjamin's historiography, and indeed Habermas turns to it for a more "radical historical thinking" than what one finds in the idea of progress (*The Philosophical Discourse of Modernity*, 14). Benjamin envisions the face of the angel of history turned toward the past as the origin of temporal dis-

ruption. (See "Theses on the Philosophy of History," in *Illuminations* [New York: Schocken, 1969], especially 257–58.) The poetics of anticipation I am describing in Romanticism constitute a historiography equally "radical," equally disruptive to linear historical thinking as is Benjamin's; one significant difference, however, is how that disruption appears more prominently future oriented in Romantic texts. Theorists of modernity, however, might look to Romanticism for a significant precursor to Benjamin's radical historical thought.

33. See Jameson, *A Singular Modernity*, 31–41.

34. Nicholas Roe, *John Keats and the Culture of Dissent* (Oxford: Oxford University Press, 1997).

35. Andrew Bennett, *Romantic Poets and the Culture of Posterity* (Cambridge: Cambridge University Press, 1999). To my knowledge, this is to date the only book-length study of Romantic anticipations from a cultural perspective. Ian Balfour's *The Rhetoric of Romantic Prophecy* (cited in note 39) is perhaps the only other book-length study on the topic of Romantic futurity, although, as Balfour shows, prophecy is not always about the future.

36. Jeffrey Cox, *Poetry and Politics in the Cockney School: Keats, Shelley, Hunt and Their Circle* (Cambridge: Cambridge University Press, 1998), 2.

37. Kevis Goodman, *Georgic Modernity and British Romanticism: Poetry and the Mediation of History* (Cambridge: Cambridge University Press, 2004), 10.

38. Deborah Elise White, *Romantic Returns: Superstition, Imagination, History* (Stanford: Stanford University Press, 2000); Mary Favret, *War at a Distance: Romanticism and the Making of Modern Wartime* (Princeton: Princeton University Press, 2010).

39. Ian Balfour, *The Rhetoric of Romantic Prophecy* (Stanford: Stanford University Press, 2002).

40. Jane Austen, *Emma*, vol. 4 of *The Novels of Jane Austen*, ed. R. W. Chapman (Oxford: Oxford University Press, 1988).

41. Jerome McGann, "High Instincts and Real Presences: Two Responses to the Death of Beauty," in *Repossessing the Romantic Past*, ed. Heather Glen and Paul Hamilton (Cambridge: Cambridge University Press, 2006), 226–43.

42. Ibid., 235, 231.

43. Ibid., 236.

44. Marc Redfield, *The Politics of Aesthetics: Nationalism, Gender, Romanticism* (Stanford: Stanford University Press, 2003), 108.

45. Ibid.

46. Harold Bloom, Paul de Man, Jacques Derrida, Geoffrey Hartman, and J. Hillis Miller, *Deconstruction and Criticism* (New York: Seabury Press, 1979), ix.

47. Ibid., 248.

48. See P. B. Shelley, *The Triumph of Life* (line 405) and Paul de Man's reading, "Shelley Disfigured," in *Deconstruction and Criticism*, 39–73.

49. Redfield, *The Politics of Aesthetics*, 108.

50. Anne Frey, *British State Romanticism: Authorship, Agency, and Bureaucratic Nationalism* (Stanford: Stanford University Press, 2010), 116–39.

51. See Deidre Lynch, introduction to *Persuasion* (Oxford: Oxford World Classics, 2004), vii–xxxix; Jillian Heydt-Stevenson, *Austen's Unbecoming Conjunctions:*

Subversive Laughter, Embodied History (New York: Palgrave, 2005); and Devoney Looser, *British Women Writers and the Writing of History, 1670–1820* (Baltimore: Johns Hopkins University Press, 2000), 178–203.

52. Habermas, *The Philosophical Discourse of Modernity*, 12.

1. From Precedents to the Unpredictable: Historiographical Futurities

1. Koselleck, *Futures Past*, 267.

2. Habermas's critique, which I cited in the introduction, is especially relevant here: "Koselleck overlooks the fact that the notion of progress served not only to render eschatological hopes profane and open up the horizon of expectation in a utopian fashion but also to close off the future as a *source* of disruption with the aid of teleological constructions of history" (*Philosophical Discourse of Modernity*, 12).

3. William Hazlitt, *The Spirit of the Age; Or, Contemporary Portraits* (Dove Cottage, Grasmere, Cumbria: The Wordsworth Trust, 2004).

4. J. G. A. Pocock, *Barbarism and Religion: Volume One, The Enlightenments of Edward Gibbon, 1737–1764* (Cambridge: Cambridge University Press, 1999), 9.

5. See Mark Salber Phillips on how eighteenth-century historians aspired to emulate the "classical ideals" of "linearity and perspicuity," while departing from classical models in other respects. Phillips, *Society and Sentiment*, 8.

6. Phillips, *Society and Sentiment*, ix.

7. For example, in Greg Kucich's searching essay on Keats's relationship to the Enlightenment histories he avidly read, Kucich refers repeatedly to the "linear narratives" of eighteenth-century historical writing; when he observes ideas of decline mixed in with ideas of progress, he still describes the "motion of humanity through time as an ongoing tension between *linear* contraries" (Kucich, "Keats's Literary Tradition and the Politics of Historiographical Invention," in *Keats and History*, ed. Nicholas Roe [Cambridge: Cambridge University Press, 1995], 246, 247, emphasis mine). Kucich addresses historical writing more as an intellectual context than as literary texts (along the lines of Hayden White) and overlooks the narrative temporalities in Enlightenment historiography that diverge from the linearity of progress or decline: simultaneity, digression, and temporal gaps, for instance.

8. Hugh Blair credited Voltaire with introducing this "improvement," which he clearly encouraged, remarking on "a more particular attention than was formerly given to laws, customs, commerce, religion, literature, and every other thing that tends to show the spirit and genius of nations. It is now understood to be the business of an able Historian to exhibit manners, as well as facts and events; and assuredly, whatever displays the state and life of mankind, in different periods, and illustrates the progress of the human mind, is more useful and interesting than the detail of sieges and battles. The person to whom we are most indebted for the introduction of this improvement into History, is the celebrated M. Voltaire" (Blair, *Lectures on Rhetoric and Belles Lettres* [Carbondale: Southern Illinois University Press, 2005], 411–12).

9. William Godwin, "Of History and Romance," in *Things as They Are; Or, The Adventures of Caleb Williams*, ed. Gary Handwerk and A. A. Markley (Peterborough,

ON: Broadview, 2000), 456–57. All subsequent quotations of "Of History and Romance" refer to this edition.

10. Ronald Meek, *Social Science and the Ignoble Savage* (Cambridge: Cambridge University Press, 1976), 2.

11. Chandler, *England in 1819*, 127.

12. Ibid., 107. On the concepts of anachronism and "uneven development" and their relation to one another, see pp. 107–35.

13. Referring to the rules of war and the employment of force for the obtainment of justice and preservation of national rights—not for gratuitously destroying the vanquished—Adam Ferguson observes: "This is, perhaps, the principal characteristic, on which, among modern nations, we bestow the epithets of *civilized* or of *polished*. But we have seen, that it did not accompany the progress of arts among the Greeks, nor keep pace with the advancement of policy, literature, and philosophy. It did not await the returns of learning and politeness among the moderns; it was found in early periods of our history, and distinguished, perhaps, more than at present, the manners of ages otherwise rude and undisciplined" (Ferguson, *An Essay on the History of Civil Society*, ed. Fania Oz-Salzberger [Cambridge: Cambridge University Press, 1995], 190).

14. Ferguson, *An Essay on the History of Civil Society*, 194–223.

15. Blair, *Lectures*, 393.

16. Jane Austen, *Northanger Abbey*, vol. 5 of *The Novels of Jane Austen*, ed. R. W. Chapman (Oxford: Oxford University Press, 1988), 197–98.

17. Ronald Meek (social scientist) and Gregory Kucich (literary historian), whose works I cited earlier, are two such examples.

18. I'm indebted to Phillips's *Society and Sentiment* for bringing Robert Henry's fascinating history and its narrative innovations to my attention.

19. Robert Henry, *History of Great Britain: From the First Invasion of It by Julius Caesar. Written on a New Plan* (London: Hodgson and Co., 1823), xxxvi.

20. Ibid., xxxvii.

21. Jane Austen to Martha Lloyd, November 12, 1800, *Jane Austen's Letters*, ed. Deirdre Le Faye (Oxford: Oxford University Press, 1995), 59.

22. Blair, *Lectures*, 398.

23. William Robertson, *The History of the Reign of the Emperor Charles V* (London: W. & W. Strahan, 1769), ix.

24. Phillips, *Society and Sentiment*, 91.

25. Blair, *Lectures*, 403, 405.

26. Ibid., 203.

27. David Hume, *An Enquiry Concerning Human Understanding*, ed. Lorne Falkenstein (Peterborough, ON: Broadview, 2011), 79. All subsequent quotations of *An Enquiry Concerning Human Understanding* refer to this edition.

28. Blair, *Lectures*, 402.

29. Ibid.

30. Hume, *An Enquiry Concerning Human Understanding*, 124.

31. Jean-Jacques Rousseau, *The Social Contract and Other Later Political Writings*, ed. Victor Gourevitch (Cambridge: Cambridge University Press, 1997), 41. All subsequent quotations of *The Social Contract* refer to this edition.

32. Koselleck, *Futures Past*, 246.

33. Robertson, *The History of the Reign of the Emperor Charles V*, xiv.

34. Godwin, "Of History and Romance,"454.

35. Ibid., 457.

36. Ibid., 454.

37. Ibid., 458.

38. Ibid., 460. In Mark Salber Phillips's recent commentary on the Romantic critique (and its misreadings) of sentiment in Enlightenment historiography, he argues, for instance, that "our image of the historical sensibility of the Enlightenment as wholly abstract and detached is in many ways a myth created by the Romantics as a foil for their own critique" (Phillips, "Relocating Inwardness: Historical Distance and the Transition from Enlightenment to Romantic Historiography," *PMLA* 118.3 [May 2003]: 446). Godwin surely contributes to that critical "myth" in "Of History and Romance," but my comparison concerns not emotional distance or intimacy but the conceptions of futurity; in that respect, Godwin's critique is consistent with what we have seen in the work of Enlightenment historiographers.

39. Godwin, "Of History and Romance,"457, 462, 458.

40. Ibid., 466.

41. Thomas Jefferson to John Jay, July 19, 1789, in *The Papers of Thomas Jefferson*, ed. Julian P. Boyd and William H. Gaines, vol. 15, *27 March 1789 to 30 November 1789* (Princeton: Princeton University Press, 1958), 290.

42. Godwin, "Of History and Romance," 466–67.

43. Williams, *Letters Written in France*, 109.

44. Edmund Burke, *Reflections on the Revolution in France* (New York: Penguin, 1969), 91.

45. Ibid., 339.

46. John Stuart Mill, "The Spirit of the Age," in *The Spirit of the Age: Victorian Essays*, ed. Gertrude Himmelfarb (New Haven, CT: Yale University Press, 2007), 51.

47. Hazlitt, *The Spirit of the Age*, 92, 99.

48. Jane Austen, *Persuasion*, vol. 5 of *The Novels of Jane Austen*, ed. R. W. Chapman (Oxford: Oxford University Press, 1988). All subsequent citations of *Persuasion* refer to this edition.

2. Dizzy Anticipations: Sonnets by Keats (and Shelley)

1. John Keats, *Complete Poems*, ed. Jack Stillinger (Cambridge, MA: Belknap, 1978). All poems by Keats subsequently quoted refer to this edition; only line numbers will appear in parentheses.

2. For the most thoroughly researched discussion to date of Keats's choice of Cortés over Balboa, see Charles Rzepka, "'Cortez: Or Balboa, or Somebody Like That': Form, Fact, and Forgetting in Keats's 'Chapman's Homer' Sonnet," *Keats-Shelley Journal* 51 (2002): 35–75. Rzepka argues that Keats's choice was not a mistake but a deliberate invoking of belatedness crucial to the sublime experience that Keats wanted to convey. I would emphasize that the speaker himself is not the

first to read "Chapman's Homer" either; Keats's poem concerns the individual subject's "breath[ing of] that pure serene," his personal registering of this world-shifting knowledge.

3. Daniel Watkins, *Keats's Poetry and the Politics of the Imagination* (Rutherford, NJ: Fairleigh Dickinson University Press, 1989), 26.

4. Jerome McGann, "Keats and the Historical Method in Literary Criticism," *The Beauty of Inflections: Literary Investigations in Historical Method & Theory* (1979; Oxford: Clarendon Press, 1988).

5. I am referring, for instance, to Roe's *John Keats and the Culture of Dissent.* I'll discuss Roe's text at more length especially in respect to "To Autumn" toward the end of chapter 3.

6. This is the sonnet as it appeared in *Poems* (1817). In October 1816, Keats and Charles Cowden Clarke had stayed up late at Clarke's reading passages aloud from Chapman. The next morning the sonnet appeared on Clarke's table and later that year was published in Leigh Hunt's *The Examiner.* Among some slight differences between the 1816 version and the 1817 one included in this chapter is a significant revision of line 7, which originally read, "Yet could I never judge what men could mean."

7. Rzepka, "'Cortez,'" 74. Rzepka's essay constitutes the most thorough discussion to date of Keats's choice of Cortés over Balboa, arguing that the belatedness of Cortés's arrival to the scene is crucial to the experience of the sublime that the poem conveys.

8. Marjorie Levinson, *Keats's Life of Allegory: The Origins of a Style* (Oxford: Basil Blackwell, 1988). Levinson writes: "We cannot help but see that 'pure serene,' a primary reification, further calls attention to itself as a fine phrase, that Keats clearly looks upon as a lover. Not only is the phrase a Miltonic construction, but more recent usage would have characterized it as a sort of translator-ese. One thinks of Pope's 'vast profound' and indeed, of Cary's own 'pure serene,' a description of Dante's ether (1814). Coleridge uses the phrase in his 'Hymn before Sunrise in the Vale of Chamouni,' in 1802. Keats's reproduction of the phrase designates both his access to the literary system and his mode of access—that of translator to Original" (12–13).

9. Roe, *John Keats and the Culture of Dissent,* 57.

10. Ibid., 58.

11. Kucich, "Keats's Literary Tradition," 243.

12. Ibid., 249. Although Kucich refers here to "form," his analysis of historiography appears almost purely thematic.

13. The poem appears, here, clearly open to the critique of eliding the suffering of others. In the writing of *Sleep and Poetry* (written around the same time or just after "Chapman's Homer" in 1816) as discussed, Keats appears to theorize this elision, as an aspect of human life he will address in a future "nobler life, / Where I may find the agonies, the strife / Of human hearts" (123–25); at present (in 1816), he is concerned with a very different notion of "the great end / Of poesy, that it should be a friend / To soothe the cares, and lift the thoughts of man" (245–47). That trajectory, indeed, seems accurate enough as a description of Keats's career insofar as the suffering of others (and the necessity of trying to address it) does later appear central to the themes of the *Hyperion* poems and the odes.

14. Peter Fritzsche, *Stranded in the Present: Modern Time and the Melancholy of History* (Cambridge, MA: Harvard University Press, 2004), 29.

15. Jane Rendall, "'The grand causes which combine to carry mankind forward': Wollstonecraft, History and Revolution," *Women's Writing* 4.2 (1997): 164.

16. Ibid., 157.

17. Habermas, *The Philosophical Discourse of Modernity*, 12.

18. These are Reinhart Koselleck's terms for the experience of time that inaugurates modernity. See *Futures Past*, 263–75.

19. Such a reading rests, I think, on what Kevis Goodman recently has called for: "a revised historicist method that reserves a place at the table for sensation and affect" (Goodman, *Georgic Modernity and British Romanticism: Poetry and the Mediation of History* [Cambridge: Cambridge University Press, 2004], 10).

20. Kucich, "Keats's Literary Tradition," 242.

21. William Robertson, *The History of America* (London: Cadell & Davies, 1808), v–vi.

22. Ibid., vi. See also Blair, *Lectures*, 390–401 on the importance of "unity" in historical writing.

23. See the introduction for an extended discussion of the nonlinear temporality of anticipation in this part of Keats's letter.

24. Roe, *John Keats and the Culture of Dissent*.

25. Ronald Sharp, *Keats, Skepticism, and the Religion of Beauty* (Athens: University of Georgia Press, 1979), 124.

26. Ibid., 119.

27. Keats was keenly aware of the various modes for representing truth available in historical writing. In "Keats's Literary Tradition," Kucich examines the poet's historical reading habits and makes us remarkably aware of what an avid, critical reader of histories, particularly those written in the eighteenth century, Keats was. Kucich observes in Keats's poetry a sense of historiographical debate not unlike what Sharp has described, a kind of negatively capable historiography: Keats's "calling attention to the indeterminate process, itself, of how we look upon the 'illimitable gulph / Of times past'" (257) as a way of resisting "that inclination in eighteenth-century historical writing to conceptualise the motion of humanity through time as an ongoing tension between linear contraries" (247). From here, Kucich introduces the issue of subjectivity, "particularly those beleaguered female subjects" (253), as the principle on which Keats turns away from universal historical paradigms, "'man's truth,' strategically constructed to elide women and other marginal groups from 'historical and political life'" (254). This gender distinction, however, does not seem apparent as an influence on, for instance, the "Chapman's Homer" sonnet as discussed earlier, and Keats's often hostile comments about women seem to tug at the tidiness of Kucich's explanation.

28. Emily Sun, *Succeeding King Lear: Literature, Exposure, and the Possibility of Politics* (New York: Fordham University Press, 2010), 81.

29. See Pyle, *Art's Undoing*, 67–70.

30. This disowning of desire would substantiate Jacques Khalip's thesis on Romantic anonymity and dispossession for which Keats is a central figure. See Khalip,

Anonymous Life: Romanticism and Dispossession (Stanford: Stanford University Press, 2009).

31. Percy Shelley, *Shelley's Poetry and Prose* (New York: Norton, 2002).

32. Chandler, *England in 1819*, 31.

33. Balfour, *The Rhetoric of Romantic Prophecy*, 37.

3. Accommodating Surprise: Keats's Odes

1. See Chandler, *England in 1819*, 389–440; and Nicholas Roe, "Keats's Commonwealth," in *Keats and History*, ed. Nicholas Roe (Cambridge: Cambridge University Press, 1995), 194–211.

2. William Cowper, *The Task*, in *The Task and Selected Other Poems*, ed. James Sambrook (New York: Longman, 1994), 285.

3. Chandler, *England in 1819*, 389–40.

4. For a description of Habermas's critique of progress, see pages 12–13.

5. Keats and Shakespeare are separated historically by, among other things, the rapid rise in print culture and literacy around 1800 that makes the kind of private reading Keats celebrates in the sonnets on Chapman's Homer and *King Lear* possible for a lower-middle-class person. This historical-cultural divide begins to explain perhaps why Keats imagines the Shakespearean legacy not for the stage but for the lyric and narrative poem, although Keats did complete one play, *Otho the Great*.

6. In an essay titled "Keats's 'Dull Rhymes' and the Making of the Ode Stanza," Jonathan Mulrooney has recently argued along these lines that it is out of Keats's dissatisfaction with the sonnet form that Keats developed an ode stanza that would accommodate a more meditative speaker. Mulrooney, "Keats's 'Dull Rhymes' and the Making of the Ode Stanza," *Literature Compass* 5.5 (2008): 935–48.

7. See, for instance, Jean Laplanche, *Life and Death in Psychoanalysis*, trans. Jeffrey Mehlman (Baltimore: Johns Hopkins University Press, 1976), 41–44.

8. Karen Swann, *"Endymion's Beautiful Dreamers,"* in *The Cambridge Companion to Keats*, ed. Susan J. Wolfson (Cambridge: Cambridge University Press, 2001), 23.

9. Stuart Sperry, *Keats the Poet* (Princeton: Princeton University Press, 1973), 258–59.

10. Helen Vendler, *The Odes of John Keats* (Cambridge, MA: Harvard University Press, 1983), 59.

11. Chandler, *England in 1819*, 416.

12. Ibid., 413.

13. Susan Wolfson's essay "Keats Enters History: Autopsy, *Adonais*, and the Fame of Keats" (in *Keats and History*, ed. Nicholas Roe [Cambridge: Cambridge University Press, 1995]) deserves mention here, though I'm less concerned in this discussion with how Keats actually did enter history than with how his anticipations structured his poetics. The essay characterizes *Adonais* as forcefully contributing to the cultural processing of Keats's death, "one of the main routes by which the 'romance' of 'Romanticism' emerged in the nineteenth century" (19). Wolfson notes that Keats was cast into the role, along with Chatterton and Henry Kirk White, of receiving public

unkindness and neglect (21); moreover, "It was not only the Tory reviewers who cast Keats in this role; it was also the script of the Keats circle itself, who sensed in his 'story' an outlet for sentimentality as well as politics" (22). I would add, further, that Keats himself, through his identification (if not on other grounds) with the mythical Psyche he characterizes as neglected, provided substance for *Adonais*'s sentimental tone.

14. Chandler, *England in 1819*, 417. Chandler's answer is Wordsworth's poetry and the "tension between enlightenment analysis and Christian superstition" that he sees animating Keats's reading of it; see *England in 1819*, 417–25.

15. Barbauld, "On the Uses of History," 286. This notion of the present's disconnection from the past, including Barbauld's view of it, is discussed in the introduction and in Chapter 1.

16. In his 1816 advertisement to the Thanksgiving Ode, a patriotic Wordsworth could not ignore the "veil" of "present distresses": "It is not to bespeak favour or indulgence, but to guard against misapprehension, that the author presumes to state that the present publication owes its existence to a patriotism, anxious to exert itself in commemorating that course of action, by which Great Britain has, for some time past, distinguished herself above all other countries. Wholly unworthy of touching upon so momentous a subject would that Poet be, before whose eyes the present distresses under which this kingdom labours, could interpose a veil sufficiently thick to hide, or even to obscure, the splendour of this great moral triumph. If the author has given way to exultation, unchecked by these distresses, it might be sufficient to protect him from a charge of insensibility, should he state his own belief that these sufferings will be transitory" (72). More overtly critical of the war and what he perceived as its direct social consequences, Percy Shelley, in his 1817 "Address to the People on the Death of Princess Charlotte," wrote of the economic distress caused by policies that took shape during the war with America and that the government extended during the war with France: "The government which the imperfect constitution of our representative assembly threw into the hands of a few aristocrats, improved the method of anticipating the taxes by loans, invented by the ministers of William III, until an enormous debt had been created. In the war against the republic of France, this policy was followed up, until now, the *mere interest* of the public debt amounts to more than twice as much as the lavish expenditure of the public treasure, for maintaining the standing army, and the royal family, and the pensioners, and the placemen. The effect of this debt is to produce such an unequal distribution of the means of living, as saps the foundation of social union and civilized life." See also Philip Shaw, *Waterloo and the Romantic Imagination* (New York: Palgrave, 2002), 1–34.

17. Shaw, *Waterloo and the Romantic Imagination*, 15.

18. Immanuel Kant, *The Critique of the Power of Judgment*, ed. Paul Guyer, trans. Paul Guyer and Eric Matthews (Cambridge: Cambridge University Press, 2000).

19. Edmund Burke, *A Philosophical Enquiry into the Sublime and Beautiful*, ed. David Womersley (New York: Penguin, 1998), 101.

20. McGann, "Keats and the Historical Method in Literary Criticism," 61.

21. Roe, *John Keats and the Culture of Dissent*, 257, 263, 264.

22. Ibid., 252–53. Roe's Godwin, and indeed Keats's, is the Godwin of *Political Justice*. But Godwin began to write in a mode more like possibility than perfectibility in the mid- and late 1790s in, for instance, the unpublished essay "Of History and Romance"; much earlier, in the *Herald of Literature* (1784), Godwin appeared to parody predictability by reviewing volumes of books, even quoting from them, before they had been written.

23. In the introduction to the 1986 special issue, Susan Wolfson aptly notes that the essays to follow significantly complicate the "general critical tendency to regard the very conjunction of 'Keats' and 'politics' as something of a metaphysical conceit" (171). Wolfson, "Introduction," *Studies in Romanticism* 25.2 (Summer 1986): 171–74.

24. William Keach, "Cockney Couplets: Keats and the Politics of Style," *Studies in Romanticism* 25.2 (Summer 1986): 190.

25. Paul Fry, "History, Existence, and 'To Autumn,'" *Studies in Romanticism* 25.2 (Summer 1986): 217.

26. Ibid., 211, 219.

27. Ibid., 211, emphasis mine.

28. Deborah White, *Romantic Returns: Superstition, Imagination, History* (Stanford: Stanford University Press, 2000), 8–9.

29. My language here of "opening onto" history is meant to suggest a more permeable boundary between the categories of "poetry" and "history" than that which many critics have tended to assume. The metaphor also, however, maintains a certain difference between poetic discourse and the political and historical discourses in whose concerns Keats's poetry intervenes; it intervenes, in part, by virtue of this very difference in kind—i.e., Keats's poetry could not enter these debates fully without fundamentally changing them in ways that the rest of this argument aims to show.

30. For instance, in *England in 1819*, James Chandler—although he describes Keats's "sense of a historical present" in the "vale of Soul-making" letter as "defined by the tension between enlightenment analysis and Christian superstition"—never mentions that, in the letter, it is Keats's meditation on Robertson's history, which Keats has lately been reading along with Voltaire, that appears to initiate Keats's alternative thinking of the world as a "vale of Soul-making" (422). Chandler's analysis of "To Autumn" also emphasizes a context of Christian redemption when he describes the poem as "the most powerful of those consolation poems that refuse to resort to Christian comfort" (431).

31. Keats never returns, in the letter, to the second "instance," Voltaire.

32. Pierre France, "Voltaire and the Necessity of Modern History," *Modern Intellectual History* 6.3 (November 2009): 469.

33. It is perhaps worth noting in relation to the metaphor of the school that Keats attended the Enfield School from 1803 until 1811. In *John Keats and the Culture of Dissent*, Nicholas Roe argues convincingly for the centrality of this experience to the formation of Keats's radical political views. Keats's time at Enfield was intellectually and socially rich, and this is where Keats developed voracious reading habits. Keats won books as prizes while at school, including Bonnycastle's *Introduction to Astronomy*, but he read primarily books that he borrowed from the school's library, as

well as some additional books borrowed from Charles Cowden Clarke. Roe writes, "Like everything else at Enfield School, the library was remarkable" (46). If we take Keats's metaphor of "reading" literally, that in school he was reading not only books he owned but also those that would circulate through the hands of others, this supports the notion of reading (of suffering and feeling in the world) as a process that is at once one's own (a private act) and social (an act that renders the reader permeable to a broader human experience of the temporal world).

34. When Keats wrote in December 1818 to his brother and sister-in-law, he clearly was using the term in this way: "I have been so little used to writing lately that I am affraid [sic] you will not smoke my meaning so I will give you an example." Again in the same letter Keats used the term more broadly, to suggest "smoking" not only as understanding but also perhaps as making fun of: "Mrs. Tighe and Beattie once delighted me—now I see through them and can find nothing in them—or weakness— and yet how many they still delight!—Perhaps a superior being may look upon Shakspeare [sic] in the same light—is it possible? No—This same inadequacy is discovered (forgive me little George you know I don't mean to put you in the mess) in Women with few exceptions—the Dress Maker, the blue Stocking, the most charming sentimentalist differ but in slight degree and are all equally smokeable" (*LJK*, 2:18–19). Keats expressed elsewhere (and with characteristic sonic play) an intention not to publish his poem "Isabella" because "It is too smokeable—I can get it smoak'd at the Carpenters shaving chimney much more cheaply" (*LJK*, 2:174). Here the term seems to be both: the poem will risk ridicule because its meanings are so transparent. For further commentary on "smokeability," see Chandler, *England in 1819*, 395–402.

35. Jacques Lacan, *The Language of the Self: The Function of Language in Psychoanalysis*, trans. Anthony Wilden (Baltimore: Johns Hopkins University Press, 1981), 63, emphasis mine.

36. Although "reading" in the "vale of Soul-making" letter is clearly figurative, it is not incidental that Keats witnesses, and dramatically benefits from, a historical moment of rapidly expanding print culture and rising literacy rates that made literal reading accessible in an unprecedented way.

37. Geoffrey Hartman, "Poem and Ideology: A Study of Keats's 'To Autumn,'" *The Fate of Reading and Other Essays* (Chicago: University of Chicago Press, 1985), 131.

38. My language here makes the subject's relations to the natural world exchangeable for relations to a social world because Keats himself appeared to think through social relations in natural terms. He wrote to J. H. Reynolds in February 1818, for instance: "Man should not dispute or assert but whisper results to his neighbor, and thus by every germ of Spirit sucking the Sap from mould ethereal every human might become great, and Humanity instead of being a wide heath of Furse and Briars with here and there a remote Oak or Pine, would become a grand democracy of Forest Trees" (*LJK*, 1:232).

39. Hartman, "Poem and Ideology," 130.

40. Habermas, for instance, refers to the "new experience of an advancing and accelerating of historical events" around this time, which means that "time becomes experienced as a scarce resource for the mastery of problems that arise—that is, as

the pressure of time. The *Zeitgeist*, or spirit of the age, one of the new words that inspired Hegel, characterizes the present as a transition that is consumed in the consciousness of a speeding up and in the expectation of the differentness of the future" (*The Philosophical Discourse of Modernity*, 6).

41. Hartman, "Poem and Ideology," 129.

42. Keats, *Complete Poems*, 64.

43. Along these lines, in "Ode on a Grecian Urn" the repetitions in "More *happy* love! more *happy*, *happy* love!" (25) elicit the reader's "panting" (27) akin to that of the urn's figured lovers.

44. Responding to Keats's sonnet "Great spirits now on earth are sojourning," the critic "Z.," John Gibson Lockhart, in however irate a tone, clearly recognized Keats's poetry as contributing to debates about the "spirit of the age" when he wrote in *Blackwood's Edinburgh Magazine* in 1817, "Mr. Keats classes together WORDS-WORTH, HUNT, and HAYDON, as the three greatest spirits of the age, and that he alludes to himself, and some others of the rising brood of Cockneys, as likely to attain hereafter an equally honorable elevation" (933).

45. Whereas in "To Autumn" the possibilities appear evenly balanced, all equally plausible, in the "Chapman's Homer" sonnet the conjunction of possibility "Or like stout Cortez" improves upon the preceding simile of the astronomer.

46. Vendler, *The Odes of John Keats*, 251.

47. Rei Terada, "Looking at the Stars Forever," *Studies in Romanticism* 50.2 (Summer 2011): 279.

48. Along these lines, Jonathan Mulrooney has written: "in the fullness of the given moment language reaches its limit: existing in time, words cannot convey simultaneity except through figuration that must, finally, recognize an experience beyond its grasp" ("Keats's 'Dull Rhymes,'" 944).

49. Remarkably, there are no leaves in Keats's "To Autumn" where we might expect to find visually mixed tones of color.

50. A number of fine critics have discussed the elaborately interwoven sound patterns. See, for instance, James O'Rourke's extensive description of them in *Keats's Odes and Contemporary Criticism* (Gainesville: University Press of Florida, 1998) and Garrett Stewart's wonderful essay, "Keats and Language," in *The Cambridge Companion to Keats*, ed. Susan Wolfson (Cambridge: Cambridge University Press, 2001).

51. Vendler, *The Odes of John Keats*, 254.

52. O'Rourke, *Keats's Odes and Contemporary Criticism*, 167.

53. Fry, "History, Existence, and 'To Autumn,'" 218.

54. Jonathan Bate, *Song of the Earth* (Cambridge, MA: Harvard University Press, 2002), 105.

55. Hartman, "Poem and Ideology," 126.

4. Contingencies of the Future Anterior: Austen's *Persuasion*

1. Austen, *Persuasion*, 252.

2. In *Northanger Abbey*, Catherine Morland explains her distaste for reading histories by describing the contents as largely devoid of the lives of women: "'The

quarrels of popes and kings, with wars and pestilences, in every page; the men all so good for nothing, and hardly any women at all—it is very tiresome'" (108). And in *Persuasion*, Anne Elliot declares in no uncertain terms who has written what is commonly accepted as history: "'Men have had every advantage of us in telling their own story'" (234).

3. Jane Austen to James Edward Austen, December 16–17, 1816, in *Jane Austen's Letters*, ed. Le Faye, 323.

4. Marilyn Butler, *Jane Austen and the War of Ideas* (Oxford: Clarendon Press, 1975).

5. Claudia Johnson, *Jane Austen: Women, Politics, and the Novel* (Chicago: University of Chicago Press, 1988), 120.

6. Favret, *War at a Distance*, 145–72; Frey, *British State Romanticism*, 116–39; William Galperin, *The Historical Austen* (Philadelphia: University of Pennsylvania Press, 2003); Lynch, introduction, vii–xxxiii. Focusing on Austen's *Northanger Abbey*, Devoney Looser's *British Women Writers and the Writing of History, 1670–1820* (Baltimore: Johns Hopkins University Press, 2000) also deserves mention here for its cogent argument that the novel presents itself as better instruction for negotiating the present than one finds in Gothic fiction or historical writing of the day; see pp. 178–203.

7. Lynch, introduction, xix. Lynch's analysis, which focuses much on the novel's reinterpretations of the past, extends the sense of agency to the act of reading: "[Austen] doesn't separate solitary reading from the public service performed by men of action; she puts them into proximity" (xxix). Focusing on questions of community building and state institutions, on the other hand, Frey's study finds that the novel emphasizes the limits of authorial agency: "Austen suggests that shared reading is not enough to form people into a large scale community: writing can *depict* networks of obligation and responsibility but not actually create them" (*British State Romanticism*, 128).

8. Lynch, introduction, ix. Similarly focusing on the novel's preoccupation with the past, Claudia Johnson observes that "Here, as in no other novel, we are constantly being pointed backwards … in short, to the inconjurable difference time makes" (*Jane Austen*, 147).

9. Ross Hamilton's wonderful commentary on the novel touches on this point; he writes of Anne's "reading" of William Elliot: "Although her skill in deciphering the man beneath the manner shields her when her cousin insinuates that his affections rest on her, her insight is of no use in making the critical leap into defining her own future." See Hamilton, *Accident: A Philosophical and Literary History* (Chicago: University of Chicago Press, 2007), 220–28.

10. In this sense, what Michal Ginsburg has written of Fanny Price in *Mansfield Park* applies equally to Anne Elliot in *Persuasion*: "If the 'true self' is not immediately visible, it is not because it is double or split, nor is its becoming visible the result of a demystification. Rather, characters become known through differences and similarities unfolded over time" (Ginsburg, *Economies of Change: Form and Transformation in the Nineteenth-Century Novel* [Stanford: Stanford University Press, 1996], 105).

11. Anne-Lise François, *Open Secrets: The Literature of Uncounted Experience* (Stanford: Stanford University Press, 2008), xxii.

12. Peter Brooks, *Reading for the Plot* (Cambridge, MA: Harvard University Press, 1992), 23.

13. This is the first time the word "immortality" (or, as far as I can tell, any words related by root, such as "immortal") appears in Austen's writings, though "immortal" appears twice in *Sanditon*, which Austen began writing soon after she finished *Persuasion*.

14. Favret, *War at a Distance*, 148.

15. This dramatic formalist reading of the subjectivity of the novel owes something to David Wagenknecht's discussion of the "window scene" in "The Turn of the Screw"; see esp. pp. 432–39 of his essay "Here's Looking at You, Peter Quint: 'The Turn of the Screw,' Freud's 'Dora,' and the Aesthetics of Hysteria," *American Imago* 55.4 (1998): 423–58.

16. See Alistair Duckworth, *The Improvement of the Estate: A Study of Jane Austen's Novels* (Baltimore: Johns Hopkins University Press, 1971), in which he describes "a new mode of communication ... in *Persuasion*" (204–8). Other commentaries on this issue include Tony Tanner, *Jane Austen* (Cambridge, MA: Harvard University Press, 1986), 235; Janis Stout, *Strategies of Reticence: Silence and Meaning in the Works of Jane Austen, Willa Cather, Katherine Anne Porter, and Joan Didion* (Charlottesville: University Press of Virginia, 1990), 60; and Tara Ghoshal Wallace, *Jane Austen and Narrative Authority* (New York: St. Martin's Press, 1995), 105–6.

17. Virginia Woolf, "Jane Austen," *The Common Reader* (New York: Harcourt Brace, 1948), 206.

18. William Wordsworth, "Preface to *Lyrical Ballads, 1800*," in *Lyrical Ballads, and Other Poems, 1797–1800*, ed. James Butler and Karen Green (Ithaca, NY: Cornell University Press, 1992), 747.

19. I am indebted to Julia Brown for drawing my attention to this aspect of historical context (and doubtless for a great many other insights into Austen's novels).

20. Gary Kelly, "Feminine Romanticism, Masculine History, and the Founding of the Modern Liberal State," in *Romanticism and Gender*, ed. Anne Janowitz (Cambridge: D. S. Brewer, 1988). As recently as 1998 in a special edition of *Essays and Studies* titled "Romanticism and Gender," Gary Kelly has argued—even while recovering earlier female authors' works as predecessors to Scott's historical novel—that unlike other female novelists of the time, Austen seals history and historiography out of her work: "[Austen's] novels appear to ignore history and historiography, apart from Catherine Morland's complaint in *Northanger Abbey*. ... Readers at the time might well feel that Austen's novels deliberately exclude and marginalize history and historiography" (13). Clearly the argument I elaborate here takes issue with Kelly's assessment, especially with respect to *Persuasion*.

21. This effect is what Paul de Man describes in "The Rhetoric of Temporality" as irony: "In the idea of fall thus conceived, a progression in self-knowledge is certainly implicit: the man who has fallen is somewhat wiser than the fool who walks around oblivious of the crack in the pavement about to trip him up. And the fallen philosopher reflecting on the discrepancy between the two successive stages is wiser still, but this does not in the least prevent him from stumbling in his turn. It seems instead that his wisdom can be gained only at the cost of such a fall. The mere fall-

ing of others does not suffice; he has to go down himself" (de Man, "The Rhetoric of Temporality," *Blindness and Insight: Essays in the Rhetoric of Contemporary Criticism*, 2nd rev. ed. [Minneapolis: University of Minnesota Press, 1983], 214). In the example of Admiral Croft that follows, Austen shows us a kind of philosopher reflecting on the successive stages who, we presume, nevertheless cannot avoid his own impending fall.

22. To see the novel as embodying the same kind of representation as the painting does—figures unwittingly about to "fall" (in their various forms) or be taken by surprise—is to suggest that its aesthetic sides not with Admiral Croft's utilitarian perspective of ostensible disillusionment but with that of the painting, whether or not the imminent "upset" the Admiral observes was intentional or not. The image of Romantic sublimity and the gentlemen's blind spots, the limits of their awareness of their situation, gives us a peculiar, evocative access to the historical moment. This claim runs against the grain of Anne Frey's recent reading of that scene in which she sees the "picturesque" of the painting as an aesthetic in contrast to—and as an escape from—the "real world." "[T]he Admiral's response is tied more to the real world than to the picturesque," she states; "viewing art temporarily removes the Admiral from engagement with the real world" (*British State Romanticism*, 132). Whereas Frey claims that "the Admiral's turning away from the picture demonstrates a firm grounding in reality," my argument suggests the opposite: that the painting gives us peculiar access to the shifting grounds of "the real world."

23. François, *Open Secrets*, 153.

24. Favret, *War at a Distance*, 145, 146, 148.

25. Galperin, *The Historical Austen*, 231, 232. Deidre Lynch, among others, echoes that pronouncement of the romance plot's "foregone conclusion" in her introduction to the Oxford edition of the novel (introduction, xi).

26. On the significance of imagining alternative lives in nineteenth-century fiction, see Andrew Miller, "Lives Unled in Realist Fiction," *Representations* 98 (Spring 2007): 118–34.

27. Harry Shaw, *Narrating Reality* (Ithaca, NY: Cornell University Press, 1999), 163.

28. Jerome de Groot, *The Historical Novel* (London: Routledge, 2010), 3.

29. Georg Lukács, *The Historical Novel*, trans. Hannah Mitchell and Stanley Mitchell (Lincoln: University of Nebraska Press, 1983), 19.

30. Ibid., 35.

31. Walter Scott, *Waverley*, ed. Susan Kubica Howard (Peterborough, ON: Broadview, 1991), 450.

32. Meek, *Social Science and the Ignoble Savage*, 61.

33. Ibid., 37.

34. John Stuart Mill, "Carlyle's French Revolution," in *Essays on French History and Historians*, ed. John M. Robson and John C. Cairns (Toronto: University of Toronto Press, 1985), 135.

35. Phillips, "Relocating Inwardness," 446.

5. The "Double Nature" of Presentness: Byron's *Don Juan*

1. Jerome McGann, *"Don Juan" in Context* (Chicago: University of Chicago Press, 1976).

2. See Chandler, *England in 1819*, 381; and Jerome Christensen, *Lord Byron›s Strength: Romantic Writing and Commercial Society* (Baltimore: Johns Hopkins University Press, 1993).

3. Brooks, *Reading for the Plot*, 23.

4. See Christensen, *Lord Byron's Strength*, 238.

5. Lord Byron, *Byron's Letters & Journals*, ed. Leslie Marchand (Cambridge, MA: Harvard University Press, 1976), 6:207 (hereafter cited as *BLJ* by volume and page number).

6. McGann, *"Don Juan" in Context*, 101.

7. Peter W. Graham, *"Don Juan" and Regency England* (Charlottesville: University of Virginia Press, 1990), 158.

8. Peter W. Graham has argued differently: that Juan "grows up" in the course of his travels and that he attains a sense of purpose and self-interest by the time he arrives in England (see *"Don Juan" and Regency England*, 159–63). That sense of psychological development seems to me not fully accurate since the poet-narrator scarcely looks inside Juan's mind. Rather, Juan appears, like a chameleon, to take on the prevailing attributes of the societies in which he moves, without the psychological depth or memory that might allow him to internalize these traits and access them once he moves on.

9. Brooks, *Reading for the Plot*, 5.

10. As Jonathan Gross reminds us, certain aspects of *Don Juan* actually *are* predictable when we know the source material; he argues cogently that Canto 5, for instance, is based on the Joseph story and unfolds predictably when read through that lens. See Gross, *The Erotic Liberal* (Oxford: Rowman and Littlefield, 2001), 55–77. Along those lines, the English cantos clearly deal in the familiar and even highly predictable tropes of Gothic romance. At the same time, however, the poem's extended structure of shifting modes with shifting geographical locales—as well as the question of what topic will fill the narrator's next digression, among other things—elicits, in ways that I have suggested, a recurrent sense of the unpredictable. The extremes of predictability and unpredictability commingle, in other words.

11. Brooks, *Reading for the Plot*, 23.

12. McGann, *"Don Juan" in Context*, 101.

13. Jerome McGann makes this point in *"Don Juan" in Context*, where he substantiates the claim by observing specifically that Byron's "experiences at Drury Lane gave him plenty of factual material to deal with this set of characters in full narrative treatment" (103).

14. Shelley, *A Defence of Poetry*, 511.

15. Friedrich Meinecke, *Historism: The Rise of a New Historical Outlook* (New York: Herder and Herder, 1972), 62.

16. Blair, *Lectures*, 397.

17. Chandler, *England in 1819*, 373.